The Medieval Filmscape

The Medieval Filmscape

Reflections of Fear and Desire in a Cinematic Mirror

WILLIAM F. WOODS

McFarland & Company, Inc., Publishers
Jefferson, North Carolina

LIBRARY OF CONGRESS CATALOGUING-IN-PUBLICATION DATA

Woods, William F., 1942–
　　The medieval filmscape : reflections of fear and desire in a cinematic mirror / William F. Woods.
　　　p.　　cm.
　　Includes bibliographical references and index.

　　ISBN 978-0-7864-4651-3 (softcover : acid free paper) ∞
　　ISBN 978-1-4766-1341-3 (ebook)

　　1. Middle Ages in motion pictures.　2. Medievalism in motion pictures.　I. Title.
PN1995.9.M52W66　2014
791.43'658207—dc23　　　　　　　　　　　　　　2013048603

BRITISH LIBRARY CATALOGUING DATA ARE AVAILABLE

© 2014 William F. Woods. All rights reserved

No part of this book may be reproduced or transmitted in any form or by any means, electronic or mechanical, including photocopying or recording, or by any information storage and retrieval system, without permission in writing from the publisher.

On the cover: Bengt Ekerot in *The Seventh Seal*, 1957 Sweden (Svensk Filmindustri/Photofest)

Manufactured in the United States of America

McFarland & Company, Inc., Publishers
　Box 611, Jefferson, North Carolina 28640
　　www.mcfarlandpub.com

For Annie, Eva, Sara and Sebastián

Amores mios

Table of Contents

Preface	1
Introduction—Our Lady of Pain: The Subgenre of Medieval Film	3

PART I

ONE: Authenticity	23
TWO: Simplicity	35
THREE: Spectacle	46

PART II

FOUR: *The Advocate*	59
FIVE: Northern Light	76
Bergman, *The Seventh Seal*	76
Dreyer, *La Passion de Jeanne d'Arc*	85
SIX: French Arthuriana	94
Rohmer, *Perceval le gallois*	94
Bresson, *Lancelot du Lac*	104
SEVEN: *The Name of the Rose*	116
EIGHT: *The Return of Martin Guerre*	135
NINE: *Kingdom of Heaven*	155
Epilogue	175
Filmography	179
Chapter Notes	181
Bibliography	194
Index	199

Preface

Medieval film has become our favorite medievalism—our preferred way of looking backward on the medieval past, enjoying its oddly familiar strangeness while projecting ourselves into it and pairing it with our own ideas, fantasies and emotional needs. The medieval film world is filled with men on horseback, edged weapons, elegant queens, and scruffy peasants, but because we can enter this world and dwell in it through the apparent reality of film, it is also a mirror for us: a shared experience dramatizing what we covertly hope and fear. This world appeals to our pride and our sense of style—isn't that what chivalry has always meant?—but threat is there as well, the plagues and wars, the veiled eye of betrayal, and, perhaps even stronger, the bitter sweetness of faraway love, the exaltation of courage, and the craving to be loyal to God and King, and (despite temptation or even torture) true to oneself.

This book has three parts:

- The introduction enters the medieval film world, describing its typical features and showing how they create a convincing sense of its time.
- Three short chapters discuss *authenticity, simplicity* and *spectacle*—the roots of film medievalism.
- Six longer chapters comment on individual films.

By the end I will have described what goes into a medieval film and how it affects its audience, while offering a few suggestions about why its themes are meaningful to us.

At present, there are few books that try to define the subgenre of medieval film by describing its features and analyzing its effects and their significance. This book is a modest, informal attempt at such a definition. I do not cover the entire spectrum of medieval film. I say little about Robin Hood movies, for instance (they have received adequate treatment elsewhere), and my choices of movies is selective. I discuss works which extend the reach of the medieval film genre, such as Dreyer's *La Passion de Jeanne D'Arc*, with its emotional range; or Bergman's *The Seventh Seal*, which creates a universal symbolism. Not all of these pictures are recent, and some might be an acquired taste. Each of them has a particular way of drawing us into the Middle Ages, confronting us with our own fears and desires, reflected strangely, deeply in the medieval mirror.

* * * * *

Parts of this book have been published elsewhere in earlier versions, and I wish to express my gratitude to the editors and publishers who have granted me permission to use again work which originally appeared under their care. An earlier draft of Chapter Four appeared as "Seeking the Human Image in *The Advocate*," *Studies in Medievalism* XII (2002): 55–78, published by Boydell & Brewer; and a different version of Chapter One appeared in Martha W. Driver and Sid Ray, ed., *The Medieval Hero on Screen: Representations from Beowulf to Buffy* (Jefferson, NC: McFarland, 2004), 38–51.

* * * * *

Thanks to the many that in so many ways helped me with this book. First, Tom Shippey, the careful and gracious editor of the article that became Chapter Four, and Nick Haydock, who chaired the section where I presented an early version of Chapter Two and had some welcome praise for it and for a draft of the Introduction. Kevin Harty also heard that early paper and helpfully let me know he liked it. Norman Hinton, having read the Introduction, kindly suggested that it might serve to begin a book. Martha Driver provided some judicious criticism and editing of an earlier version of Chapter One. John Ganim's early interest in medieval film and his subsequent essays on it have been important influences, and his encouragement meant much.

A respectful nod as well to the Fairmount College of Arts and Sciences at Wichita State University for the sabbatical that brought most of the book into being, and to my fine, movie-wise students in the classes I taught on medieval film. Thanks also to Kristie Bixby, whose editorial wit has been a constant inspiration; Ramesh Devineni, without whose patient computer expertise this book would have no pictures; and Dennis Bishop, who saw many of these movies with me, discussed them, and gave helpful readings to some of the chapters.

But *muchísimas gracias* to my daughters Eva and Sara, who helped in heartfelt ways, to Sebastián, man of letters, and especially to my wife Annie, who read every word of this book and deserves most praise for that of it which is good.

Introduction—Our Lady of Pain: The Subgenre of Medieval Film

Blood-soaked epic, mystical sword and sorcery, legalistic monkish psychodrama—these are the medieval movies. Watching them we open ourselves to the medieval past, but sooner or later comes the question: What's medieval about them? And its corollary: Why should we care? Given time, we might rephrase these questions a bit: What is it in these films that we associate with medieval times, and why do we identify with these associations—why do these old images and themes fire the imagination and touch our hearts? And finally, what cares of our own do we project into this "medieval" vision to make it our own?

These are the core questions of cinematic medievalism. Like any medievalism, it ponders how moderns conceive the Middle Ages—how we connect with those times through the medium of medieval film. This book will attempt to identify some images, characters and situations that we tend to accept as authentically and compellingly medieval, not so much to establish their historical authenticity—these are stories, after all, not documentaries—but to determine what allows us to enter this virtual medieval experience, to live for an hour or two as a warrior king or a philosophic monk. Let us consider Arthur, torn between Lancelot, his right hand, and Guinevere, his heart. Drawn by his crisis of loyalty and identity, we bow to his necessities, share his burdens, and, feeling the weight of a harder world than our own, we too are torn. Thus we confront ourselves within the dark truth of Arthur's agony, testing it upon our own sensibility and shouldering the weight of medieval necessity, if only as the once and future king, and until the final credits.

The images, characters and whatever there is on screen that we associate with Arthur's times are, in effect, authenticating features. Potentially infinite in number, these peasants, princes, castles and huts form an ever-growing, open-ended list, but they are not an index of historical accuracy. They merely tell us "this is a world, a surrogate experience which we have agreed to recognize as medieval." Taken together, these content features allow us to identify the movie—to "read" it—as belonging to a narrative subgenre we typically call "medieval film." Arthur's crisis, on the other hand, is a less-tangible generic feature which could be called "formal" (as opposed to features of content), "syntactic" (not a "semantic" sign of the medieval), or perhaps simply "inner form" (as opposed to "outer form," which would be images or characters).[1] As a feature of inner form, Arthur's placement between Lancelot and Guinevere produces the "medieval" theme of the tortured Man-King, and its emotional dynamic draws us to invest ourselves once more in Arthur's painful but by now well known experience.

These inner and outer features place us in the medieval world (they are the answer to "What's medieval about it?"). By making possible our identification with the problems of that world, they show us "why we should care," for as we consider them, the generic outlines of these films begin to emerge, and we begin to gain a sense of how we ourselves react to these movies, how cinematic medievalism has its way with us. I will begin by examining some of the common details, techniques and assumptions that make up the world of medieval film, and then move to the characters and their stories. They will lead us to the obsessive ideas and ideals that also, and even more powerfully, assert the experiential authenticity we seek in these films.

Ground Rules

"Once upon a time..." That is how fairy tales begin, and if they did not, we wouldn't know how to respond to them.[2] Fairy tales are generic. In other words, we bring to them a rich context of remembered motifs, rhythms, and plot lines that help us enter the world of each tale. Medieval movies are somewhat the same, a loose genre that is always being subverted; but even those changes are understood in terms of the generic space we already know so well. This space has a frame. The beginning of practically any medieval film is, of course, its music, and often it is old music, played on medieval or Renaissance instruments, which tells us that we have entered an historical context—an olden time before our time, with very different constraints and freedoms. Probably at the same instant, a text begins crawling up the screen, telling us when this action took place, what wars and other difficulties these people were having to face. This is the medieval version of "Once upon a time," or "Long, long ago, in a galaxy far, far away." This frame story covertly implies that the action and our participation in it shares in the "truth" of an historical event. To put it another way, the framing text makes a truth claim, a claim to authenticity:

we are told that this movie recovers history, we have as yet no reason to doubt it, and thus are inclined to acceptance.

The world we enter, the background for the opening credits flashing onto the screen, appears in a visceral, half-conscious way to be a medieval world because immediately we are close to the earth. *The Return of Martin Guerre* begins as the camera follows a rider across a brook and inside the walls of a small peasant village, through streets that are rutted and none too clean. *The Advocate*'s initial scene is a coach—really just a large, roofed wagon—jolting along through the French countryside, and watching it we can practically feel the bumps ourselves. The people in these landscapes do not have that scrubbed look. Their faces may be dirty, especially if they are children. Their clothes look lived in, not dusty, perhaps, but authentically unwashed—a connection with the dirt floors and smoky interiors of their homes, not an insulation from them.

The people themselves, not so much the princes and priests but the peasants, tradesmen, housewives, and soldiers, contribute significantly to the medieval effect of these initial scenes. In *The Name of the Rose*, most of the film takes place within the walls of a Benedictine monastery, but we are continually reminded of the scruffy villagers who live below the walls. It is hard to forget them: they come in droves to scavenge the abbey's garbage heap, they find their way in at night to trade (or in one girl's case, to sell her body), and at the end they arrive just in time to save that girl from burning, and to push the Holy Inquisitor and his carriage off a cliff. *The Lion in Winter* is essentially a stage drama with most of its scenes indoors, but when Eleanor of Aquitaine arrives at Henry's castle by water we get a good look at the boatmen, soldiers and other folks who labor so that these princes can play their vicious politics. Indeed, it often seems in medieval movies that The People should appear in capital letters. One thinks of *The Peasants' Revolt*: Wat Tyler, about to torch a pile of documents in the Tower of London, draws himself up as only Anthony Hopkins can do and shouts as though the whole town could hear him, "Let might make right; let the people speak!" Wherever it is made, if we discount the occasional art film like Eric Rohmer's *Perceval le gallois*, a medieval movie is likely to have a populist flavor and probably will not urge us to identify with the effete upper class. In *A Knight's Tale*, Ulrich von Lichtenstein may pretend to be a knight, but we are expected to like him because he is, after all, a thatcher's son.

But what are these medieval movie people like? Usually "the people" live a brutally hard life. They seem politically oppressed and economically destitute. England may have been called a "nation of shopkeepers" at various periods in its history, but if there are shopkeepers in medieval movies, they tend not to be the princes of trade. Guildsmen and great merchants like Nicholas Brembre, the wealthy grocer and Lord Mayor of London (1377) who lent money to Richard II until going to the scaffold (1388), do not appear often in medieval film, perhaps because they have too many choices, which somehow seems modern, urban, democratic. Medieval film people, by contrast, are so cruelly constrained that we find it believable they should leave the fields, burst from their shops and tiny houses to celebrate, get drunk, make merry, or start a riot. They are sensual, earthy and vital,[3] like Chaucer's Wife of Bath; but unlike her, they can seem morally uncomplicated, even childlike, strangely liberated by their grinding toil, and more like Perkyn Reveller, the irrepressible anti-hero of the *Cook's Tale* ("At every bridale wolde he singe and hoppe; / He loved bet the taverne than the shoppe" [I:4375–6]).[4] Yet if there is something regressive or infantile about the simple pleasures enjoyed in *A Knight's Tale*, for instance, with its farting contest, or in *The Advocate*, whose bedroom scene had to be severely edited to merit even an R rating, we should not be surprised. These motifs of sensual innocence are enormously accessible; thus, at a basic level, they seem "real." They are what I would call the common denominator of cinematic medievalism, accounting for the peculiar rooted feel of the medieval world on film, as well as its modest but steady box-office draw.

Someone might object at this point that primal pleasures are what movies—any movies—are all about, and that is true. But in medieval film, the raw sensuality of drinking, loving, and fighting belongs to a much larger ambience which is overtly tangible and sensible, the intimate caress of felt experience. In the world of medieval movies, one is not insulated from feeling anything. Clothing is uncomplicated and hand-made, and artificial textiles are unimaginable. The roughness of woven cloth alternates instead with the oriental mystery of silk, and with animal fur. None of these fabrics are waterproof: people get wet in medieval film. Or they are burned by the sun, and they smell. These characters are in touch with the world, perhaps painfully so, and no modern magic, no drug store, no insurance policy can prevent them from dealing directly with it.[5] Colin Firth, as the Advocate Courtois, leaves Paris for the much smaller town of Abbeville because he wants to be among real people, to help those who have a genuine need for him. Like Henry Thoreau, he would prefer to "live deliberately," and that is more or less what is promised by the world of medieval film, a post-romantic world, an unmediated confrontation with nature and oneself.

Needless to say, the felt experience of this world is seldom gentle. Violence is immanent, and in a stylized way has become virtually the trademark of medieval movies. For what is a medieval film without a joust—blood and iron, horses thundering, banners snapping in the wind, women privileged, imperiled, scheming? The fascination of the joust comes down to one point: the point of a lance "that may skewer me—or you," as Gawain tells Lancelot in Bresson's

Lancelot du Lac. The danger is direct and mortal. Precisely because we ourselves are so seldom threatened in this way, we want to see it. There is similar danger and fascination in the edged weapons that have always been necessary to this kind of film, the swords and knives that are continually at someone's throat, the staffs that bruise, the maces that break heads. Some sort of ritual activity is required to bring these keen tools into play, and so there are cold-blooded duels (Tim Roth, in *Rob Roy*, is to me the most frightening of these smiling assassins), as well as battle frenzy and the bitterness of the long siege. The most terrible violence is torture, the forcing of a person's will as the body becomes traitor and no mercy can come from anywhere. Elaine Scarry has written about torture with a relentless lucidity, concluding that it is done mainly to enhance the appearance, as well as the feeling, of power in those who torture.[6] But in medieval film, as in saints' lives, the power we feel is in the moral victory of the tortured. Examples abound, most vividly Mel Gibson as William Wallace in *Braveheart*, who is racked, eviscerated and finally hanged as the camera keeps rolling. But the burning of Joan of Arc, the Maid of Orleans, seems the quintessence of torture, perhaps because, having given herself utterly to obeying her "voices" and making France one, she seems to embody youthful innocence doubly betrayed by church and state. In any case, there have been many Joans in these movies, and it probably says something about the genre of medieval film that it has told her story more frequently than that of any other medieval person.

Joan of Arc's story compels our attention for many reasons, but chiefly, I believe, because there is no way out for her. She is doomed and therefore representative of the human condition as it is understood in medieval film. That seems a bit strong, no doubt, but the "doom" I am talking about is closer to its old sense of "judgment" than to apocalypse. The people of medieval film are "doomed" to be themselves and suffer the consequences thereof. This is what has been called the "tragic sense of life," as we encounter it in *Oedipus Rex* or in the *Iliad*; it has the difficulty of making human life hard, unforgiving and short, and the virtue of freeing that brief, glorious or shameful life from lingering guilt and grief over what one should have done.[7] You might object, and rightly, that Joan of Arc cannot be a tragic character because, after all, she becomes St. Joan, ascends to heaven, and by definition can have no tragic flaw. But in the worldly sense implied by her role as soldier to the French king, and by Cecil B. DeMille's silent film *Joan the Woman*, there is considerable sorrow and pity (and perhaps fear) in seeing this young life cut short by official cruelty, and every film about Joan exploits this aspect of her story in some way.

The inevitability of Joan's death at the stake is expressed in a more general way by the movies that have been made of Mark Twain's *A Connecticut Yankee in King Arthur's Court*, where the narrative ends with the hero's return to the

American present, as the English Middle Ages darken and fade beneath the appalling gloom of the Interdict, as Twain calls it. Twain has difficulty with endings—think of the end of *Huckleberry Finn*, or of his last work, *Letters from the Earth*[8]—but for the *Connecticut Yankee* films, it seems appropriate that medieval times end in stasis, while the inventive, pragmatic narrator returns to the challenge of his technological present.

For the world of medieval movies is not supposed to change, and its people are what they are: that is their mortal flaw and the main reason we love them. Whether they like it or not, there is "No Exit" for these characters. Their Middle Ages cannot be improved, but only reborn as the Renaissance, and so as medieval people they must deal with the way things are.[9] Our own culture tells us that there is always a better way, and so we contemplate the inescapable necessities of the medieval film world with a vague horror, but covertly admire the characters who can and will bear those burdens to the end of their short lives. Consequently, even though the quest narrative is the heart of medieval romance, in medieval movies it is the *failed* quest that most powerfully conveys their ethic of doomed strength. The crusades are probably the fundamental story of medieval failure, and I suspect that they resonate all the more strongly for us because the holy warriors return with the terrible awareness that they have only scars and the memories of war to show for their wasted years. One thinks of Antonius Block, the idealist, God-deserted knight of Bergman's *The Seventh Seal*, who has not found an echo to his faith, and now comes home where plague and death await him. In the Arthurian narratives, Arthur's Round Table is scattered by the fruitless Grail Quest, and the kingdom itself falls apart as Arthur loses Guinevere. But only when the director tries to graft a happy ending onto this tragic action, as in *First Knight*, do we feel that somehow we have been cheated. In this often ironic view of the Arthurian age, Richard Gere plays Lancelot, a (relatively) young soldier of fortune who inherits Guinevere once Arthur—played by a much older Sean Connery—has been shot full of arrows during the climactic siege of Camelot. The fortunate couple then rides away, rather pointlessly, into the future, leaving us to wonder what this story was about, since it was apparently *not* about the passing of all things, the fall of illustrious men, or the greatness of human endeavor in an imperfect world.

In their way, the Monty Python troupe gives us the most unmistakable sense of an unchangeably imperfect medieval world, because in their *Grail* movie they so relentlessly expose what must be the absurdity of medieval necessity when it is upstaged by the antic postmodern reality of consumer capitalism.[10] From this comic point of view, Arthur's grief over the Round Table is merely obsessive—he should lighten up, maybe go into the tourist business. But in medieval film, the failure of Arthur, the debacle of the crusades, the burning of the great Benedictine library in *The Name of the Rose*, which nearly breaks the heart of Brother William of Baskerville—these judgments on the human condition tell us that indeed men are mortal, sinful, and prone to error. Their works do not endure, their deeds live only in story. We go to the medieval movies partly to be reassured that we too are imperfect, necessarily so, but that with Arthur, Brother William, and St. Joan in mind, we too can endure our imperfection with the same desperate humility and strength.

Nel Mezzo del Cammin

Life is a journey, and nowhere more than in the medieval movies, where now is typically the middle of life's road, as Dante says. So many of these films begin with an arrival along this route.[11] *The Name of the Rose* opens as Brother William and young Adso ride slowly across the mountain meadows of northern Italy, headed for a brooding Benedictine Abbey on the skyline; *Ivanhoe* begins with Robert Taylor riding up to the walls of one more (this time, Austrian) castle, searching for Richard Lionheart, who is now a royal hostage; *The Advocate* begins with Richard Courtois riding a coach into the Norman French countryside, away from Paris to Abbeville, where (he thinks) people are innocent and the air is clear. Katharine Hepburn, Eleanor of Aquitaine in *The Lion in Winter*, arrives by boat; and at the beginning of *Excalibur*, the robed figure in silhouette against the flare of a burning town is Merlin as he strides purposefully toward Camelot, reason come to Uther's darkened mind. Let us concede that arrival is a convenient way to begin a narrative because it automatically creates complications, and medieval movies share this motif with many other films. Still, I would insist that travel is a key feature of medieval film because it is intimate and physical. There can be no significant movement without horses (of which, more later); walking is a real part of medieval life; and for Viking films like *The Thirteenth Warrior*, so is sailing. All of these modes have us lurching, limping, rolling along with the characters on screen, directly feeling the roughness of the ground or the surge of groundswell; and so once again we are "grounded" in medieval experience, vulnerable to it, and committed to the struggle at a fundamental level.

Travel in medieval movies is also social. Wagons are a slow, uncomfortable ride, and the people in them are forced to live at close quarters. The coach wagon bearing the Advocate Courtois to Abbeville also contains his dour law clerk, a little boy, his buxom, middle-aged, matter-of-fact mother, all of their baggage, as well as some chickens they are taking to town. Courtois falls asleep during the long hot ride, and upon waking realizes that everyone knows he has been having a nightmare. Even two men riding together are sharing an experience that practically requires them to communicate in some way, talking, planning, complaining, singing. In *The Seventh Seal*, Antonius Block and his squire Jöns do all of this and more as they ride up the Swedish coast, home from the crusades. Soon they will encounter a landscape devastated by the black plague—movement generally brings new opportunities and threats—but basically, travel in medieval films means new and continued interaction between people. It does not give us the High Plains Drifter, a lone rider out of nowhere, or the Road Warrior, moving alone through the sand and rust of a post-nuclear desert, or even a solitary boy and his sentient, post-nuclear dog. Medieval films are haunted not by the figure of Shane, but by Chaucer's pilgrims headed for Canterbury, and maybe headed for trouble on their easy three-day ride, but determined to assert themselves, in story, along the way.

In our own time, it is about an hour by train from London to Canterbury, but in Chaucer's day, and in all medieval films, the slow pace of travel means that space and time are immensely expanded, resulting in the increased importance of the here and now. When the horizon is a good part of a day's journey distant, one thinks twice before setting out for it. Villages and even towns are more isolated, more their own place. Roads, rivers, bridges and paths acquire a crucial importance; instead of being simply the way from here to there, each becomes problematic, a significant locus for events, almost an agent for generating narrative action. For the characters involved, this intensified sense of local place within an extended and largely inaccessible landscape means that the responsibility for action lies more heavily upon the individual and his or her group.[12] Leelee Sobieski, who played Joan of Arc in a recent movie with that title, may see that her friend Jean, and Pierre, her captain, have penetrated the English-held castle in disguise, but we know that it is much too late, the friendly troops cannot arrive in time. Riding toward the castle, they see a dark plume of smoke—the martyrdom is taking place, and it might as well be a thousand miles away.

In this kind of landscape, minutes and hours are displaced by days, weeks and even years. Messages arrive somehow—by foot, horse or boat—and coming from a relatively remote reach of space and time, they assume the character of mystery, promise or prophecy, each one a dim text emerging from past time, more puzzle than communication. Michael Crichton's novel *Timeline*,[13] which became a film, exploits this motif of remote communication through the device of time travel—a perilous journey, after which one's molecular structure can resemble a bad Xerox copy. And even beyond this liminal threat, the sense of isolation continues to grow. Lost eyeglasses become instant artifacts. Worn only yesterday in the twenty-first century, then lost today in the fourteenth, they could be found later this afternoon, back in the future, buried deep in a medieval ruin, having lain there for over 600 years. Remoteness in time is linked to distance in space. In every medieval film there is the unspoken yet felt sense of a limited, tangible, immediate, and usually endangered present surrounded at an uncertain distance by other towns, reaches of land, provinces, and kingdoms whose reality for those present exists largely as rumor or myth. The holy land is out there, to the East, somewhere. For the Gypsies in *The Advocate*, their home has been India, Egypt, and more recently Perpignan, all of them lying somewhere behind on the road of their endless wandering. In that sense, place in medieval movies is, as it were, intertextual but not contiguous, contextual (that is, lending a sense of place) but not much connected with other places.

What is it like to be in place in medieval movies? For the viewer, the experience may seem sensible and well-defined, yet isolated and existential, or, if that is too arcane, then archetypical, representative in its isolation and tending toward allegory. Where, after all, is Arthur's court, where is Camelot? It is the center, the heart of the realm, and who would ask further? In *The Return of Martin Guerre*, Gerard Depardieu plays Martin, come home from the wars. In fact, he is Pansette, a peasant imposter from another town in the region, but who would know such a thing? The village is its own place, and one lives there in a little world, in most ways separate from other lives outside. The hero in medieval movies is not alone in the landscape, but emplaced—embattled—in a social world of limited extent where relations and necessities are direct and pressing, and he (or she) is central to them.

To Horse

For the medieval movie, horses are the landscape come to life. If medieval heroes like William Wallace are icons of loyalty and truth, horses are iconic for chivalry and agriculture, in somewhat the same way that cathedrals are for the Church. As I said earlier, there can be no significant movement in medieval film without the horse. Movement, in turn, enables plots, for it creates potency, choice, possibility and connection. More than any other single motif, horses constitute both a practical and metaphoric bond between what Kenneth Burke called Actor and Scene, and I suspect they are fundamental as well to the ways in which viewers gain emotional and reflexive (that is, kinetic, physically reflexive) access to the experience of the film.

The importance of horses to medieval film is signaled by their invisibility. As in western movies, we expect to see horses, we know pretty much how they will appear, how they will be used, and so we take them for granted. As viewers, we tend to focus on pieces of architecture in long shots, and on people in mid-range or close shots, so the horses are simply there, part of the medieval scene, a little below our level of full awareness. Their impact on our reception of the film is enabled precisely by the transparent commonality of their presence.[14] For it is through the horse that the knight, the soldier, the fighting man or woman connects with the action and, as it were, enters the landscape. "The man on horseback" has been a cultural icon for many thousands of years because together they are an arresting sight—much taller than any man, and infinitely more powerful, faster, and dangerous. The man and his horse dominate their part of the landscape, and because it is possible that at any moment they could swiftly invade even more of its space, they represent potential action and are automatically the focus of our attention. The man, of course, is the real danger, for his intentionality makes the horse a weapon, and so it is that the man shares, and in a sense acquires, the beauty and power of his mount. (If the horse somehow takes control, throws the man or becomes a "runaway horse," the effect is reversed, and the man's loss of power is the source of comedy.)

The writers of epic and romance understood these practical and emotional bonds between man and horse. On Babieca, El Cid rides out of Valencia to meet Doña Jimena, and his great horse serves him well, now and always.[15] Gawain begins to recover himself, after three days of dalliance with Bertilak's wife, at about the time he recovers Gringolet, taking simple joy in how the people of the magic castle have fed him well and brushed down his coat.[16] An even more direct example drawn from film would be the recent *King Arthur*, a *Band of Brothers* sort of film where Arthur's Late-Roman Round Table are the medieval equivalent of the Magnificent Seven. Tristan is actually a Cossack, and Lancelot hails from the Russian steppes. In this film, swords ring from their scabbards with relentless frequency, and horses are big, rough and often at a run. At the end, though, with Lancelot and Tristan dead, closure is achieved at sunset through a voice-over—"It is said that the souls of great knights enter the lives of noble horses"—while we watch a final slow motion zoom shot of two remarkably beautiful horses in fluid gallop over the splendid green plains of Ireland. Together with their horses, then, the chivalric heroes of these films seem all the more beautiful, powerful, and noble. And because there are horses we also have the indispensable rituals of jousting and charging into battle.

The most stylish and realistic jousting I have seen in medieval film appears in *A Knight's Tale*, where Heath Ledger, as Will Thatcher, earns his skills with scrapes and bruises before he enters the lists. Perhaps because earlier in the film we have been shown, or at least told, what to look for in a joust, and certainly because the camera is closer, sometimes lower, the horses seem to leap into action, the men appear to be aiming their lances, and when they fall, they fall hard. The result is galvanizing. It is hard not to allow even the arrogant

Charleton Heston as Rodrigo Díaz de Vivar on Babieca in Anthony Mann's *El Cid* (1961).

young villain his measure of respect, for he has just been doing things on a horse that take our breath away. Still, the joust is a ritual, both in Will Thatcher's fourteenth century and in our medieval films. Its purpose was and is to showcase the hero, privilege his skill and courage, and, of course, to make him bleed a bit so as to deserve the attentions of his lady. Occasionally in medieval film, the irony of this purpose shows through. In Bresson's *Lancelot du lac*, a few Round Table knights have returned, disconsolate, from the hopeless grail quest, but then they are challenged to a tournament by the knights of Escalot. We watch them training with swords, tilting, exercising the horses. "Look at them," says Arthur, "they are happy now—it has given them something to do."

It would be reductive and cynical to describe medieval battle as "something for the knights to do," yet there is an edge of truth to that, and on film, the battlefield speeches, the charges (always at a hard run), the arrows, the mêlée and its bloody work—these motifs seem to repeat themselves ever more faithfully, picture after picture. Like true fans, however, we react by looking for new kinds of carnage we haven't seen before. I was surprised, for instance, when in *Joan of Arc*, Leelee Sobieski's horse fell down a bank, rolling completely over her (or over someone) in the process. Can horses do that? How could someone not be crushed if a horse rolled over on her?

But, in fact, horses play a deeper role in medieval battles. The archery that was decisive in the hundred years war had its terrible effect on men, but it was aimed primarily at the horses: without them, the heavily armed knights were helpless. Worse, fallen horses and men effectively halted the advance of the mounted knights behind them. As these cold-blooded truths begin to enter the films, we will probably see many a horse hit with arrows—something uncommon in earlier medieval movies, where shooting someone's horse was considered bad form, as it usually was in westerns. Indeed, the forbidden pain of horses in those early films implies another aspect of what I have called their invisible presence. Knights are supposed to bear pain quietly. Lancelot is the representative Arthurian knight in part because he carries out his duties to Arthur, and even Guinevere, without a murmur of complaint. In his exemplary self-denial we see the ascetic edge of the crusader knight, the soldier saint.[17] Unlike these self-sufficient warriors they carry, however, the horses in medieval movies need care. It is tacitly understood that they get tired, and cannot run or even walk forever without rest and food. They are easily wounded, feel pain and have emotions. We do not often see a knight caring for his horse, but we know without being told that the man on horseback is the head, and the horse—immensely stronger, yet more dependent, physical and vulnerable than he—is the heart of this ancient pairing.[18] In *Sir Gawain and the Green Knight*, Gawain's care for Gringolet tells us that his own conflict between body and soul, head and heart, can be resolved. In Bresson's *Lancelot du Lac*, Arthur's court occupies a minimalist set, some of it resembling a converted stable. But most striking is the frightened neigh, almost a cry from a horse somewhere off camera, a sound which conveys, if anything could, the oppressive anxiety of these knights whose goal is lost, whose king has lost the will to lead them, and who are waiting restlessly for their deaths. Bresson repeats this cry at intervals, using exactly the same taped sound each time, so that we begin to hear it as a leitmotif, an emotional marker in this tightly written, highly controlled film.

Historically, it is no accident that "chivalry" is derived from "cheval," the Old French word for horse. Chivalry was a way of life made possible by horses, and if its striking power and mobility were sustained by them, so were its vivid sense of style, its not-so-subtle eroticism and emotional resonance. To see how this ancient truth appears in movies, try an experiment: try to imagine a medieval movie without horses. No man on horseback, his mount circling and rearing its head, as he himself grows more impatient; no riders against the skyline, or ladies riding to the hunt; no teams breaking the sod on a spring day, no jousts, no mounted knights, swords drawn, thundering into battle. It is just impossibly flat without horses. Take them away and you deprive the medieval movie of its subconscious; and you deny the medieval film hero an understated, deeply felt counterpart to his identity.

Fables of Identity

In a way it is difficult to grasp the identity of the medieval hero. Yes, this one is Guenevere, that is Ivanhoe, Arthur, Eleanor. But what are they like, these distant mirrors of our selves? How shall we know how they feel, what they wish for, what drives them into battle, into exile, to the cloister? The traditional answer is that Ivanhoe, for example, is Robert Taylor the movie star: he is, in outline, what every man wants to be, what every woman wants; and "Ivanhoe" adds color to his figure, giving him a world, a life and a story line. In recent years, the construction of star identity has diminished to a degree, and younger actors play the ancient roles. So is it the rising star who defines the hero? Or the tension of a good script? Or is it a combination of meticulous production qualities—great photography, authentic costumes, good casting, a well-constructed set, big scenes shot on location, and careful attention to what seems historical detail? These emphases are the concerns of movie mavens and historians, and certainly they are helpful in judging the quality of a picture. But are we really any closer to cinematic medievalism—the way moderns conceive the Middle Ages through the medium of medieval film? What is so compelling about the hero of a good medieval movie, and why do we care?

This question targets the viewer as much as the medieval hero, for we experience the film narrative by adopting the perspective of the hero. His cause must be our cause, but also, less obviously, our cause must be his. Perhaps a story can guide us here. A few years ago I attended a performance of *Othello*, a Shakespeare in the Park production where the players acted on a raised platform, and we spectators sat around on blankets or folding chairs. The play began around eight p.m., near sunset, when the heat of the day began to fade. As we waited for the play to open, I was aware that a small group of people from the Society for Creative Anachronism had entered the park and passed behind us, but that is not unusual in our parks. It was later, when Othello was dead and the play over that I looked back and realized that the Society members had formed a tableau in a small field, beyond an arch of trees. They had carried in two high-backed wooden thrones, one for the "king," a fat young man in his robes, one for the queen, and to either side their attendants stood in elegant, mannered poses, like young men at court. There was still enough light to see them in dark outline, motionless, as they had been throughout the entire performance. What were they doing there? They were not part of the play, and were too far away to hear any of it. Later, it occurred to me that the playing of *Othello* had created an historical space, and the society members had extended that space through their own presence—a royal audience, of a sort, and the better for being distant, solitary and silent. They wanted not to see Elizabethan drama, but to dwell in it somehow, and this they could do *by being seen* as inhabitants of its historical space.

Those young people had found a practical way of being in the medieval world. Using their example as an entry, let us speculate about what it is in such a world that they, or any viewer, might be seeking. I imagine that what the Society members were acting out in their sunset tableau was fundamentally an attitude, an endorsing of commitment. To be king, to serve a king, or to be married to him is to give oneself to an institution, at least (but more likely) to a purpose—no, the imagination is not content with that—to an *ideal* of some kind. In so doing we escape, or possibly transcend, ourselves. That is really what medievalism, or any -ism, is about. But even an imaginative commitment to an ideal is only possible through tangible things, common materials but resonant of another world, in this case the Middle Ages. To put it a different way, the ideals of medievalism are reified, made perceptible and apparently brought closer to us through material things, through swords and other weapons, and through the fighting, work and pleasure—drinking and dancing, for instance—that we associate with medieval people.

But the material world is only the beginning of cinematic medievalism. So far we have laid the ground for a good costume drama about the Middle Ages, but I don't think we have scratched, or rather pierced, the skin of the medieval hero. Let us think about medieval necessity, beginning with the physical—hunger and cold will do nicely. In the recent Joan of Arc movies, one may expect to see Joan's breath smoking in the winter chill of northern France, and this tiny detail brings us into the landscape with her. Banquets are, of course, an old standby of medieval movies, just as eating and drinking are an important part of detective thrillers; in each case, food compensates for what is felt to be the bleakness of life outside the castle, or out there in the mean streets. Then there is the necessity of making a living in the unforgiving medieval economy. Every sou, every penny is precious, we see. *The Advocate* begins with Richard Courtois arriving at the Abbeville Inn, where he is met by Madame Langlois, the Innkeeper, a forbidding, flint-eyed woman with a vast girth and a certain amount of sardonic wit. "Beans and sausage?" she offers. He makes the mistake of quoting a few lines about the beautiful simplicity of pastoral fare. "No sausage," she concludes, turning ponderously toward the kitchen.[19]

Our feeling for medieval movies begins with simple needs like these, the sensory details of physical being, which have us identifying with the medieval hero without consciously thinking about it. Danger and threat are also faces of necessity, of course, and so are pain and death. Medieval movies are compelling because they make these fears tangible and perceptible—the medieval hero can't get out of it, must face the threat, and we with him. Of course, when the tangible threat is denied us, when there is something unexplainably wrong in the town of Abbeville—small boys are dying, and no one will talk about it—then the threat is even worse, for who knows whether the Gypsies might be part of it, or the malice of Satan, embodied in a murderous black pig. The Middle Ages, in such movies, are an inner state. The dark superstitions that haunt *The Advocate*, the fear of the plague and God's judgment that torture Sweden in *The Seventh Seal*—these are fears that begin in tangible threats and work their way inward to form habits of mind, and here we have come a little closer to what it means for us to lift the burdens and briefly share the lives of Richard Courtois, Antonius Block, and the other medieval heroes.

We might say, then, that the marvelously solid, in some ways primitive, surface of medieval movies—a life where taxes are paid in coin, paper is rare, and light comes from candles—creates our feel for the medieval world, and we understand the general anxiety when that solid surface does not explain the event, as when the Benedictine monks of the great mountain abbey begin to die in *The Name of the Rose*. But it is equally true that the weight of familiar things by themselves would be oppressive, like a tedious documentary, if not for a compensatory move toward the intangible, the world of medieval fear, faith and imagination. The commission of sin may be as ordinary as cursing a neighbor or stealing a loaf of bread, but its significance is inward, requiring absolution, the ministrations of a priest, perhaps even a formula—a charm—pronounced in the Latin language. As medievalists, we know the medieval penchant for symbolic thinking, whereby practically everything must be understood as meaning something beyond itself, so that even normal objects and events are perceived as an integument, or cover, beneath which lies the hidden reality they manifest. Medieval movies satisfy this human hunger for meaning in a different, perhaps simpler way. Comforted by the familiar, we must then be threatened, blessed, or charmed by the strange.

For instance, given the ordinary greed and lust of King Uther in *Excalibur*, we are more than ready for the ambivalently canny Merlin, who has much more on his mind than this barbarous dark age monarch. Merlin is wise—better, he is wisdom incarnate. Being nearly immortal, he has a long learning curve. Not a warrior, not even a human being, he is somehow mysteriously one with the woods and waters, and with the Dragon whose spirit runs beneath the world and binds its substance. Unlike Uther, Merlin can take the long view, and through him, the rustic, almost clownish chivalry in which Arthur grows up gives way to a sober dream of justice and order. The plot needs Merlin, all right, but so does everything else in this gorgeous but rather heavy-handed movie. Asked why he played Merlin the way he did, with goofy chuckles and blank gazes in between moments of dark prophecy, Nicol Williamson said he thought Merlin had to be unpredictable and a bit other to be a convincing wizard, so if his humor is not that of Arthur and the court, so much the better.[20] Merlin, with his uncanny humor and fey wisdom, gives the crowded *Excalibur* enough space and air for our imagination to breathe properly. Gandalf, the wizard in the *Lord of the Rings* trilogy, has a similar elfish wit, and he isn't really human either. Even Sean Connery, as Brother William in *The Name of the Rose*, is a bit strange, being an intellectual, as most of the monks are not, and an elderly Franciscan in love with Aristotle, as Christian Slater's teenage Adso is, at this point, not. There are many other figures of wisdom in medieval movies, for cinematic medievalism would be incomplete, would seem airless, rootless, and not a very satisfying world at all, without their infinite reach.

From wisdom, I should like to pass on to love, for that too is intangible and necessary, but to my own surprise, love in the medieval movies seems more an alloy with loyalty and identity. One of the great love stories of medieval film is that of Lancelot and Guinevere. But story after story, as we go from *The Sword of Lancelot* to *Camelot*, *Lancelot du lac*, *Excalibur* and *First Knight*, we find that the major theme is Lancelot's love and loyalty to *both* Guinevere and Arthur. Yes, of course he loves her, but *who* he is depends upon being true to both of them, just as in Malory. In *The Name of the Rose*, the boyish Adso falls in love with a girl from the peasant village below the abbey. When she escapes burning, she wants him (*we* want him!) to stay with her, but of course he turns his donkey and follows his master, William of Baskerville, into a monastic future. Richard Courtois, in *The Advocate*, falls in love with Samira ("Summer Wind"), a Gypsy girl, but finally she will not go with him to Paris. She could love him, but she thinks she is not quite human for him, not a beast, as the villagers imagine, but a splendid fine creature to have by his fire and in his bed. The film that comes closest to presenting a real love story is, of all things, *The Seventh Seal*—not Antonius Block's exhausted return to his wife after ten years, but the married love of Jof and Mia, the two players who travel Sweden in their little wagon with their baby Mikael. Their story is simple, intimate and sweet, a fairy tale come to life. Yet the significance of this love for the rest of the film lies partly in the obvious parallel with Joseph, Mary and Jesus (Jof sees visions of the Holy Mother and her child), and partly in the famous scene where Mia offers Block some strawberries and a bowl of fresh milk. And with the milk, this weary, disillusioned man seems to gather innocence and strength into himself—enough to go on, enough for one more turn at chess with Death. So I will not argue that love is a theme that dominates medieval film, even though its men and women care for each other and do many things for love. Loyalty, however, is a dominant theme in these movies. Not that we ourselves lack it, perhaps, but in a world that is harder, and in some ways simpler than our own, loyalty often seems absolute, a human ideal come to life.

So the medieval hero is wise and loyal? If so, he would be monstrous—worse, he would be dull. Yet wisdom and loyalty are issues for every medieval hero, and as he struggles with them we are insensibly drawn into his story—it becomes "medieval" for us. The same is true for faith, the last great intangible, for it begins in the ordinary places of life, but extends beyond wisdom and loyalty—and, of course, beyond life itself. In our fairly secular age, it is hard to discuss faith without being mired in religious politics, so let us go back to Thomas Becket, in the film of that name, where Richard Burton plays the thorny, ambitious young Saxon who becomes Lord Chancellor of England. But then, through the extravagant folly of Henry II, he is also appointed Archbishop of Canterbury. Becket tries to refuse this high ecclesiastical appointment; but once he has accepted it, he bows to the will of no man, not even his king. Is he merely stubborn, is this yet another of his clever political schemes? The truth is even stranger than the cynical Henry (Peter O'Toole) could have predicted. Becket, having become Archbishop, lives and dies as the servant of God and the Pope in Rome, for this clerical post is more real for him than politics: it is connected to something that is, for him, most real. Henry is surprised, and possibly so is Becket.

As viewers, we struggle to imagine this kind of stubborn faith in a hard-nosed political man like Thomas Becket, and I suppose we wonder if we ourselves are capable of it. But if we attend medieval movies, we will often contend with this doubt because so many of them resemble, in one way or another, the agon of a saint's life. This is the context in which we can best understand Antonius Block, the searcher for God in a desert of stones. Or Brother William, in *The Name of the Rose*, called once more to serve the Holy Inquisition for purposes he cannot accept, but with the assurance of being its victim if he does not. Or Bertrande, the wife of Martin Guerre, who finally gives up their ruse and exposes him to justice, surely because that is how she can save her children, but perhaps also because it is simply wrong, before man and God, to take from another person the name, the identity—indeed, the "substance" of who he is. These are terrible choices, but none worse than that of Joan of Arc. Renée Falconetti's Joan in Carl Dreyer's *La Passion de Jeanne d'Arc* seems the most innocent of all martyrs, and that she should be burned for believing in God and King Charles questions our faith in justice itself.

In some ways the most touching trial of faith, and one that involves a professional experience, is the struggle of Richard Courtois, the Advocate, to reconcile the local politics of church, state and the landed gentry with his faith in the law. Does it make sense to hang a pig for the death of a child, when it is obvious that the real killer is still at large? What logic is there in hanging a pig at all, unless under *lex naturalis* both pigs and men are subject to God's law, and that society be made whole and its fears banished, no crime can remain unpunished. When as viewers we begin to worry about monstrous crimes, natural law, and what it is to be human, then we have entered the world of medieval film, and we begin to see what part it might play for us beyond the final credits.

Our Lady of Pain

In movies where life is a journey punctuated by adventure, we enter the country of romance, where disguise and recognition entertain us until the final disclosure of identity.[21] Identity is excruciatingly important for the medieval hero. Always he is tempted by companions, by women, sometimes by the promise of happiness, and occasionally by the promise of life itself. But the heroes of these movies remain frighteningly true to their ideals—to *themselves*—despite their difficult tasks, which more often than not involve enormous pain.[22] Shortly I will discuss our own central need to identify with someone true to him or herself, for that, I believe, is why we find these movies so peculiarly compelling; but first let us think about the hero's difficulties and the pain they bring him.

Early in her extended meditation on pain, *The Body in Pain: The Making and Unmaking of the World*, Elaine Scarry argues that the fundamental truth for those who suffer is isolation. In pain, we dwell in a world where no one else can be. That is, in part, its terror.[23] But for the purposes of medieval film, pain's isolation of the hero helps us accept the reality of his or her situation, and to empathize. On screen, as in life, our eyes are drawn to the person, or even the animal in pain, and we are swift to suspend disbelief. In effect, pain becomes a feature of authenticating realism in narratives of all kinds; we respect its awful need at a level somewhere beneath our conscious attention.[24] Perhaps for this reason, Freud linked pain with what he called "the reality principle," which has first claim on our attention, distinctly before "the pleasure principle."[25] Our response to others' pain probably derives from our underlying fear of it, and our superstitious wish to fend it away from ourselves by giving serious attention, at least, to the one who suffers.

Living a harder life than our own in most cases, medieval heroes are not onscreen long before they are troubled, afflicted, and wounded by the world. And because they are representative figures, their suffering is meaningful and significant beyond their own lives. Like the martyred saints, medieval heroes undergo a *trial* of faith, religious faith for some, and for the rest, being true to an ideal or to themselves.[26] Hence their suffering becomes "a sign that points to a realm of eternal truth beyond the perishable body" (129), as David Morris says.[27] In a sense, they suffer for us, just as the saints, enduring their agonies, were understood to be reenacting Christ's passion, a pain that redeemed others.

The most egregious example of a hero suffering for an ideal is probably Mel Gibson's William Wallace, whose torturings in *Braveheart* take up so much of the film that Wallace's pain begins to seem its main point. Surely his ordeal at the hands of the English is metonymic, a metaphor suggesting the iron fist of the aging King Edward I. But mainly the grudge is personal for Wallace, who has seen his father and other villagers hanging from the rafters of a barn. In *The Advocate*, Maître Richard Courtois endures a pained bewilderment at the human condition as he observes Abbeville's ignorant yet crafty townspeople being preyed upon by the nobles, the church, and, not least, the men of law. Isolated from the townspeople by his profession and from those in power by his idealism, he reels through a drunken nightmare, an infernal vision shot through with dark imaginings of who or what is preying upon the boy children of the town. His struggles to understand Abbeville are like our own groping attempts to fathom his fifteenth-century angst, and to find our own position on human identity as it is reflected in the mirror of legal and political philosophy. What, after all, is man, when pigs and "witches" are hanged as scapegoats?

But the pain of heroes and martyrs has another dimension, and that is its "power to transcend the world and the flesh."[28] In pain, one is alone, but its very isolation may become a visionary experience beyond the material world, a communion with the divine or with transcendent truth. For visionary saints like St. Catherine or St. Teresa, pain is "a sign that always points beyond itself. It gestures toward an ecstatic union with God in which suffering is finally indistinguishable from love."[29] Such is the typical film ending of Joan of Arc, who looks toward heaven as the flames begin to climb and leap, her face expressing a kind of joy. And in the strange, ambivalent ending of Bergman's *Seventh Seal*, at the apocalyptic moment when death comes to take them all, and almost all are silent in fear, the young servant girl looks directly into the camera, her face rapt, innocent, shining with light, speaking for them all—"It is finished." Whatever the hero's pain in medieval film, the experience is likely to build toward transcendence, not necessarily a wisdom beyond what we can know, but a kind of cursed/blessed state, earned by more than human endurance, in which the hero has somehow risen above the importunate demands of the world—its cold, hunger, exhaustion and disease, not to mention the mailed glove of power and the knife of betrayal.

The medieval hero is torn and suffers in these ways, and we care about it, not only because we feel the pain of William Wallace, but because we ourselves need to be torn, and to suffer the consequences of being who we are and doing as we must.[30] It may be that more than any other kind of film, medieval movies cause us to invest ourselves in the identity of the hero because, having entered the experience of Lancelot, St. Joan, or even Richard Courtois or William of Baskerville, we are steadied: within the matrix of their trials and temptations, we are able to confront ourselves. Held by the medieval moment, we import our own burdens, the faiths and ideals we quietly stand for, and defend them within the charmed reality of its film-historical space. The heroes and their fraught medieval situations make life's necessities tangible and pressing, rendering possible and visible the idealism and self-sacrifice that thrill and frighten us. For us, as for them, the greatest need is to transcend ourselves. And once having tasted the hard-won freedom, having walked with Lancelot and the rest, we are closer to going that way on our own.

PART I

Chapter One

Authenticity

What are the authenticating features of medieval film, the ways it leads us to accept what we see on screen as a convincing version of the medieval world? Let us begin with the realism of Johan Huizinga's historical narrative in his classic *The Waning of the Middle* Ages, then pass to its close cousin, cinematic medievalism. Both of them attract us on sensible but also spiritual levels, and are constructed from mundane details that yield a realistic narrative surface. I will try to show how such details enhance the image, character and thematic force of the film hero, whose reflective, painful life reveals our own, as if in shadow.

"To the world when it was half a thousand years younger," Huizinga begins, "all experience had yet to the minds of men the directness and absoluteness of the pleasure and pain of child-life .... We, at the present day, can hardly understand the keenness with which a fur coat, a good fire on the hearth, a soft bed, a glass of wine, were formerly enjoyed."[1] From sensations he moves to sentiments, for emotions, too, were closer to the surface in medieval times: everyday life had a "tone of excitement and ... passion," veering as it did "between despair and distracted joy, between cruelty and pious tenderness."[2] Huizinga's great history presents medieval life as sensuous and immediate—thus, in a basic sense, authentic. The close attention to tiny details of mundane experience, the emphasis on human suffering, on the emotional extremes of terror, exaltation, or joy, the sense that a meaning, indeed a complex of meanings lay behind ordinary acts and perceptions, lending them a significance beyond themselves and a kind of order—these and other authenticating devices are the means by which Huizinga creates a medieval world which has the density and immediacy of lived experience. Consequently, the affect of his historical narrative is very like that of cinematic realism.

For despite their mythic overtones and romance coloring, medieval movies, like medieval histories, have to deliver a convincing picture of life.

Costume dramas and sword and sorcery fantasies we reject out of hand, just as we smile at the paradings of the Society for Creative Anachronism. Nonetheless, the authenticity we suppose we are looking for proves elusive. Would we recognize real medieval life even if we saw it? And if medieval reality appeared to us like a living photograph, what would be the charm of that artless, unaesthetic view? Some films do indeed gain our assent, but it is not necessarily historical accuracy that moves our acceptance, or brilliant dialogue or camera work. We connect with the world of the film when we can share some difficulty, some desire that is simplified, made a little strange, and in a way vitalized by *what we can accept* as authentically medieval. With that, our resistance fades and the scene breaks upon us with the force of real experience.

The best medieval films have this kind of power because they invite us to collaborate with them in what could be called a shared cinematic medievalism. For a discussion of medieval movies, we can use a visual metaphor and define medievalism as simply looking backward and, as Cervantes put it, imagining our past. When medieval films are made and when they are viewed, modern ideas and sensibilities are projected backward into the past, shaping and being shaped by what is known of the medieval world. What is constructed in this kind of activity is a communal fantasy, since writers, directors, viewers, and even historical consultants tacitly agree to accept—if only within the purview of the movie—the same version of medieval reality. This agreed upon fantasy is the core truth of every medieval film. Something that lived in the imaginations of writers and directors is brought to the screen in such a way that it breaches the walls of our disbelief, and, insensibly, we begin to contribute from our own experience, adapting the shared vision to create our own perception of the medieval world.

The medieval film world comes to us as a romantic vision, then, in a sense that Wordsworth would have recognized. But what is it, exactly, that enables us to suspend our disbelief? In a basic sense, medieval film, like Huizinga's narrative, engages the senses and the emotions directly, heightening our perception of common life. Yet it is not merely, or not only, a version of primitivism— neither a pastoral idyll nor what Eco has called "shaggy medievalism."[3] Searching for immediacy in medieval experience, and for authenticating features that suggest it, will lead us not only through the blood and mire of medieval battles (e.g., *Henry V*), the dark, smoky interiors of peasants' huts (*The Return of Martin Guerre*), or exuberant barnyard sex (*The Advocate*), but also into experience one might call spiritual or intellectual. There can be a piercing emotional quality to the lives of saints—Saint Joan (*Jeanne d'Arc*), for instance, or Saint Francis, to mention two frequently filmed stories. Even Brother William of Baskerville (Sean Connery in *The Name of the Rose*), despite his deft intellectual style, is drawn into a crisis of identity and potential self-sacrifice.

The characteristic immediacy of medieval film attracts us on two levels, then: first through the senses and emotions, but, more importantly, also through the linked problems of loyalty, faith and identity. Medieval film privileges felt experience but also subjectivity—the sense of self—which is problematized in the best of these movies, so that characters, as well as the viewers who identify with them, must struggle intimately with the hard questions of who we are, what we serve, and why. Films like *The Advocate*, *The Return of Martin Guerre*, and *The Seventh Seal* retain their peculiar impact of authentic medieval experience because their problems are, in real and insistent ways, our own. Forced to confront them *within the historical world of these movies*, we shed much of our protective armor—our enabling insensibility—and battle our/their problems as if we were peasants, princes, saints ... people for whom identity had an immediate, tangible importance. It is the sensible and spiritual poignancy of their human experience that makes the best medieval films feel authentic; and this particular form of authenticity—realistic yet reflective—is the definitive quality of cinematic medievalism.

"Definitive quality?" That high, clear vision is like viewing distant peaks before the climb. If medieval movies have such qualities, they derive from the infinite ordinary details that help create the illusion of the "medieval" on film. These authenticating features that we are about to examine—some of them elementary and scarcely noticeable—provide us with a practical means, perhaps a kind of vocabulary for discussing medieval films and their heroes.

What seems real or authentically medieval in a film depends largely upon perceptual realism—what we see there. Still, our first impression in a medieval film is generally formed by what we are told. There will be a voice-over or perhaps a text moving up the screen that frames the upcoming story, telling us when and where it occurred and what the complications were—war, plague, hunger, for example—and how people were reacting to them. Every medieval movie has a frame story. To a degree, the framing statement establishes genre, just as fairy tales have to begin with "Once upon a time." Implicit is the assumption that we will be testing our own experience against this tale of olden times, and that is part of the fun. It invites our *interaction* with what we encounter in the story, which in turn creates a bias in favor of accepting it as a substitute for real experience. Also understood in a peripheral way is the framing assertion's truth claim. Merely by making the statement (i.e. "These are medieval times"), the narrator asserts its truth, thereby bringing to bear what Grodal, in his study of "Realism in Audio-Visual Representation," has called "a central means of transmitting a feeling of reality and factuality."[4] In effect, because at the very beginning we are told it is going to be authentically medieval, we become willing to suspend our disbelief.

Very quickly the framing statement ends (the more quickly for films with broad demographics), and some kind of action begins, if it has not been in progress since the beginning. Often the opening shot places us in company with someone on a journey—such as monks riding slowly across mountain meadows toward a forbidding Benedictine abbey, as in *The Name of the Rose.* Or my own guilty pleasure, the opening of *Excalibur*, where, waiting in the Wagner-tormented dark, we see a point of brightness out in the barren lands, a torch—Merlin!—coming to shed some light on Uther's benighted realm. The need for onscreen action is so obvious as to escape notice if we were not scrutinizing what feeds the roots of medieval film realism. The perceptual processes which create our basic sense of reality are linked to our "motor-based relations to the world.... Those things, those perceptions are real that can guide our (re)actions."5 In other words, we tend to see something as real when we have already had the experience of reacting to it or something like it. In extreme cases we find our muscles twitching as we watch, as if we ourselves had to ward off a sword stroke or enter the dance. This basic reactivity is fundamental to our response to most movies, and when the range of action is severely restricted, as it is in Bresson's *Le Procès de Jeanne d'Arc*, where Joan and her prosecutor recite the words of the trial with frozen faces, their bodies rigid, we are acutely aware of its lack. Furthermore, given our preconceptions of the medieval world, we probably associate the authentically medieval with particular kinds of physical action—men on horseback, for instance, or swordplay, plowing, and prayer.

Going further with this topic would require a list of prototypical acts, an iconography of deeds that say "medieval." But that would have to be an open-ended list, for there is really no end to medieval activities—and would that endless list bring us any closer to the origin of our sense of the authentic? In medieval film narratives, as in medieval romances, the jousting, feasting, journeying seize one's attention, yet our ultimate concern is not the events themselves but the inner logic which determines the sequence, severity, tonality and finally the significance of events. The logic, or relevance of the action, depends upon the character or, to be precise, the agency of the medieval protagonist. That is why a discussion of cinematic medievalism must focus not merely on the experience represented by the film, but on heroic experience, the ways in which the action expresses the subjectivity—the identity, abilities, background, problems and desires—of the film's hero.

One might suppose the hero creates the action merely by riding out boldly into the landscape, but that is exactly wrong. In heroic narratives, the action occurs in precisely the ways which best demonstrate the hero's courage and limitations, and reveal the inevitability of the conclusion. The mechanism is that he or she must make choices. The need for Bertrande to choose between the two men who claim to be Martin Guerre, her husband, is paradigmatic for all heroes that we care about. Such choices demonstrate the inner logic of the narrative, but—and this is important for our sense of the authentic—they also dramatize the problematic nature of the medieval experience. Given a hostile world and their own resurgent weaknesses, human beings must make hard choices, plan carefully, deny their fears and defer desires. Hence the primary way we participate in medieval film is by taking upon ourselves the hero's problems, planning, feeling his or her hesitation—trying to figure out what we would do in Lancelot's place, for example, had we his beauty and strength, that touching loyalty, and Guinevere.

Perhaps this is the moment for a procession of our medieval heroes—the somber knights (*The Seventh Seal*), tragic queens (*The Lion in Winter*), exalted saints (*La Passion de Jeanne d'Arc*) ... even an idealistic lawyer or a philosophic monk (*The Advocate, The Name of the Rose*). They pass in review and they are splendid. They are the main reason we came to the medieval movies in the first place. And yet the range of medieval film heroes is not as broad as that of, say, detectives in mainstream films. It is as hard to imagine a medieval anti-hero as it is a cowboy with a dark heart. It might be argued, certainly, that Robin Hood can sustain a negative role, but perhaps that is only because we like him better when he can cause real trouble for an unjust state. A sardonic Robin Hood might play well as a satiric figure, but medieval film satire tends to be, like Monty Python's work, an unheroic medium. Still, ironic heroism would create some interesting possibilities, and the unlikely heroes of *A Knight's Tale* and *First Knight* may indicate a move toward that kind of authenticity.

What about women as heroes in medieval film? Some have said the female heroes are rather predictable—martyred saints, yes, and tragic Guineveres and Iseults, but Marjory Kempe? Margaret Paston? Perhaps that is unfair, but as with the male heroes, the range of roles does not seem especially broad. It would be interesting if we had a film about mad Margery Kempe, but the world of medieval movies is deeply dyed in the colors of romance and folktale, and it is most unlikely (although much to be hoped) that we will soon see films like *The Return of Martin Guerre* starring heroes like Margery (Judi Dench would play her well, though). What we do have at present is an intriguing variety of mostly aristocratic or saintly female heroes, at least one of them dark-hearted, if that is what one could call Morgana, the tarty villainess of *Arthur's Quest*, who is a kind of anti–Wonder Woman.

More important is the general principle that whoever the hero happens to be, he or she tends to be reflective by nature and will probably suffer considerable pain of some kind in the course of the film. Let us look at some heroes, then. At the beginning of *The Advocate*, just after the framing statement and the opening credits, we are treated to a close-up of ... a crow. This fellow darts his head here, there, behind, with a bird's impossible quickness, while the sound track plays a brooding theme we soon come to know as "the lawyer's music." CUT to the coach entering town, where the Advocate Courtois, recently of Paris, has fallen asleep; and as he peers out into the dark, drizzling night of his dream, we see the first of his long, pondering, brown-eyed gazes. These long looks recur throughout the film, helping to create the rhythm of its scenes and keying its major themes (the idealistic Courtois, having left the wicked city for the small, unhappy town of Abbeville, is there to see and sift *everything*, even if he can't improve it). The crow moves us toward the idea of Courtois as an eagle-eyed representative of truth and justice, and Courtois himself shows us that there is much to ponder in fifteenth-century France.

For the viewer, these long, thoughtful glances are an invitation to enter the film, to interact by pondering along with the Advocate questions of natural law and human identity that in the context of the film seem unavoidable. As we commit ourselves to weighing these questions and their context, the town of Abbeville—with its corrupt prosecutor, the lord with his frigid humor, the compromised priest—becomes real for us. Other examples of silent, expressive eyes come easily to mind, the most striking of them being Renée Falconetti's heartbreaking gazes aloft in *La Passion de Jeanne d'Arc*, and Tilda Swinton's very long, ambivalent gazes into the camera in *Orlando*, but also Richard Burton's quandaries in *Becket*, Sean Connery's puzzling in *The Name of the Rose*, or even Richard Harris's Arthur (*Camelot*), whose agony of indecision shows us the tragic necessity of his role, giving it a credibility that is mostly lacking in Malory.

Arthur is reflective, but he is also in pain, torn between Guinevere, his heart, and Lancelot, who is his right hand. Let us acknowledge at once that pain can hardly be separate from jousting, medieval warfare, or even the ravages of medieval weather, hunger, and disease. Courtly love (or any love!) is almost sure to involve pain, and so is death, abandonment, and the seven deadly sins. But pain is more than an incidental result of authentic medieval life; pain is itself a primary authenticating feature. We tend to take narrative seriously, we consider it more lifelike, more authentic "when vital human (or animal) concerns [are] at stake," Grodal says.[6] And pain, or the possibility of it, raises the stakes without our even thinking about it. Grodal's analysis of this equation is illuminating:

> [Because] a strong feeling of reality [requires] that vital human or animal concerns be at stake, "realism" is more often attributed to representations that portray negative emotions than those that portray positive emotions. This is perhaps based on the assumption that "pain" is more real than "pleasure," thus evoking more genuine behavior.[7]

One. Authenticity   29

We remember, he adds, that Freud called the associative mechanisms linked to pain the "reality principle," as opposed to the "pleasure principle."[8]

But if pain signifies the harsh reality of the human condition, is it also an authenticating force in medieval film? Examples do come to mind, beginning with the trivial and leading quickly to the excruciating scenes that have

Kirk Douglas as Einar on his dragon ship in Richard Fleischer's *The Vikings*, MGM (1958).

over time become synecdochic for what viewers expect in medieval film. The trivial, for me, would be a sad group of extras—old men, women, young children and youths—standing miserably in a cold Norwegian rain, their rough clothing soaked, breaths smoking as they watch Kirk Douglas's Viking ship row up the fjord (*The Vikings*). It *did* seem authentic. As for the excruciating, various scenes are contenders, but being burned at the stake has a ritual starkness that gives it pride of place over the other agonies. One thinks of the many Joan of Arcs who have died thus in medieval film (and no, it would be hideous to think about which deaths were most realistic, affecting, or noble). But this motif has been used in other contexts—the burning of the fool, the peasant girl and the heretic monk in *The Name of the Rose*, for example, or the young girl who is burned in *The Seventh Seal*. Antonius Block, the weary, God-deserted knight, kneels over the condemned girl and, with an exhausted pity which amplifies our sense of her death's blind pointlessness, gives her an anodyne before she is burned.

If we think of medieval life as vulnerable to cold, hunger, war and pestilence, it probably seems natural to accept its promise of pain, the pain lending weight to that experience, a burden of the real. Virtually every medieval film provides additional examples. We have only to remember that the pain does not have to be bloody or physical to create authenticity. In the best of these films, pain can be subtle indeed.

More commonly, however, the pain in medieval movies *is* physical and bloody, and that is because our sense of the real is fundamentally visual: we tend to believe what we see. And we can extend this foundation. Herakleitos said, in a kind of mantra, "For to know and to be are the same." But if that is true, since seeing and knowing are so closely linked, perhaps we could say that seeing and being are also similar. Seeing tells us not only where we are, but also, in a basic sense, who we are. Since we are reactive entities, our identity derives from our surroundings, what we move toward, against, or away from. For film, perceptual realism is central. We watch something happen on screen, and whether it is the fifteenth century or the Old West, it becomes reality for us: we live it for about 100 minutes, and we live it partly as Lancelot or Joan of Arc, because we unconsciously react to the perceptual world as he or she (like any hero) focuses it for us.

How do we judge the visual authenticity of a medieval film—why does *The Return of Martin Guerre* look real while *Excalibur* does not (*pace*, fans of that gloriously bad movie!)? That judgment depends largely on the viewer's knowledge, but first let us address the aspects of perceptual reality that seem universal. "All other things being equal," Grodal says, "*perceptual uniqueness and complexity enhance the feeling of realism*, because the representation is directly simulated in our brains as if we were confronted with reality."⁹ Stones are an idea to us, but a small oval stone polished by a mountain brook, gray granite flecked with mica, this is the stone in hand, both in life and on film. In a perceptual sense, realistic castle walls and convincing heroes are like that stone. And the more we enjoy the hero's looks and mannerisms, the better established and more particular his character must also be to sustain the illusion of authenticity.

In *The Seventh Seal*, for instance, Antonius Block is a tall, fine looking knight whose role tends toward the allegorical—he plays chess with Death, after all. But his face reflects an endless quest, and close-up shots reveal his emptiness. The face of William Wallace in *Braveheart* is constantly before us in close-up, whether he is weeping, raging, or wearing barbaric face paint. Here we identify with the man, not so much the idea. We want him real and beautiful in close-up—hence the long hair, the face paint, the mask of battle-rage as the ragged ranks of Scots and English race toward each other with axes and claymores held high—and we require consistency in his role. We need to see the emotions in that face translated into body language (notice how Wallace *walks* in this movie, every stride strong, as if he were advancing against an enemy). His every action must imply the reach and depth of his character.

"Perceptual uniqueness" is crucial. We go to medieval movies for chivalric gore, for smoky banquet halls and elegant women, darkly bright. Many of us will never forget the unearthly beauty of Elizabeth Taylor as Rebecca in *Ivanhoe*. Others will remember Olivia Hussey in the same role, or Michelle Pfeiffer in *Ladyhawke*. It isn't only that we fall in love with Taylor's face, or identify with it, though these responses are strong and instinctive. It is more that her face gives emotional strength to what seems authentic and meaningful in her life. In the battles, banquet halls and bedrooms, but far more in the faces of these medieval heroes, we feel what William Wallace feels for Scotland under England's iron fist, and we sense the pride and sadness of medieval Jews wherever they were. In the best of our movies, a face can have a layered strength that underlies the illusion of medieval realism.

But when viewers argue the authenticity of a film, or (more often) the lack of it, they often mean realism based on decorum, or fittingness. One hesitates to complain that a director put a fifteenth-century bridle on a fourteenth-century horse (although critics can be pretentious in that way), but some flaws—a prominent anachronism, or an accent which strongly reminds us of a modern time or place (one thinks of Kevin Costner's casual surfer-boy inflection in *Robin Hood, Prince of Thieves*)—do tend to destroy the illusion: the perceptual complexity is compromised, historical depth disappears, and we are left looking at a movie set.

Hollywood often makes these mistakes (experts tell us that very little of what we see is historically accurate), but how seldom it is that a lapse of authenticity tears the fabric of the viewer's *sense* of the authentic. We are quite tolerant of inconsistencies, perhaps because our feeling for the authentic is sustained by what seems *typical*, the *kinds* of clothes, gestures, and so forth that we expect of medieval reality. Our prior knowledge of the medieval, built up from watching films and from other sources, allows for a range of specificity in the unique image. There is a register of descriptive features for a castle in *Ivanhoe*—or for Ivanhoe himself—and we quietly accept any version that does not clearly violate that category: many versions of a peasant's jacket would seem authentic, in other words, but not one trimmed in sumptuous fur.

Our sense of the typical in medieval life deserves special attention because it is the foundation of cinematic medievalism—the paradoxical way modern viewers conceive of the Middle Ages. This film medievalism is both comforting and an implicit threat. Presented with Camelot, we are suddenly at ease. We know pretty well what to expect from Gawain, Guinevere and the rest. Lancelot can be Cornel Wilde (*The Sword of Lancelot*) or Franco Nero (*Camelot*), but the ground rules are the same: the loyalties and betrayals we love are replayed on the violent medieval turf, where men's lives and women's fates depend on the edge of a sword. What we can accept as the medieval authentic, in other words, is partly what we think we know, and partly what we need to think and feel about that dim medieval twilight where death and taxes are so much closer to the bone. The stereotypes in *this* open-ended list—medieval life was dirty, dangerous, sexy, ignorant, passionate, doomed, and so on—are essential: they index the deepest level of audience appeal. If these medieval stereotypes strike us as regressive, too easy, like an infantile projection, remember that they are a common denominator, a simple but effective device for accessing our emotions. Those who think this an unfair remark should consider the farting contest at the end of that very successful film *A Knight's Tale*.

But if we acknowledge the murky, underlying attractions of the medieval stereotypes—the excremental humor, the barnyard sex (*The Advocate* had to be edited even to achieve an R rating)—we must also give attention to medievalism at the other end of the scale, the over-arching themes, the structures of obsessive ideas which are equally a source of authenticity in medieval movies. This is where the medieval hero, the focusing presence of the film, matters most, and this is where we feel the implicit threat. For we live the film's events and emotions through our heroic surrogate, and the blows of fortune, the lovers, the loneliness and joy are viscerally powerful for that reason. Moreover, the ideology of the medieval film world, its organizing necessities and unexamined assumptions (mingled, naturally, with modern ideologies projected by its makers and viewers) depends upon the embattled situation of the hero. This is where character matters, and tradition, God and King. This kind of realism is less perceptual than cognitive, because concepts like freedom, dignity, loyalty and identity are abstractions (Locke called them "complex ideas") derived from many levels and varieties of cultural experience. Grodal associates these "schemas" of film realism with Plato's idealist tradition:

> The schemas are the mentally pertinent features in the experience of the ever-changing phenomenal world. [Their] ... "schematic salience" ... provides a feeling of reality that is abstract and atemporal ... the power of which comes from being the mental essence of many different experiences, in contrast to the feeling of perceptual salience that is connected to the temporal, specific and unique.[10]

As Grodal explains, the perceptual and the schematic are complementary in a film. What we see creates perceptual realism, while what we know (the organizing concepts that govern what we see) creates our sense of its reality.[11]

In some films, visual realism may seem to dominate, in others, the cognitive sense of reality. *First Knight* has been criticized as—if not a mindless film, then a film distinguished by "the irresolute flatness of [its] characterizations."[12] Yet the aging Richard Gere still has about him the aura of his earlier, wilder roles, and *watching* him as he casually wins at swordplay, or rides (unhelmeted) into battle, we are entertained. *The Seventh Seal*, on the other hand, moves toward allegory. And in Bresson's *Le Procès de Jeanne d'Arc* the burden of ideas presses so heavily as to move the film toward a kind of moral didacticism. Joan sits motionless under the scrutiny of the inquisitors, returning her answers without hesitation, but also without inflection or facial expression, so that finally she seems more a representative of the idea of righteous innocence than an innocent peasant girl cruelly examined.

Loyalty, faith, and identity are abstract schemas, then, and have their own sense of reality, but in medieval movies we do not experience them in the abstract. They are, after all, real to the hero, in ways that cause him or her enormous pain. But surely our need to see the hero torn between loyalties, faiths, and identities does not arise from sadism but from a need to be torn ourselves, transfixed inescapably by the necessity of doing what we must, believing as we do and being who we are. Medieval films, like most stories, are fables of identity—but in a harder world than ours, where the demands of loyalty and faith are absolute, and the hero bears an appalling weight of self-investment. This is not the unbearable lightness of being—a modern affliction—but its opposite, where being is the still center, and all other things fall into orbit around it, transient and relative to the ineluctable identity of the self. We need such hyperbolic terms to describe the martyrdom of St. Joan or, for that matter, Thomas Becket or William Wallace. We sense that with Richard Courtois, the Advocate, in his quest for justice, or William of Baskerville, in his quest for the truths of earth and heaven, the hero holds to his own truth with all the force of his being, despite enormous difficulties, which often—no, *always*—offer the truly frightening opportunity of recantation, betrayal, and the abandonment of self. In such ways medieval movies call upon us to be authentically ourselves, if only in the person of Martin Guerre and until the final credits.

CHAPTER TWO

Simplicity

Loyalty, faith, identity ... yes ... but shall we be candid? That is not why you have come to the medieval movies. Not at first. When the lights go down and the medieval world blossoms on the screen, what you may very well be feeling is *relief*, having left behind the complexity of the present to enter what you half-consciously agree to accept as the simplicity of the deep past. Globalism, annual growth percentages, actuarial statistics (your multiplex insurance set-up), none of it matters here. Genes, stress, GPS, therapy—no, vanished, and in their place the hard impact of physical experience lived moment by moment (no one wears a watch) while life lasts. We have insulated ourselves from threat—hence our lives are long, full of words, voices, images—and so we crave the simplicity of mere being, just as Thoreau did, and, in his time, St. Francis. That too is what we seek in medieval film.

Simplicity, however, turns out to be multiform, since we seek it in different ways and at various levels. Let us turn immediately to the very lowest level, the surging carnal bloodbeat of conquest and desire. Conan the Barbarian speaks with slow difficulty—Arnold Schwarzenegger's English really is better than that!—but he moves cat-quickly through mountain forests teeming with savage half-men, his axe or spear a blur of motion, swung by an arm ridged with striated muscle and stained with old blood. His woman? She's not a wordy type either, but her feral sexuality pierces your gut like a terrible cry—this is what *Amazon* means, friend, and she can send an arrow through your neck before you take your next breath.[1]

Well, that is a bit over the top, but you get the idea—not so much an idea as a feeling, though, a regressive, atavistic yearning for a timeless racial past. Our animal past. Have you ever wondered what the curse means in *Ladyhawke*, where Michelle Pfeiffer (Iseault) becomes a bird of prey at sunrise, while Rutger Hauer, her former lover, turns into a black wolf at the dying of the light? The twelfth-century Breton Lais of Marie de France favored such transformations (e.g., Bisclavret, another wolf-man), and they seem equally at home in medieval film,² perhaps because even now, man the hunter feels kinship with the animal Other—"The wolves ran on through the evergreen forests," Auden writes, and part of us has always run with them.³ In any case, animals are frequent in medieval film. In *The Advocate*, a pig is indicted for murder, dog-victims are nailed to trees, and an ass is nearly hanged for indecent sexual relations with her owner—but in such a tale, how can we not reflect upon the animal behavior of the men? In *The Seventh Seal*, poor Jof, who is Mia's husband and a harmless actor, has to dance like a bear over the flames, and our instant pity derives partly from knowing that even though he is *not* a bear of a man, his suffering is like that of a wordless animal. Even *The Return of Martin Guerre* courses with the vigor of animal life, not through direct parallels but because animals are everywhere, pigs wallowing in mud holes along the street, and dogs, chickens, cattle and horses mingling intimately with daily life. When Martin Guerre and Uncle Pierre disagree over money, they circle each other, eyes narrowed and heads drawn down between their shoulders—a dog fight. Later, when Martin believes Pierre will give up the profits he owes, he runs off happily across the farmyard with a bouncing gait, his big shoulders heaving as he jogs sideways, just missing the rear end of a cow. An intelligent, resourceful man, he is nevertheless bound to the land and livestock, and lives close with them.

Fear, desire, anger, aggression—the dogs of war—lie waking and ready for action: remember your last faculty meeting? We deplore and love them, for they waste us and it feels, in Homer's words, like "a sweet smoke within the heart."⁴ Somehow we know that a medieval movie will loose these dogs from their depths, and in a part of ourselves we want that. But the animal world we have entered opens everywhere into the world of men, into the fifteenth-century French peasantry, for instance, as in *The Return of Martin Guerre*, or into a fourteenth-century Benedictine abbey, as in *The Name of the Rose*. And men have codes, they are social beings subject to laws. These men are angry and passionate, but instead of falling upon each other with fang and claw, we know they will fight by the rules, and this too satisfies our hunger for simplicity. Knights fight, monks pray and peasants toil. That is how the twelfth century saw it, and however inadequate this division might have been as social theory, much work was put into devising protocols for each of these estates (i.e. states, or conditions, of life): for the knights, chivalry; for the monks, the Benedictine Rule (and other rules); for the peasants, the iron rule of custom—the way of our fathers. Each of these coded ways of life described what was acceptable to those who lived it; in medieval movies we see them as *typical* ways of being, and anything resembling them strikes us as acceptably authentic.

Chivalry is a good place to begin because knights, or at least some of them—Geoffroi de Charny,⁵ for instance, or William Marshall⁶—believed chivalry was a high calling and left evidence that they lived by its code. Malory, whatever his actual behavior, seems to have felt the same, and he left behind him a voluminous account of Arthur's knights of the round table, taken from thirteenth-century French prose romances but simplified and heightened—re-idealized, if you will—in his somberly nostalgic *Le Morte d'Arthur*.[7] Alas, Arthur. John Steinbeck fell in love with him and retranslated Malory's tales into mid–twentieth-century American English.[8] Movie makers have made their own translations, bringing Arthur to the screen in many versions, every one of them vividly simple. His round table, for example, makes complexity seem charmingly manageable, the many neatly collapsed into the universal one (Latin *uni-*, one; *versus*, turned: thus "turned into one"), an idea medieval people liked so well they made it their schooling. To us it probably implies the democratic way, seen in a softly positive light ("one for all," etc.). Then Arthur himself—"one king to rule them all," to echo Tolkien,[9] because unity is the bright political face of simplicity and we worship it, whatever nice things we may say about diversity.

Arthur's knights present a bewildering complexity (Malory has fun making up whole lists of fanciful names), allowing an author to explore any number of divergent themes based on their adventures; and so it is not the knights we come to see on film but the one great adventure, Arthur's death. Arthur has to die, that's clear, for if not, his rule seems indeterminate and his enchanted realm is mere geography. This king is defined by our seeing him in retrospect, and his greatness is that of a martyred myth. So Arthur needs to be played by someone who can make us sorry he will die—not Nigel Terry, who makes a good teenage (pre–Merlin) Arthur in *Excalibur* but an embarrassing monarch, and perhaps not even Sean Connery, although one might argue that both Connery and Arthur were wasted in *First Knight*. I think Richard Harris played him best in *Camelot*. Despite its staged campyness, that imaginary garden allowed Arthur his agony as a king and his pathos as a husband, and as a man born to die.

In some ways Arthur's youth offers a more promising narrative than his reign, for in those early years, promise is all, and we delight in seeing glimmers of the King in the boy's progress. T.H. White capitalized on this theme in *The Once and Future King*,[10] but in a general sense it was a theme already popularized by chivalric culture, which codified and romanticized the apprenticeship of knights-to-be. At seven years, one becomes a page, at fourteen a squire, then finally a bachelor knight (yes, like a B.A). In any case, medieval movies and their audiences have internalized this ritual (for us, apprenticeship precedes being knighted into professional life), and it has become a key to understanding the elaborately developed world of chivalry. In *A Knight's Tale*, Will Thatcher (Heath Ledger) is a low-born attendant (not even a squire) to an aging knight, a tournament contender until he dies, and Will must become a counterfeit

Franco Nero as Lancelot, Richard Harris as Arthur and Vanessa Redgrave as Guinevere in Joshua Logan's *Camelot* (1967), The Academy of Motion Picture Arts and Sciences.

knight or go hungry. His once-impossible apprenticeship then begins as he assumes a knightly rank (Sir Ulrich von Lichtenstein), learns painfully to joust, engages an armorer he can trust (a woman armorer!) and gains entry to the lists, thanks to some smooth language by the always delightful Geoffrey Chaucer (Paul Bettany). *A Knight's Tale* is a spoof of medieval men and movies that works and is funny precisely because we know very well the ritual of knightly becoming and appreciate this light-hearted, democratic variation on it.

Kingdom of Heaven is another kind of film, and, accordingly, its apprenticeship formula has different work to do. Balian is a blacksmith, miserable in his tiny French town because his wife has killed herself (her child was stillborn), his brother the priest wants his lands enough to call his grief heresy, and an itinerant crusader knight (Sir Godfrey of Ibelin) tells him he is a bastard (Godfrey and the blacksmith's wife, all those years ago). Unbearably provoked (his wife's body was beheaded before interment), he kills his brother, gallops away from the village and joins his father who is returning to his fiefdom in the Holy Land. Balian will learn to be a lord, but this infernal beginning creates a story arc that recurrently comes near to destroying him, body and spirit, before the ambivalent ending. The Holy Land promises riches to some, death to many, and a new identity for those who wish it. Godfrey and Baldwin IV, King of Jerusalem, have given their lives to form a Kingdom of the Just. Soon they are dead, however, and though Balian proves his worth in combat and in love, he finds that the only kingdom of heaven to be had here or anywhere is the one man seeks within himself. At the end, Ibelin is lost to the Saracens, he marries a princess (but she is no longer Queen of Jerusalem), and we sense that his French village is no home for them. Indeed, his kingdom lies within or nowhere. Simple, no?

Of course, it is not simple at all. The medieval movies have had their way with us once more, offering a taste of blood, rage, fear, the keen edge of desire, then leading us through an apprenticeship that seems to make easy sense of it all, but finally leaving us right back where we started, like Dante, grounded in real life at the end of the *Paradiso. The Name of the Rose* is such an apprentice program, with Christian Slater (Adso) learning from Sean Connery (Brother William of Baskerville) how to parse clues and deal with the Benedictine monks. At first, as we follow William and Adso from their cell to the refectory, then up to the scriptorium, to the library, and down the cliff below the walls where Italian villagers are picking through the monks' leavings, doesn't it seem like travelogue, an adventurous feast for the eyes but little more than that?

There is much more. Adso falls in love with a village girl as she looks up from the field of garbage and seizes him with her remarkable eyes. William, the former Inquisitor, was tortured and fled those heretical issues—until heresy seeps into the ancient abbey and he must again be its judge. Ah, ruin! Adso, a German baron's son, has vowed to become a Franciscan monk. How can he (a novice!) save this girl from burning? But if she lives, how can he save her from her poverty, and how can he leave her, as he must? For William, who better applies his vast intellect and demonstrates impressive self-control, it means trying to explain to the abbot and Bernardo Gui, the Grand Inquisitor, that the witchcraft and heresy revealed within the abbey must be understood as the inevitable results of superstition and poverty as seen by a culture of privileged, ignorant and politically manipulated monks. It is impossible. William and Adso find the murderer, but each in his way is overwhelmed by the problems of the early fourteenth century.

We have sought simplicity in the chivalric world and among the monks; now let us try the third estate—the peasants of town and country. In *The Advocate* Maître Richard Courtois, a young Advocate at Law, has done well in Paris but now wishes to live away from town, among real people whose problems he can deal with directly. And so he goes to Abbeville, a smaller, Norman town where simple folk live under a confounding mixture of Roman law and ancient custom (*coutume*). Well, at least the fare is simple at the Abbeville Inn, and the chamber maid willing; village dogs smile at Courtois, as he thinks (toothy smiles), and the local mad-woman is accused of inciting the rats to bite her neighbor. He deals with such things with a townsman's light irony, but the public baths are a convenient trope for Courtois's deepening immersion in the real difficulties of this country life. The civil court, to begin with, is dominated by the local Seigneur whose payoffs to the Prosecutor far exceed his yearly pay. The priest of Abbeville, a wise and cultured man, has also been compromised: his pastoral care has come to mean absolution of the country wives, and he is careful not to contradict the superstitions confirmed by spies of the Inquisition. Courtois, moreover, has fallen in love. Worse, he loves Samira, from the camp of local Gypsies who poach game and perform at banquets for the Seigneur, Jehan d'Auferre in the castle, which this wealthy businessman bought along with his title. Courtois manages to find the murderer (as in *The Name of the Rose*, a detective plot is an illusive promise of clarity), but in the end the labyrinthine nature of this country town seems foreign to him, and he gets back on the coach for Paris.

But the peasants, surely *they* are simple? In *The Return of Martin Guerre*, we enter the southern French village of Artigat, following the visiting notary who will write a marriage contract for the young Martin Guerre and his bride, Bertrande de Rols. He is fourteen years old, she less. Entering town, we pass a dung heap and a hog wallow. Chickens run across the path, and people are out in the street cooking and carrying things. With their sturdy legs and bent postures, they remind us of peasants in the paintings of Pieter Brueghel the Elder. Soon we are inside the home of Mathurin Guerre, father of Martin, who has (of course!) arranged the marriage and signs the contract by drawing a tiny chicken (his mark), since, like most of the people in Artigat, he does not read or write. The family, neighbors, and friends gathered about him laugh and cheer—a new couple has been woven into their social fabric. If you like country towns, it feels good here—earthy, connected ... *real*. This film deserved its French Academy Award for excellence in production design, for the illusion of authenticity is deeply, tangibly solid. CUT to the bedroom where Martin and Bertrande lie beneath the covers of (her dowry) bed, the village priest blesses them and makes his little joke ("Martin, make sure these pretty flowers are well watered ..."), and everyone goes out. "Martin"—she touches his shoulder, but he has turned away, and mercifully we CUT to another scene, far in the future, when Martin has run away from his village and family: he did not like living under his father's roof, he was not a happy husband and father, he wanted another life. And so he went off to fight in the king's wars (there were so many), becoming, in essence, a different man.

The life of peasants, it seems, was a simple one, and yet not so simple. The crops in 1548 were better than they had been in the fourteenth century, with its bad weather, and the plagues and wars that devastated the human harvest. But precisely because the population had now rebounded, the family lands were divided into increasingly smaller parcels, and it became harder for a person to live on his inheritance. So families fell together, living under the father's roof and submitting to his authority; the family lands were worked in common.[11] Young men had less freedom to do as they wished under these circumstances, and few secrets could be kept, either from the extended family or from the village at large. Men and women worked, ate, socialized and even slept in close groups; their occupations were traditional and their play ritualized. If your wife did not bear children—for eight years Martin's wife did not—it was considered your responsibility (or your neighbor's, or someone's) to ride an ass through town facing backwards in the Charivari ritual, announcing and reaffirming the village's obsession with fertility.[12] In real life and in the movie made about him, Martin Guerre was a rather contrary, introverted person, and we can understand why he and men like him might have wanted a new start—an escape, even, to the adventure of soldiering, or seafaring, perhaps to the new world somewhere to the west.[13] Seen thus, *The Return of Martin Guerre* becomes a fable of identity, or "self-fashioning," as Stephen Greenblatt says[14]—doubly so, since Martin's self is reconstructed before our eyes by Arnaud de Tilh, another soldier who came home, not to his native village but to Artigat to *become* Martin Guerre, to farm his lands, enjoy his family and friends, and live with his wife. As so often with medieval films, we return to Chaucer's (Arcite's) great questions: "What is this world? What asketh men to have?"[15] These medieval worlds have turned out to be anything but simple, but in the end, simplicity would not have been enough for us. Our deepest craving is for problems we cannot solve.

That leads us to the otherworldly in medieval film, which does involve questions of faith and ontology (let us simply call it "being"); but are we able to confront them? Faced with the martyrdom of Jeanne d'Arc, the quest of Antonius Block (*The Seventh Seal*) or the faith of a Franciscan monk like William of Baskerville (*The Name of the Rose*), we are tempted to take medieval faith and being for granted—"It is an age when faith is always already assumed; even heretics have faith in *something*; surely no one could imagine *being* that is not simultaneously being-in-the-world and being part of God's creation, however many worlds it might contain, including heaven, earth and hell itself." In other words, to be is to believe, in medieval film, and being is simply to be part of the Whole—for nothing can exist beyond or apart from God. If I have stated these implicit assumptions correctly, they are probably comforting: here is a world where people can agree on what is and is not real, where faith is unquestioned, perhaps thoughtless, but in any case not a problem.

Best to say, right up front, that the simplicities of faith, being and love do endure in the medieval movies—at the end, they retain their power to bring us to silence—but for the faithful, as for lovers, being in the world is a complicated business; that simplicity is hard earned. As *La Passion de Jeanne d'Arc* opens, for instance, we pan across the courtroom (one of Dreyer's famous long shots) past soldiers standing guard and setting up a stool for the defendant, priests filing into their jury box, everyone bustling, until at the far right door we see a small, plain person shuffle in (her feet are shackled) with enormous haunted eyes that take in the busy room with apprehension and horror. This is Joan, the Maid of Orleans, but where is her armor, her captains and faithful troops? She is utterly alone in this trial; we see it from the beginning. A young, female French peasant accused of witchcraft (and of fighting the English, of course), she will be subject to the questions and machinations of the cleverest, most devious clerical men Burgundy can provide. She must die, we never doubt it. The only question is whether she can be true to her *voices*, retaining her simple dignity in the face of inhuman prosecution and the severe, unfathomable demand of her faith.

As the trial progresses, every scene with a more sophisticated cruelty, we realize that Joan's strength is her very simplicity. "Who taught you the Catechism?" "My mother," she says quietly, and a tear begins its way down her cheek. The visual complexity of these scenes lies in the naked close-ups of the judges' faces—scheming, raging, gloating—shot in black and white, without make-up, so that each one is an engraved portrait of what medieval people would probably have called sin. Joan's face, too, is often in close up, but her quiet features imply an inner purity deeper than the fear and sorrow being wrung from her. She tells what she knows about the voices; she wants to hear Mass, to take Communion; and she believes that the forged letter signed by her king is real. She is defenseless, really, but after being frightened into recanting what she heard (the angel Gabriel and other voices of God), she returns to her cell and immediately realizes she has lost her way. Christ died, and so must she. Simple. This is the turning point of the film. After that, her taking communion and even her immolation, unbearable as it is, are celebrations of victory over every worldly force that would deny the truth revealed to her in its unanswerable clarity.

Antonius Block is another matter—unyielding, dense, one critic thought—and even ten years of obscene war in the Holy Land have only made him search more desperately for evidence that God exists. A good man, married, with a castle and its responsibilities, he heard the call to crusade and left to serve God and be filled by the divine presence. The priest he heard stayed behind to become a corpse robber and rapist (the plague enables a certain freedom), but Block, still with his emptiness, has come back to Sweden where he has one emblematic day to live.

Block's simplicity is not a lack of brains and know-how. He survived the battles, the hunger, the disease-ridden camps, and after long weeks at sea is waking, praying, rousing his squire to take the road again. This tall, thin blade of a man once had a life, we imagine, but now his face shows little expression; he deals with life but seems to have lost the ability to care about it. He has carried his emptiness until it eroded him, and nothing remains but the bleak core of pure being and the endless, perhaps hopeless search for God's answer. His squire Jöns, in many ways an opposite, shows us the other side of life. This strong, soldierly man does have expressions, swearing, singing, drinking with various people along their way. Death is all about them—he knows it just as Block does—but after a few drinks and a bitter joke or two he can laugh at death and God, then draw a satirical cartoon of Jöns, a man who travels light. While Block has nothing left but his craving for an answer, Jöns cares for nothing but whatever the next moment will bring. These paired, contrasting men work together perfectly, however, and their mutual support is unquestioned—indeed, to the death. We know them; we are like them both.

Each of these typical men—these *archetypes*—is complete and unchangeable, for they represent two different understandings of life. At the end of the film, when death, the Great Lord, appears to them in Block's castle, Block is still searching for answers, while Jöns, absurdly, will stop talking "only under protest." All are silent then as the servant girl kneels, her face full of light—"it is finished." Life is, and then it is gone, however you might understand it: that is the message in its stark simplicity.

And yet, and yet ... the substance of the film—the cruel, silly, insane, delightful antics of those we pass on the way to the castle—gives the two archetypes their depth of meaning, at the same time that they frame every activity, forcing it under the eye of eternity. The complexity of motives, faiths and delusions we see in the flagellants' procession, or the soldiers burning the "witch" girl is indeed the stuff of life, just as confused and blindly sought as anything in our own lives. The confusion is unchanging, eternally human, and it constitutes what might fairly be called Bergman's uncompromising view of the medieval world as well as our own.

Still, the movie offers what I have called the love story of Jof and Mia, their charmed marriage idyll that includes baby Mikael and even the horse and the little pageant wagon (their house). Both are adorably simple, Jof the actor/acrobat who writes songs for his Mia and sees visions of the Blessed Mother and Child, Mia the unassumingly lovely wife and mother who represents the future's eternal promise. After the death-storm has passed away with the night, the little family emerges to face the bright day, and there is only Jof's vision of the knight, the squire, the smith and his wife ... a line of them, led toward the dark lands by death with his scythe—shadows to recall their little lives.

It seems fitting to close this discussion of simplicity by returning to *The Name of the Rose*, since William of Baskerville and Adso of Melk belong to an order founded by a man drawn so powerfully to the simple life that he gave away all his possessions and begged to sustain himself while he preached. St. Francis has been called a genius of the religious life. He was not a learned man, and the directives (Rules) he left for his order were brief but clear: the brethren were to live as Christ had lived, in simple poverty, which meant that they could own nothing beyond a begging bowl, a habit of ordinary woolen cloth, and a pair of sandals. Francis's own habit (which has been preserved) was famously decrepit—it was full of holes—but people swarmed to him when he preached, perhaps because he spoke as someone who lived his convictions. When he talked of following in the steps of Christ, no one doubted that he gave himself entirely to the *usus pauper* ("poor use"), nor could he do otherwise, for the kingdom of heaven was tangibly, necessarily at hand: one had only to shrug off the contemptible burdens of the world and live to serve others.

But when William and Adso enter the great Benedictine abbey in the mountains of north Italy in November 1327, Francis has been dead for a century, and the Franciscan order has split. The Spirituals continue more or less in the way Francis laid down in his final Rule (1223), but the Conventuals, as their name implies, are content to own buildings and many other things, participating in the local economy. Pope John XXII (the Frenchman Jean de Cahors) has taken the side of the Conventuals, and some Spirituals who persisted arrogantly in their discipline have been burned. Soon the abbot will host a debate between Spiritual representatives and the papal legate (an Italian cardinal), sent from Avignon to represent the Pope. As for William, he is here to represent the position of the Holy Roman Emperor Louis IV of Austria, who (like a good Machiavellian) has taken the weaker (Spiritual) side, hoping

Two. *Simplicity*   45

to blunt the political thrust of John XXII. It is all quite confusing, yet the issue at hand is simple poverty, the life of Jesus and his disciples.

Adso? In love by this time, with that Italian girl. Obstacles to this love include the Italian language (he speaks German and Latin), the desperate poverty of her family (they steal from the abbey and glean its garbage), Adso's vows (including chastity), and two cultures as different as Columbus and the natives of the new world. But—he loves her, she him, and with love's terrible simplicity.

William counsels the boy as well as anyone can, for he is no simple monk but a man with a past. Like many Franciscans, he was drawn to Oxford, studied with Roger Bacon, became the friend of William of Ockham, the great dialectician, then was taken up by the Inquisition in its early days until he could no longer distinguish between heresy and the need of poor people to hope for better life. Tortured, he recanted and returned to Oxford to study Nature (astronomy, optics, natural philosophy) and to heal. What remains of the former man is an inquiring mind and (like Bacon and Ockham) a consuming love of what is real and true. That is William's simplicity. He will find the murderer (Adso helps, in his way), but he cannot resolve the debate about Christ's poverty, any more than Adso can bridge the abyss that separates him from "his only earthly love," though love sprang across it in a heartbeat. William suffers the burning of the books—one of the greatest research libraries in Christendom, its voices lost in flame—and Adso must leave the girl and his own youth behind as he rides slowly after William into a long, monastic life.

Simplicity is a dream, of course, and so we seek it always.

CHAPTER THREE

Spectacle

Authenticity, simplicity ... spectacle. In his *Poetics*, Aristotle says that spectacle (*opsis*, from *ops*, eye) is, of all the six parts of tragedy, the least integral to the poet's art.[1] Aristotle cared most for plot structure, the "soul" of tragedy, and he lived during a time when Athenian tragic poets felt they had less control over the productions of their plays than ever before.[2] Still, he is able to add that spectacle is *psychagogikon*—"stirring, seductive" (from *psyche*, soul, heart; *agogos*, leading, guiding)—a word he uses earlier in Chapter Six to describe the (to him) more important effects of tragic reversal and recognition.[3] Medieval film bears little resemblance to the virtually bare stage of Greek drama, but *stirring* and *seductive* ("leading the heart") may help us understand some of its characteristic visual pleasures.

Let us begin with that most medieval of all sights—*castles*—somber and immense, their battlements crenellated like giant teeth where men have fallen, dying, into the moat or onto a pile of bodies seared by burning oil. Castles are ancient, storied: their dungeons and *oubliettes* hold the bones of forgotten favorites, their courts the splendor of exiled kings. Young women come of age in castles, marry—or not—and live out their lives in endless intrigues; little pages come to receive their proper upbringing, learning to bow, play the flute, say their piece like gentlefolk; princes learn to watch the skyline and, during the hunger and sickness of long siege, watch the soldiers grow restless. Castles are iconic. They stand for feudal might, the iron crown, but they also imply the ritualized elegance of chivalric life, with its coded amours and deadly pride.

The castle of Burgos, seat of Sancho II, King of Castile and León, lies dark against the dawn. "This is Spain," begins the narration, but the castle already implies what we soon will know. The world of *El Cid* revolves about the honor of kings, which the Cid and many others will die defending. Now France: *The Lion in Winter* opens as Eleanor of Aquitaine is rowed up river to the castle of Chinon, where Henry II, still her husband after all these years, will hold Christmas court. Within those great stone ramparts, within the cold

The Alcázar de Segovia, used for Lancelot's castle of Joyous Garde in *Camelot* (1967; courtesy the Academy of Motion Picture Arts and Sciences).

stone rooms with their tapestries and hard furniture, she and Henry will exercise their practiced cruelty, tearing away at each other until both are exhausted and their sons are bewildered once more by these willful monarchs. France again, near Abbeville: the ironized castle of the Seigneur Jehan d'Auferre, now a lord but earlier a merchant wealthy enough to buy a title and all that goes with it. The Maître Richard Courtois, the Advocate in the film of that name, visits him there, thinking it a good thing to praise the tapestries in the great

Peter O'Toole as Henry II and Richard Burton as Becket, his advisor, in Peter Glenville's *Becket* (1964; courtesy the Academy of Motion Picture Arts and Sciences).

room. "Don't try to please me, Courtois, my wife chose them, I'm a simple businessman." It is the fifteenth century, after all, and the middle class is rising. And Italy, with further irony: William of Baskerville and his novice Adso of Melk ride up through the foothills of the Apennines toward the Benedictine abbey which is home to many frightened monks and one of the greatest libraries in Christendom. The massive tower with its narrow windows looms before them on its cliff. During the long ages of barbarism it was a fortress; now it defends pagan (i.e. Aristotelian) learning against the prying eyes of monks who should not know it, and against laymen everywhere.

Castles, yes, and *kings*. For medieval movies, as for medieval life, they are the symbolic center, the source of power, politics, law and taxes. A king is the head, if not always the heart, of the land—he is French, English, Spanish *identity* in human form, his court the world in little. You can say we've put our kings behind us; we are democratic, but on film, at least, their spectacle moves us. As *Becket* opens, Henry II of England, Ireland, Normandy, Anjou and Aquitaine climbs alone up the broad steps of Canterbury Cathedral, his gold crown and red cape the focal point of this enormous open scene, while off to the side masses of soldiers, retainers and priests stand waiting. The king has come to do penance for the death of Thomas Becket, once Lord Chancellor of England and (by Henry's order) Archbishop of Canterbury. Peter O'Toole plays Henry seamlessly, as if born to his easy sarcasm and arrogant pride. Soon he will descend to the crypt and, laying his hands on the sarcophagus, speak to the dead man privately, as if the church were empty. Like all kings, Henry dwells apart: for better or worse, and whatever the difficulties might be, his will is absolute and weighs upon him alone. He unties the cape, lifts it negligently from his naked shoulders: he finds the scourging absurd and contemptible, but it will sway public opinion his way and increase his power over the Saxon pigs (priests!) who hold the whips. Like him or not, this king has style and presence, a razor wit and endless guile. He can manipulate anyone in a hundred ways; he is melancholy, humorous, scheming and supercilious, all at once. This first man of the realm, is he more than man or a pampered, neurotic monster? *Mientras en mi casa estoy, rey me soy.* He is us.

The queens are another matter, not less wise and willful, certainly, but as sometime sweethearts, wives and mothers, they offer different possibilities. Guinevere, for instance. In *Camelot* she is Vanessa Redgrave, who charms the round table knights with her Scandinavian good looks and salty talk ("In fact I'll bleed inside if you don't guide me to ... the ... show"). She is more than a match for Franco Nero's Lancelot, and a sadly perfect wife for Arthur; who else had the beauty, confidence and mature sadness for the scene where she and Arthur bathe together, "like simple folks do." Jean Wallace made it entirely forgivable that Lancelot (Cornel Wilde) should fall for such a woman in *The Sword of Lancelot* (she was actually Wilde's wife); and in *Excalibur*, Helena Bonham Carter gives a convincingly energetic portrait of the lady when young (it was 1981, and Guinevere needed personhood). Laura Duke Condominas is the Guinevere of Bresson's *Lancelot du Lac*; her quiet, intense presence reminds us that queens, no less than kings, have an inner life, weigh alternatives, and suffer the consequence. And Keira Knightley, who plays Guinevere in *King Arthur*, is the daughter of a barbaric Woad chieftain. She shares her father's loyalties—through her, Arthur develops British roots—and being a good archer she enters battle in revealing leather armor.

Guinevere's thematic possibilities are probably endless, but given the story line, she is a queen who never rules. Elizabeth the first did reign, giving rise to some excellent films, but in earlier times we look to the medieval queen of queens, Katharine Hepburn, who is Eleanor of Aquitaine in *The Lion in Winter*. Eleanor inherited the southern French Duchy of Aquitaine from her father, and when she married Henry II of England he added those lands to the duchies of Normandy and Anjou, which he already held. But Eleanor was not content to be idle. Having borne Henry eight children, she meant to do as she liked with her influence as duchess, and since that did not suit Henry's ambitions, he imprisoned her at various places, mostly in England. Aside from brief excursions, she has been confined for ten years before the film begins: she wants out, he says no, and they reach again for weapons.

Kevin J. Harty calls this film "a feast for the eyes—and ears," and so it is, a brilliant screen adaptation of James Goldman's play of 1968.[4] Hepburn/Eleanor is, of course, an older woman, swathed in silk, rings on her aging hands, but ramrod straight as she walks off the boat, and that famous voice could cut sheet steel. Weeping, cajoling, commanding, sweetly reminiscing, lying, she is every moment in control and every inch a queen—not the nicest woman who ever wore a crown, but as solidly convincing a female monarch as Peter O'Toole (both times) as Henry. Scene after scene they hone their skills, cutting and thrusting, knowing exactly how to invoke the pain of memory, regret, loss, frustration, and every word draws blood. The three sons are already like their parents, the family greed for power well developed even in teenaged John, but their youthful snatching at the crown is at best a foil for the layered craftiness of their parents, who have played this game so many times before. This royal pair is not at all like friends of ours; no, they are frightening. But onscreen, they allow us to sound the depths of what it means to play with power at this level, be scarred by it and still survive to laugh at it all. They *are* a feast, a spectacle of emotional strength and mental finesse, and whatever it says about us, we admire them tremendously.

Broader and infinitely more varied than this tight monarchical scene is the world of chivalry, and is it not the all-purpose blazon of medieval film? Knights in clashing armor, their rippling surcoats and caparisons crimson, blue, black and gold, the big French *destriers* (or English Clydesdales) snorting deep and dancing their heavy, dangerous, spike-shod hooves—surely we are at the medieval movies now! Chivalry was more than show, it was a way of life, and many were those who gladly gave their lives to it. Practically every film offers a different version, erotic and violent beneath its striking visual appeal. In *The Thirteenth Warrior*, Antonio Banderas is an Arab prince exiled for loving a veiled beauty married to a man of influence. As ambassador to the barbarous north, he encounters a band of Vikings and, wanting to preserve good international relations, joins their Beowulf-style quest. His tastes are delicate, theirs are not. His horse is an elegant Arabian, but small, and the Vikings ask, "Why bring a dog to war?" In short, his chivalry does not suit theirs, so we are spectators as he learns Danish, puts his horse through its paces ("The dog can jump!"), forges a deadly scimitar from a heavy two-handed sword, and at length shows himself worthy. His changing into a northern warrior is, in effect, a variation on chivalric apprenticeship, so often a feature of medieval film because it anatomizes chivalric complexity, constructing the knight identity in satisfying detail. And if the learning process is painful, so much the better!

Katharine Hepburn as Eleanor of Aquitaine in Anthony Harvey's *The Lion in Winter* (1968; courtesy the Academy of Motion Picture Arts and Sciences.

We enter chivalric life most intimately, however, when realism gives way to suggestion, as it does in *Perceval le gallois* and *Lancelot du Lac*. Erich Rohmer's *Perceval* is like a manuscript illumination come to life, filling the whole screen with its brightly painted, graceful world of mannered gesture and aristocratic flair. The carpeted stage, aluminum trees and tiny castles made of plywood seem childish at first, and Fabrice Luchini too boyish to become a knight. Yet gradually, carried along by the narrative (Chrétien's verse!) sung by a small chorus of amiable, elegantly dressed young French women and men, we begin to see Perceval as a real man in the imaginary garden lightly suggested by the music and trees and other props. His perplexity and simple goodness are real to us because they are not realistic, but, like everything in this film, a mimetic mirror of a boy's learning to love and become a man. Rohmer used non-actors for every part but Perceval, producing an unstudied effect which is oddly more accessible than smooth professionalism. In its unassuming way, this film shows us what chivalry may have been like for Chrétien's own audience: for these players are not unlike ourselves, and the joys and sorrows they draw from a heroic past enter our hearts like ancient song.

Bresson's *Lancelot du Lac* is a darker chivalry. The horses, the armor, the people and their emotions are realistic enough—the horses and men are vulnerable, they bleed and die, and in the oppressive aftermath of the ruinous grail-quest, everyone seems confused—but as this bleak drama unfolds, we recognize it as a kind of impressionism. Night has fallen, and Lancelot is returning from his quest; he comes upon Gawain, who does not recognize him. In the stables nearby a horse's neigh is a frightened cry, and the same exact sound repeats at intervals in the film. The knights are lodged outside the castle in tents buffeted by wind and rain. Guinevere, "our only woman" (as Gawain points out), has a window. Knights stare at it wordlessly. Lancelot meets Guinevere, they stand as if frozen, each word seems lifeless, painful to utter.

The knight archetype. Rutger Hauer as Étienne de Navarre in Richard Donner's *Ladyhawke* (1985).

Three. Spectacle

Enough! The Arthurian tragedy of Arthur-Guinevere-Mordred provides the basis for an atmosphere of hopelessness, and perhaps meaninglessness, frightening the men who look to Arthur for encouragement and purpose he cannot offer. It is clear that practice at arms and the tournament are mere distractions filling the time before they die. This failure of the chivalric ideal has its own purpose, however, intensifying the agony of indecision shared by Lancelot and Guinevere. She lives for him, he for her. Nothing else gives purpose to either of them, and although Lancelot still defends his pride as Arthur's champion, he knows it is pointless. Guinevere is finally ready to lose even pride to have Lancelot. It is more an existential crisis than a story of unhappy love. Bresson might have preferred to call it a crisis of ethics. In any case, we are able to watch Guinevere driven back from every hope until she cannot bear to be responsible for more deaths. At that point she returns to Arthur, a moral victory of sorts, in exchange for a life without warmth or meaning. Lancelot, Arthur and the rest of the round table then die, ambushed by Mordred. *Fin.* If this is spectacle (not the ambushing of the knights, but the struggle of Guinevere), it is a battle that takes place on the interior landscape that stretches between the mind's rocky hills and the wind-wracked gulf we call the heart.

What about the other (some would say better) part of chivalry's spectacle? Yes, the chivalric world of women. Women delay, are elusive, curry favor, harbor secrets—and they wait, eternally, for their men to return from crusade, or to turn from overgrown horse-loving boys into men. Women and love-longing—*amor de lonh, sehnsucht*—a fiction of courtly love that was real to many. Jealousy, too, and passion that ensnares the mind. More? Intrigue for power. The marriage market. Aging. The art of fashioning a dream of beauty and pleasure in a desert, in war time, despite an unhappy marriage. In medieval film these things are rare, but when they are well done they give us a world in little. In *Kingdom of Heaven*, Sibylla is Queen of Jerusalem (*Al-Quds*, she calls it, in her fluent Arabic), and she is wife to Guy de Lusignan, another French colonial who will trade his fifty Templar Knights for the crown. She hates him. The marriage was arranged by her ambitious mother, and now she waits to see what she will do with young Balian, the new Baron of Ibelin, just come from France.

Balian is in his courtyard (his father's house in Jerusalem, where he is learning the subtle manners of the East). He is gentling a horse, seeing to its hoof (he was a blacksmith once), when greyhounds streak through the gate, and after them Sibylla, wheeling her horse and taking in the courtyard as if she owned it. "Where is your master?" This is the voice of command, arrogance grown from a century of occupation, challenging his manhood. "I have none." Now she would like a drink of water, and as she drinks she studies him from the corner of her lovely, intelligent eye, dark with mascara.

Of course there is more. Balian is at his father's small dusty fief at Ibelin, where he guards the trade route to the sea. As before, Sibylla sweeps in from the road, asking shelter on her way to Cana (where this road does not go). "It is given." Balian's servants are ecstatic—at last, a woman at Ibelin! She settles in and bathes, and as her women begin to set out the beautiful, delicate things that belong in an aristocratic woman's boudoir, we realize that she is making his world her own. She peers out at him through the window's lacework of stone, she has rose water to wash the dust from his face after work. Soon he will yield to her entirely, and we are glad, we want there to be gardens in this desert (he knows how to dig wells) and love in the midst of the obscenity that greedy political churchmen and lords are pleased to call Holy War. Ridley Scott, the director of this film, once said his own strength was the ability to create a world. In this case it is the rich and subtle world of an eastern woman which captures our senses as it has Balian's, providing the chivalric spectacle with its indispensable other half.

We are about to enter the world of the church, with its grand cathedrals and wealth of busy priests, but let's pause a moment and give Nature her due respect. *Natura*. As much, perhaps more, a part of medieval films as others because we need to be reminded that half a thousand years ago the sun shone, brooks ran, leaves fell and winter set in. Different as life was for medieval people, nature cared for them, or opposed them, just as for us, and so the medieval retains its ambivalent distance—so far yet so near—enabling the perception we call medievalism. Of nature's spectacle we never tire. The south of France, the plains and hills of the Midi in the county of Foix, between Toulouse and the Pyrenèes: here is the village of Artigat in early morning. Beyond the narrow French poplars, the fields and valleys are lavender-green, just beginning to take the sun, and the hills are blue in the distance. In this Edenic quiet, Martin Guerre and his wife Bertrande sleep on.

Northward! *The Thirteenth Warrior*, another morning. In the valley below us, framed by hills capped in mist, a Viking ship lies in the river, dragon-beaked; its long curving seaworthy gunwales were built for the North Sea, but here they answer the lines of the hills, the bending of the stream. Now the Apennines of north Italy, a range of snow-flecked peaks beyond the long valley where, far below, William and Adso ride slowly toward us past grazing horses and small flocks of sheep on their way to the abbey on its cliff. Now the broad green fields of Irish horse country (*King Arthur*)—another long shot—two stallions galloping flat out, muscles bunching and flowing in eloquent slow motion to end the film, nature again. And finally, Becket and Henry sitting their horses head to head as they sift their bitter past, the broad flat sands of Dover stretching far away in both directions, and before them on this bleak and sunless day, the gray reaches of the Channel.

Like every spectacle, the array of the Church is both seen and felt. Here is *human* nature, tutored, tortured—indeed, crucified—tempted, beatified and humbled. The vast whispering naves of cathedrals are a largeness within us, an inner dimension, their spires our spiritual aspiration, if not our hidden pride. We dwell in them, they in us. The same might be said of the many clerics (*clerks*) we come upon in medieval film, men (less frequently, women) of every stamp, bending somehow to discipline and living their obedience, each in their own way. Each one is the face of the Church. *The Name of the Rose* is a triumph of imaginative casting, an anatomy of monastic life by means of its fascinating monkish faces. The abbot, with his frozen, well-fed face and suspicious, frightened eyes; Brother Severinus, the herbalist/mortician, with his coarse face and clever eyes; Ubertino da Casale, skeletal, eyes that melt you with a glance or drive ice through your heart with his prophecies of the last days—and that is only three! We see all of them sitting together in the enormous dark refectory, candles burning up and down the long tables; and as they fall to eating, the Lector reads them a section of the Benedictine Rule.

Really, we find priests everywhere in medieval film because they manifest a reality we lack. *Kingdom of Heaven* has a priest, and it is Balian's younger brother, disinherited, angry and treacherous, scuttling about town in his black robes. Hovering over the glow of Balian's forge one night, he is a satanic presence, tempting and threatening his brother until Balian realizes what happened to his wife (a suicide, beheaded before burial) and impales him with a white hot sword. Another priest in *Kingdom of Heaven* is the unnamed Hospitaler Knight of the Order of St. John who becomes a quiet mentor for Balian, steadying him as his father dies and he comes to live in the crusader snake pit that is Jerusalem. This man is a counselor to Balian's father, an armed and mounted retainer, then a healer, and finally a giver of last rites. His alert, genial face is a constant presence in a film where the church is seldom a positive force, and when he dies in the battle of Hattin, we feel that something of him lives on in the man Balian has become. "You ride to certain death," Balian says. "All death is certain," he replies, and rides away to die with his order. The spectacle of morality is invisible, yet we are acutely aware of it when it appears.

Or when it is compromised. The village priests in *The Advocate* and *The Return of Martin Guerre* are, in their different ways, good men overcome by circumstance. The priest who marries Martin and Bertrande grew up in the village. He is as much a part of its social fabric as anyone, and when Martin comes to trial, he sides with Uncle Pierre, for Pierre has power and money and is someone he has known since childhood. Father Albertus in *The Advocate* is a learned priest and no villager, but his posting to the country town of Abbeville has sapped his will. A good friend and confidant to the young advocate Courtois, he is also friendly with the country wives, and to protect himself testifies for the Prosecutor. Ian Holm as Albertus is probably impossible not to like. Wisdom, humor, irony, and self-deprecation linger in the weathered face of this kind, intelligent man—he is nearly the archetype of what we want priests to be in medieval film. When he is weak we cringe a bit, but these little vices (and some greater ones) are exactly the point of this interesting film. Perhaps the moral spectacle of the Church is deeper and truer, with more to teach us, when it is flawed.

What's that? Saints? Yes, medieval film loves them as it does no others. More films have been made about Joan of Arc than about any other medieval person, including King Arthur and Robin Hood. The life of St. Francis, too, has been filmed more often than one would think possible. Once in a conference session about Joan on Film, I saw a little woman stand up and demand to know why people were so drawn to this saint. A silence ensued, and forgivably so. We pay Joan our respect, and finally it matters little whether she is Jean Seberg, Ingrid Bergman, Leelee Sobieski, Sandrine Bonnaire ... it is the death that matters. As Carl Dreyer understood, the *life* of Jeanne d'Arc joins that of many visited by voices or visions, but her death haunts us with ultimate questions. She was so young and innocent, a French patriot loyal to her king, and her death was so carefully and meticulously arranged—*by priests*. True, medieval people turned out in droves to see executions, and we are not entirely immune to this, yet the spectacle of Joan's martyrdom moves us differently. Dreyer's tortuous filming of Joan's *passion* includes her burning, of course, but finally we better remember the interior agony he was able to wring from Renée Falconetti, registered by long close-ups of that strong, tear-stained, strangely beautiful face.

Leaving for last the medieval film vision of the countryside and the peasants who toiled there probably makes sense, considering that most people want to see movies about the medieval elite. But with the renewed interest in social history, peasants have begun to swim into focus, the first among them Gerard Depardieu and Nathalie Baye in *The Return of Martin Guerre*. These are not "peasant faces." Rather, they seem authentic and hold our interest because their clothing, gestures, attitudes and intimate feelings are opposed to those of Artigat, a village where life is so closely shared. Bertrande is married to Martin before she is fourteen, and the marriage is cold. The family knows it, but the village does too, and so they perform a Charivari, dressing up in animal skins ("warriors") or big false breasts. Martin has to wear a bearskin: the bear must be caught and emasculated (big stuffed balls) to guard their women. Poor Martin. He runs away from the village, and the village mourns; his father dies of sorrow and shame. He returns (it seems), and the villagers are happy; they drink and dance like the peasants in paintings we have seen. The new Martin, an imposter, grows into the life of Artigat. We see him telling stories and jokes, charming the girls who believe they are his sisters, and loving the wife who waited eight years for a man she knew did not love her. It is a heartwarming spectacle, a man and his village enjoying life together as they have always done.

The new Martin is also a hard worker—we see him scything grain with the other men in his farmer's cap, his big shoulders rolling as he leans into the stroke. Yet he is also a rural businessman and wants to collect debts, sell a field and buy another. He is doing what any clever, ambitious small farmer did in the mid–sixteenth century, but money is tight and so is the grip of custom. Is this what our fathers have done? Distrust is born, Martin is accused, and, divided in whom they support, the whole village attends the trial.

As events unfold, we are starting to know the people of Artigat, their loyalties and weaknesses. We come to admire Bertrande, who works like any peasant wife but has learned to manipulate both her relatives and the men of law to protect the life of her family. In the end we have been shown a panorama of the intricate social manners and behaviors of a tightly-knit rural community, its group identity different from anything we have seen in the Church or in chivalric life. Led by the silver-tongued Martin, they are at the same time primitive and sensitive, earthy yet calculating and acute. More perhaps than other films, this social spectacle gives us a feeling for the communal life of medieval country people, with its infinite risks and limited possibilities. And as we move toward a deeper understanding of their lives, we begin to examine more closely our own.

PART II

CHAPTER FOUR

The Advocate

A useful taxonomy for medievalism, and one often quoted, is Umberto Eco's "Dreaming of the Middle Ages," a chapter in *Travels in Hyperreality* (1986).[1] Eco offers "Ten Little Middle Ages"—ten kinds of medievalism, as he sees it—including "The Middle Ages as the site of an *ironical visitation*" (like *Monty Python and the Holy Grail*), "The Middle Ages as a *barbaric age*" (early Bergman, "shaggy medievalism"), "The Middle Ages of *Romanticism*" ("stormy castles and their ghosts"), and so on. This handlist describing common preconceived visions of the past suggests where these attitudes are rooted, some springing from popular culture, some from academia, others from political or artistic nostalgia, or from an interest in the occult. For assessing the quality of an historical film, Eco's first category, "The Middle Ages as a *pretext*," appears to be central. In works that serve this vision, "there is no real interest in the historical background; the Middle Ages are taken as a sort of mythological stage on which to place contemporary characters" (68).

Eco distinguishes between novels—or films—in which the Middle Ages are the substance of the work, and those where the Middle Ages are accidental, mere decoration. This distinction works nicely for bad or obvious films. It works less well for good ones, I think, yet it leads to the question of what a movie is really about. One of the best films about fifteenth century France, in regard to casting, quality of dialogue, accuracy of setting, the substantial treatment of fifteenth-century themes and problems, and the hard-to-define quality of "ambiance," is the relatively unknown British/French production originally released in Europe as *The Hour of the Pig* and retitled *The Advocate* (1994) for distribution in the U.S.[2] But is this a good historical film about the Middle Ages, or is it merely an "historically accurate" medieval package for modern themes? I am going to end up arguing that it is, and very likely must be, both things, and that Eco's distinction forces us to redefine our notion of a good historical film. But since definitions are more enjoyable, more "sweet to bear away" (as the prologue to *Everyman* tells us), when they follow the agon of

59

discussion, I will first try to show how the film develops its view of the human image, then return to what and who and *when* it is about, and how that relates to the ways we—movie makers and all—turn our historical cameras backward, focused variously on the Middle Ages.

The Advocate is about a young lawyer in mid–fifteenth century Paris who, seeking the pastoral ideal of simplicity and innocence, moves to the country town of Abbeville to practice and, as Henry Thoreau might have said, live deliberately. Needless to say, his brief encounter with country life offers one comic disillusionment after another. The people of Abbeville are anything but simple, and as the tragicomic murder mystery sub-plot unfolds, innocence begins to seem an essentially unreachable ideal. The murder plot involves the lawyer's defense of a pig, accused of murdering a small boy, and this incongruous image, drawn from actual cases tried in fifteenth-century France, is where the various themes of the film converge. The local lord, covertly supported by the civil court, would like to execute the pig and close the case. Something is being covered up, but whatever it is, no one is telling. The parish priest silently guards the secrets of the confessional, the peasants are superstitious and fearful, and the local prosecutor coaches the witnesses. Moreover, the pig belongs to a family of gypsies and is their meat for the winter. None of this would interest the Paris lawyer very much, except that one of the gypsies, Samira ("summer wind"), is beautiful, stubborn, and able to rouse in him feelings both of love and ethical conscience.

Courtois's uncertain pursuit of love, truth, justice and a sense of purpose (he is young, remember) takes him from his berth at the Abbeville Inn to the drama of court appearances like his defense of Abbeville's prophetic madwoman ("look to the boy, Maitre..."); meetings with the tight-lipped lord in his gloomy castle; reflective, often sardonic conversations with the parish priest; liaisons with two women, one noble, one not, and both comic, embodying the realities of Abbeville; and, in time, infatuation with the dark, mysterious Samira. But little progress is made solving the murder until Courtois finds himself running through the night streets, trying desperately, as if in yet another dream sequence, to save a stable boy from an anonymous hooded horseman. The presumed murderer escapes on his fine black horse, but Courtois, armed with the evidence, confronts the priest ("look to the boy") then indicts the lord's degenerate son. By now, of course, *that* boy is safely out of town. Empty-handed and now thoroughly disillusioned, Courtois contrives to free the pig so it can be the gypsies' winter bacon (he finds another one with similar markings and a bad disposition), but Samira—more aware of their differences than he—will not come away with him to Paris. So he boards the coach for town, while behind him in Abbeville another "liberator" arrives in the form of a knight errant whose gleaming armor hides a mass of plague sores.

The contrived neatness of Abbeville's pestilential deliverance from ignorance and moral twilight suggests a modern audience's Rage for Order, but the significance of the film depends upon the likelihood, reinforced by the director's proto–Shavian epilogue, that life in Abbeville will continue much as before, for pigs and men as well. The inconsequential pig trial is merely a vehicle for Courtois's descent into a grimly matter-of-fact ambivalence toward civil law and social governance, and so the film leaves us with questions unanswered, to the probable discomfort of viewers for whom the ironic plague-finale seems to have been invented.

If it is puzzling how such a movie ever came to be made or what mass audience would want to see it,[3] we can sympathize with the marketing subdivision at Miramax, which had acquired a beautifully photographed, well-cast film, shot on location and full of strong acting, but not really a comedy and with no discernable selling point. A reviewer for the *Los Angeles Times* wondered if, after Monty Python, we can really take this medieval stuff seriously?[4] A reviewer for the *New York Post* was more sympathetic, calling it one of the wisest films of the season, but, like other reviewers, she thought that the murder mystery plot didn't really carry the film, and that its "unraveling ... becomes increasingly messy."[5] But Miramax saw the murder plot as a recognizable feature, and their posters begged those who had seen the film not to reveal what was, in actuality, a fairly predictable ending. The poster graphic featured women and men in erotic poses, but these figures did not appear in the movie and had no connection with it. The major concern at Miramax was that initially, because of a graphic bedroom sequence at the Abbeville Inn, *The Advocate* received an NC-17 rating, and that was too much of a good thing; when selective editing qualified the film for an R rating, medieval nudity would constitute at least one sort of broad spectrum appeal.

The Advocate grossed only a little over a half million dollars ($581,762 as of October 30, 1994)[6] during its first year of distribution in the U.S., a disappointing figure for those who had hoped barnyard sex and pig-wickedness would sell better to an American audience. Was this box-office failure a good film from any other point of view? In the opinion of one fairly typical European reviewer, "More in tune with the strangeness of medieval belief system than the similar but solemnly arty *Anchoress*, this is full of intriguing historical detail."[7] A reviewer for *Variety* said, "The interracial romance between Firth and Annabi smacks a little too much of twentieth-century posturing, but this (and a slightly overlong conclusion) is the only false note in the comic, intellectually stimulating proceedings."[8] The London-based *Film Review* called the film "a Renaissance drama"—apparently without grasping some of the "historical detail"—but gave it three stars.⁹ Most of the reviewers would probably have agreed with the writer from *Variety* who suspected *The Hour of the Pig* might do well at "international art houses."¹⁰ This being the case, why would an academic writing for the *American Historical Review* be moved to label its view of the medieval world "mean-spirited" and "shallow?"¹¹ Of this, more later. But enough has been said to justify an inquiry into the quality of medievalism presented by a "mean-spirited" movie which *Film Review* called "immensely watchable."

The quest for an R rating might seem a shallow kind of medievalism, but, *per accidens*, it is not. In a movie which relentlessly demands "What Is Man?" there is thematic relevance and relevant visual interest in human bodies nude, partially nude, old, young, male, female, European and Oriental, dressed in every variety of medieval costume, up and down the social hierarchy and across the three estates. This makes the film sound like a *National Geographic* article, but that is not a wholly inaccurate impression. Like pictures in a magazine, the bodies, costumes and faces in the film blend together, reinforce each other, and seem to imply a larger, less-tangible reality—medieval culture, certainly, but, perhaps better, medieval sensibility or even medieval consciousness. For something is seriously wrong in Abbeville, a kind of social malaise. The lawyer from Paris senses this, so we too are aware of it, discovering that the attitudes of people in this country town, and even the murder of a child, have their roots in something as fundamental and hard to define as the quality of human nature itself. It isn't the murder that carries the movie, nor is it the costumes or even the nudity. Instead, as in a few other good medieval films where costumes and settings, though splendid, are not themselves the point, we are held by the possibility that this medieval mirror will tell us a little more deeply and truly who we are.

But we must look carefully. In perhaps no other medieval film are audiences so insistently invited to scrutinize, evaluate, and go beyond the information given. This visual mandate appears with the opening credits. Colin Firth plays Richard Courtois, the Advocate at Law from Paris, but when his name appears, the image that dominates the screen is a close-up of a raven, with piercing eyes and long sharp beak, darting his head here, there, behind, impossibly quick, while the sound track plays the somber, brooding theme we soon come to know as the "lawyer's music." Then we are in the coach carrying him and his clerk to Abbeville, but almost immediately he "wakes" into a dream sequence—for it is a long, sleepy ride through the French countryside—and now, suddenly, as Firth's enormous brown eyes peer out into the dark, drizzling night of his dream, we know what his role will be in the film. The Advocate is there to *see everything*. Nothing will escape the gaze of this enlightened, intelligent, idealistic young man who has come to the country because he loves justice and wants to live and work with "real" people. We will not lose this impression of him because these long, open, pondering looks become a recurrent, identifying feature of the Advocate's character; they help to create the rhythm of the scenes and affect the way we participate in the film, pondering along with him.

It is probably obvious by now that this legal idealist is not well suited to life in a country town. From the opening scene he stands out as different from the peasants, the gentry, the parish priest. All of these people, including his law clerk, accommodate themselves in some way to the local necessities of life, but Courtois is at the same time above their compromises and comically below their level of small-town cleverness. Practically every major character calls attention to this friction in some way, but the local lord (Nicol Williamson), having failed to bribe him, says it best: "I feel that somehow, Courtois, you're not at ease with us yet."

Courtois is scarcely at ease with the local law—not Roman Law, as it is practiced in Paris, but a strange mingling of Roman Law with the regional law (actually, "custom") of Ponthieu, which "can be rather confounding," as the local prosecutor says, because for one thing, it makes less-than-clear distinctions between the jurisdictions of church and state.[12] He is amused, and a bit uneasy, with the parish priest, Father Albertus (Ian Holm), a learned Franciscan who nevertheless likes the country because the country wives are amenable to his kind of absolution. And certainly he is ill at ease with the Seigneur Jehan d'Auferre. One of the "new lords," d'Auferre is a wealthy merchant who bought his title along with his lands, and uses his power to fix prices throughout the region—in addition, naturally, to making his influence felt, when necessary, in the civil court of Abbeville. Yet there is also a kind of uneasiness in Abbeville itself, an undercurrent of dread. Surely it has something to do with the murder of a child, a few days after the Advocate arrives in town, yet it appears also to be connected with the high-handedness of the Seigneur d' Auferre, or with the Church's cruel treatment of those accused of witchery (*maleficium*), or the ravages of the Black Death in the south of France, or the spies for the Inquisition, which like the plague itself, threatens everyone indiscriminately.

People go about their business in Abbeville, to be sure, and life goes on in its countrified way, for the fields must be plowed and the animals fed; the builders are behind schedule with the Advocate's new house, as is normal; and everyone, it seems, makes use of the public baths. But still, the people are afraid, and there is something very like what Johan Huizinga, writing about fifteenth-century France in *The Waning of the Middle Ages*, called a "feeling of general insecurity."[13] Indeed, given the emotional tone of the film, its music, and the darkness of several of the scenes, it would not be misleading to quote Huizinga a little further:

Colin Firth as Maître Richard Courtois in Lesley Megahey's *The Advocate* (1994).

The feeling of general insecurity which was caused by the chronic form wars were apt to take, by the constant menace of the dangerous classes, by the mistrust of justice, was further aggravated by the obsession of the coming end of the world, and by the fear of hell, of sorcerers and of devils. The background of all life in the world seems black. Everywhere the flames of hatred arise and injustice reigns. Satan covers a gloomy earth with his sombre wings.[14]

In this town, with its country wisdom and vague despair, the Advocate would like to be a bringer of light—the knight in shining armor that the people talk about—but for the most part he simply tries to penetrate the darkness. He defends his humble clients, learns from his mistakes, listens to the priest, the lord, and the more experienced (if somewhat compromised) prosecutor and judge, and he watches endlessly ... trying to put it all together. Why do people fear the dark streets, the evil eye, gypsies, Satan in his many forms? Courtois is ever the camera's eye in this, for whenever he pauses to look, we follow his gaze, and his concerned watchfulness becomes a shared point of view—an implied commentary, even, with its undertone of apprehension and a kind of melancholy. One scene in particular demonstrates how this narrative filtration is created.[15] Courtois is standing on his balcony at night, looking down at the street as faint noise from the ale-house drifts up to him. A sequence of brief shots follows that replicates and thus reinforces his gaze: an owl peers searchingly down from a nearby railing—CUT to a barrelhead below the balcony, where some mice (his prey?) are scratching for grain—CUT to the street and the mysterious, darkly-clad stranger who so intrigues Courtois (he will turn out to be a spy for the Inquisition) ... listening, he pauses in a doorway, his eyes directed far down the street—CUT to Courtois, who takes one more look around as he turns to go back into his room, and realizes—CUT to Samira the gypsy girl who has come up the stairs to the balcony and all this time, perhaps, has been watching him. And so it is, in this tense little town where private life is obviously hard to come by, that the priest watches the townswomen, the lord gazes coldly upon the peasants, the peasants keep their nervous and suspicious eyes on the gypsies, and the gypsies watch ... the Advocate. For, as you remember, he is the defense lawyer for a murderous pig, and the pig belongs to the gypsies.

Of course it is unnatural—worse, it is unjust—to try a pig for murder. The Advocate protests, but this would not be the first medieval French animal to be executed for harboring Satan[16]; and furthermore, a surprising number of people would feel relieved if the pig were simply hanged for the child's death and an end put to the matter. Here, in fact, is the crux: the town wants the pig dead, and Courtois wants justice. Not only because he did not study law to become a defender of pigs, nor even because, as he sees it, hanging a pig for murder makes a mockery of the law, and Courtois loves the law. In Abbeville, he imagined, law could be practiced without cynicism or self-interest, in the service of people whose essential goodness it would guard and preserve. But if reasonable intent is assumed in pigs—even those influenced by Satan—then the law is not a mirror of reason,[17] and the image it reflects is no longer human.

Or is it? An historical film can stage great events "accurately" and still remain lifeless, a mere construction. Yet when great questions of history are implied indirectly by the dramatic situation, when they are quietly yet unmistakably implicit in what we recognize as normal, "realistic" human behavior, then we may find the action gripping, for its significance presses in upon us. To give Eco his due, his phrase "fictional characters [who] help one to understand the past" may entail this kind of historical realism. In any case, the question implicit in this film is a legal and a theological one. Ever since Cicero and the stoics, the basis for justice (*iustitia*), both in canon and civil law, had been God's reason as it is manifested in Nature (*ius naturale*).[18] The same natural law, the same complex idea of divine reason, had applied to Adam and Eve in their primitive state, and to all of the animals in God's harmonious creation as well. But with the fall of man, man's nature was changed and darkened, and the *ius naturale* became for man the *ius gentium*, the law of peoples. In its actual codification and administration by men, the *ius gentium*, the idea of God's reason as manifested in human nature, was called the *ius positiva*, or the *ius civile*, the Law of the State. Thus the law practiced by Richard Courtois, the law based on Justinian's *Corpus Iuris Civilis* and its glossators (especially the *Glossa Ordinaria* of Accursius), is an example of *ius civile*. Under some circumstances, the *ius civile* may appear to contradict the *ius naturale*, even though the one was derived from the other. To avoid such contradictions, and to preserve access to the authority of first principles, was the object of interpretation. Yet it follows that since animals are necessarily governed by the *ius naturale*, and men are indirectly governed by its first principles, it might be difficult to draw absolute distinctions between the prosecution of men and the prosecution of animals under the *ius civile*, derived as it is from the *ius naturale*.

Not many viewers, one may assume, can bring to bear a knowledge of the *Corpus Iuris* (here, at least, Courtois has the advantage of us), and it would be misleading to suggest that an appreciation of the pig trial presupposes an awareness of the problematic relationship between *ius naturale* and *ius gentium*. Nevertheless, the very incongruity of trying a pig for murder forces us to consider the borderland between human and animal behavior, between the reign of kings and the animal kingdom. However the law may read, we feel it is somehow deeply wrong to prosecute a pig, and this doubt casts its shadow over the apparent but murkier *human* wrong inherent in keeping silent about the hunting of male children as if they were wild game. It is a consequence of such feelings that the stern, if somewhat ambivalent, question of what is Natural lends resonance to all of the sometimes cruel, sometimes comic courtroom scenes in the film.

Indeed, one of the major goals of the film is to create a setting so dominated by images of animals, animal behavior, humans who look like animals, humans who behave like animals, and especially humans who treat other humans as animals, that finally the peculiar custom of prosecuting pigs, dogs, cats, rats, or even flies for harboring in them the evil of Satan seems not so much bizarre idiocy but rather a kind of protocol, which may or may not be convenient under the circumstances. We have our first sight of Abbeville, for instance, when the camera pans across a field outside the town, picking up a horse, some mules, scattered people, then the edge of a crowd, which turns out to be watching a scaffold. On the scaffold is a donkey, and someone is slipping a noose around its head, for the donkey (her name is Virginie) has been convicted, along with her owner, of the capital offense of sodomy, and they are about to be hanged side by side, two partners in crime. At the last moment, however, a friar arrives breathlessly with a reprieve—not for the owner, but for Virginie: their neighbors have signed a petition attesting to her good character. Her complicity in the evil act could not, therefore, have been by her consent, so the donkey goes free, the crowd cheers, the man is hanged, and the neighbors profit. I should add that Rogier Landrier, the owner, is hanged wearing only a breechclout. He is a small man with gross features but well-defined muscles. He says nothing throughout the scene, and his expression suggests nothing beyond a dully concerned awareness of what is going on. We see him mainly as a physical specimen, defined by an animal act, and the crowd accepts his death in silence.

There are other protocols, other accommodations. The local herbalist, wet-nurse and madwoman is accused of *maleficium*—to wit, inciting the rats in her dwelling to bite her neighbor, who then fell sick and died. The Advocate clears her of the rat charge—really he is quite brilliant—but she is then hanged for a prior confession to the holy fathers of the Inquisition that she made a pact with Satan.[19] Her lands, naturally, are confiscated by the civil court. Or consider the Seigneur Jehan d'Auferre, who enjoys hunting. Once he organized a chase after human quarry—not to the death, mind you, and, after all, they were well paid for their scrapes and bruises. He is trying to marry off his daughter Roseline, nicknamed Filette, who is tall and shapely but has an unfortunate laugh—"She brays like a she-ass," says the lord, "and she comes with 500 hectares of land." Nicol Williamson's d'Auferre is dispassionate and controlling, but not entirely humorless. He comes from an old Cathar family—his grandfather had his legs burned off for heresy—and he secretly maintains a Cathar brotherhood, not for religious reasons but as a means of fixing tithes and tariffs for the entire province.[20] This engagingly icy lord doesn't hate peasants, or gypsies, or pigs, or lawyers, but, as he tells Courtois, sometimes it is necessary that gypsies be driven out, pigs hanged, lawyers bribed and peasants oppressed for the sake of Order and Rule. He does not mean divine order or the rule of the law.

Nevertheless, the church and the law are also dedicated to maintaining human order in this small town,[21] and, for better or worse, they work together. On the one hand, the Inquisition is all eyes and ears, which means that anything disturbing, irritating, or simply different can be denounced as the work of Satan. Father Albertus privately thinks witch trials are preposterous. Would he testify to that in court? "Richard," he replies rather testily, "I like it here. It's a good life, and having my balls burned off in public might take some of the pleasure from it." In fact, he does testify in the pig trial, but as a witness for the prosecution. Asked if he thinks it is futile to put an animal to death for a crime, he hesitates—for this is dangerous ground—then makes what he surely knows is a self-serving distinction: "We execute not the animal itself, but Satan in it." As for the law itself, it helps to know that Pincheon, the prosecutor, earns more than his salary in payoffs from the local Seigneur. Whatever may be the truth about this pig trial, he knows more than he is willing to say, and he too is anxious to have done with it. Nonetheless, this rheumy, aging man of law, played by Donald Pleasance, compels our attention and our sympathy. His summation in the pig trial is probably the most powerful speech in the film. Its appeal goes beyond the needs of those who wish to bury the issue, and addresses the terrible need for justice and for laws that acknowledge human weakness, levy punishment, close the book, and make us whole. He himself was a successful Paris lawyer once, but now, after twenty years of country law practice and so many compromises ... "Look at me, Maître," he says to Courtois, "I am what you will become in twenty—well, thirty years."

That leaves the Advocate himself, the vigilant idealist and reformer, building a house, a new life in the country, but also, of course, the romantic under full sail who's headed for the pragmatic rocks. Courtois imagines himself a realist, not a dreamer, yet he dreams constantly, and in his dream visions he confronts—as we might expect—the specters of violence and brutality, and the ecstasies of love. He bitterly resents having to represent a pig; he dislikes losing debates with Pincheon, who plays the judge by invoking *lex talionis*—"An eye for an eye, a tooth for a tooth, a stripe for a stripe; there's a case to answer!" But most of all, he hates the idea of losing this case, for by now it represents everything that opposes him and that he can't understand in this unenlightened, superstitious town. That, and the fact that the pig's gypsy owner, Samira, has great dark luminous eyes—observant eyes, just like the Advocate himself. Also like him, she is not one to accept a compromise. The gypsies need the meat, and besides, it is obvious that Courtois will help her.

But we must be fair. The Advocate is young, yet the film takes him seriously (for the most part), and the film is more satire than comedy. Courtois dreams, it is true, but his final vision is a surreal gallery of verbal and visual clues that torment his sleeping mind as he dreams of justice. He never brings the killer to trial—indeed, the killer is another avid hunter, d'Auferre's monstrous son, whose bad habits include nailing dogs to trees—but the boy flees to England, and the people's fear is reduced thereby.[22] As for the pig, it is acquitted, finally, when Courtois, disgusted with the whole business, locates another, similar pig and rigs its "confession."

What Courtois cannot, and could never, do is to change the way these people see themselves and others. The peasants, the lord, the priest, the civil court, the gypsies—all of them fear the Black Death and the Inquisition, but they also fear each other. They are continually on watch, not just for small-town gossip, but for any small thing that will give them an advantage. This could be the stuff of comedy, as in Chaucer's *Miller's Tale*, but it is not: they fear each other because they prey upon each other, so that each one is at the same time hunter and victim. The lord abuses the gypsies, for example, and uses their pig as a scapegoat, but the pheasants and other illegal game in the gypsies' wagon end up at d'Auferre's castle, and when the gypsy girl dances at his festival banquet, it is implied that other commercial relationships might be possible—if not with this woman, then with another. The constant emphasis on animals in this film is ultimately a way of focusing on man the hunter and his human quarry. The Seigneur d'Auferre is matter of fact about it, the church would deny it (but what, after all, is the Inquisition), and the men of law, in trying to prevent it, become the most sophisticated and self-serving of all the hunters.

And so, at the end, Courtois goes back to Paris. He belongs there. Everybody knows it, and finally he accepts it too. He doesn't say good-bye to the maid at the local Inn—that was over long ago, and it turns out that he was paying for it anyway, since the Abbeville Inn is covertly the Abbeville whorehouse, and her fee was the room tax. More hunters, more victims. But Samira is another matter. He loves her, and in many ways they are similar—outcasts both, and given to those long, profoundly watchful brown-eyed gazes. But she will not go with him, not that she could not love him, but because she thinks she is not quite human in his eyes. Not an animal, a beast, as the townspeople think of her, but a strange fine creature to have in his house and in his bed. For them, as for all the characters in Abbeville, making a life depends upon knowing who you are and recognizing that identity in others. Augustine found this correspondence reflected in the Holy Trinity. The people of Abbeville, it seems, find it by living a kind of human beast fable. And as for Courtois—the Advocate goes back to Paris, where he will become the most distinguished lawyer of his time, the credits tell us, by defending two-legged clients—like himself.

Stepping away from the film a bit, we can see that there are in Abbeville two main attitudes—call them theories—regarding human behavior, and Courtois's idealism shuns both of them. First, it is generally assumed (and the film amplifies this assumption) that animals are, in effect, a revealing mirror of human life, and that anyone who doubts this correspondence is naïve or quite unrealistic. People's appetites, aggressions, fears and even cleverness are constantly shadowed by animal parallels and thus appear to have a kind of innocence—as if doing what comes naturally (usually, some kind of hunting behavior) is inevitable and not really blameworthy. Yet on the other hand, since there have to be customs, laws, and prohibitions for society to exist at all (and the film's emphasis on legal affairs underscores this theme), there is a general need for control, and virtually every character in the film demonstrates some small ability to control his or her own immediate social environment. The nobility, the church and the civil courts are obviously engaged in imposing order, but the same manipulative tendencies are plainly to be seen at a lower level in the pigherd (who pricks his pig to make it "speak" its confession), the jailer/torturer (who pricks a female prisoner, producing skin lesions that are taken as evidence of Satan's influence), the maid at the Inn, the mother of Filette, Samira (who lacerates Courtois's idealistic conscience)—each has found a way. But if control is an absolute necessity, and the law imposes control through punishment (an eye for an eye, etc.), then any behavior that violates the law must be punished, whether the guilty one is human or not. Hence the animal trials.

These two assumptions are complementary opposites. Together they imply that life in Abbeville is to control or be controlled, and very often both at the same time. But Courtois, who has come to Abbeville to bring the spirit of the law to "real" people, would like to think that humans are defined neither by animal urges nor by rigid and arbitrary codes of law. He loves the law because it seems to him impartial but also reasonable, a protection and a guide enabling people to live as they are meant to live—by choosing their way freely according to their needs and their ideals. Surely, although he does not say so in the film, he thinks that they are meant to live by *ius gentium*, not as slaves to their appetites, yet not under tyranny either, nor by the law of fang and claw.

At this point, moviegoers may wonder whether people like Courtois actually lived in the fifteenth century—but, of course, idealists and reformers spring up in every time and place. A better question is whether human and animal behavior was indeed conflated during that period, as the movie, in its schematic way, suggests. Were there really animal trials, and if so, does the film treat them accurately? The trials did occur, lawyers like Courtois became known for participating in them,[23] and there was even a kind of precedent for these odd events, if one considers that their key assumptions have an imaginative quality that recalls the *Roman de Renart*, and mimics the kind of reasoning that guided the trials of the Inquisition. These sobering parallels are implicit in the movie and seem the more powerful for being understated. The filmscript is also rich in legalistic anecdotes, phrases, ironies, and problems, all of which has the effect of keeping our attention on "order and rule"—what Chaucer might have called questions of "governaunce"—which seem genuinely compelling, given the frightening instability and disorder that characterize not only the film but the historical time and place it reflects.

For the most impressive historical aspect of the picture is not the animal trial, though it provides plot structure and directs us recurrently to the main question (*What is Man?*), but the accuracy, immediacy and variety of features which reflect the unsettled fifteenth century in France. This turbulence is central to the movie; it is, I believe, what the film is really about, just as Barbara Tuchman's *A Distant Mirror* was really about her subtitle, *The Calamitous Fourteenth Century*, which seemed to her fully as afflicted as the calamitous twentieth.[24] I mentioned above that there was a kind of social malaise in Abbeville, and yet it seems a normal, recognizable country town. Courtois wants to know who murdered a Jewish boy, but our sense of there being something deeply, intangibly wrong derives more from realizing that the many disorders referenced in the film are linked and cumulative, and that if we breathed that country air, we too would be quick-witted, hyper-vigilant, apprehensive, and suspicious.

The church, for example, is obviously in need of reform (Father Albertus is evidence for this), and the counter-reformation (as some would call the Inquisition) is an organized, vigorous answer to that threat. There are no peasants' revolts in this film, but there is evidence of growth in the little Norman town of Abbeville (Paris lawyers are moving in), and the middle-class builders, at least, are amassing capital. The Seigneur Jehan d'Auferre is himself a capitalist noble, and his heretical Catharist grandfather probably came from the South—where the plague comes from, and the gypsies, "spreading like rats," as the law clerk says. The Hundred Years War is not overtly mentioned, but its last great battle took place at Agincourt, which is not far from Abbeville, and the war will end the very next year, in 1453. Furthermore, it is a "wandering knight at-arms" who brings Abbeville deliverance from its worldly cares at the end of the film, insofar as he carries the plague. Less explicit (but typical of the film's texture and its rewardingly broad, if barely visible, historical horizons) is that Courtois himself, the university-trained civil jurist, represents the spread of the (written) Roman law into northern France, where it will displace the many unwritten and partially written customs (*coutûmes*) that were inherited from feudal practices and a tradition of Germanic law.[25]

With French law will come French rule. By 1470, Abbeville and Ponthieu (the valley of the Somme), which are at this point still subject to the Duke of Burgundy, will have become part of the Couronne de France, and the relative absolutism of the French crown will endure for nearly 300 years.[26] War and its effects, then, plague, capitalist monopoly, witch trials, animal trials, political absolutism—these are severe constraints offering a very dark glass indeed in which to seek the human image.

The Advocate is far better at stating the human problems of fifteenth-century Abbeville than it is at finding solutions, or even at tracing historical consequences, and that, surely, is its strength as an historical film. Richard Courtois is not presented as a "Renaissance Man" to save this or any other world. He ultimately returns to an urban version of the same problems, concerned, like any other man, with "making a living." And yet there is something in Courtois to which we respond. We probably like the animal exuberance of life in Abbeville, and we pretty certainly understand the often invisible but binding network of controls that accompany it; but this airless dialectic is not enough for us. Like Courtois, we want more, more choices—freedom, dignity, *identity*. And this is how the film can be about the fifteenth century and about us at the same time. Trapped (for 101 minutes) in Abbeville, involved in the animal trials, and with animal behavior a constant parallel, we are forced to question what is human; but this is a question to which we are already accustomed and have been for some time. We are like Courtois because, in our own way, we too are suburbanites, fleeing urban sprawl. In this, Henry Thoreau is still our strongest voice:

> I went to the woods because I wished to live deliberately, to front only the essential facts of life, and see if I could learn what it had to teach, and not when I came to die, discover I had not lived. I did not wish to live what was not life, living is so dear.[27]

For Thoreau, Walden Pond is a mirror, not only of heaven but of man. Nature for him is an entity, a guide, a pattern for human living, just as it was—although in a more abstract, systematic, and "realist" sense—for Courtois; it offers "higher laws" for those who are equipped to understand them. And so he goes to Walden, where the angelic pickerel, with their "cool and even temperament," swim on through "perennial waveless serenity" under the ice of the pond in winter (189).

So far we have heard the transcendentalist Thoreau, but he has other voices, and in them we may begin to recognize the conflicted, animal-haunted vision of man that we saw in Abbeville. Thoreau had few visitors in the woods, but one of these, a French Canadian wood chopper and post-maker, becomes for him an example of "natural" man: "Such an exuberance of animal spirits had he that he sometimes tumbled down and rolled on the ground with laughter at anything which made him think and tickled him" (102). And more directly: "In him the animal man chiefly was developed" (102). Thoreau both respects and patronizes this man, in somewhat the same way that Courtois treats his unfortunate clients in Abbeville. This lumberman is strengthened by his life in nature, but also, Thoreau feels, is limited by it: "When Nature made him, she gave him a strong body and contentment for his portion, and propped him on every side with reverence and reliance, that he might live out his threescore years and ten a child" (102). In a later chapter ("Higher Laws"), we see Thoreau's fully developed attitude toward man's two natures:

> We are conscious of an animal in us, which awakens in proportion as our higher nature slumbers. It is reptile and sensual, and perhaps cannot be wholly expelled; like the worms which, even in life and health, occupy our bodies. Possibly we may withdraw from it, but it never changes its nature. I fear that it may enjoy a certain health of its own; that we may be well, yet not pure [149].

We come away from Thoreau having witnessed the same struggle between natural and reasonable man that is dramatized in the movie by the character of Courtois. Nature, for Thoreau, is a great teacher and a high example (remember the pickerel), but nature *within* man is ambivalent and problematic. He feels that boys should be allowed to fish, but considers them stunted if they don't eventually leave the fishpole behind and become, as it were, fishers of men (144).

It would be tidy to conclude that Thoreau, the nineteenth-century dualist Romantic, is carrying on the same struggle between ape and angel that Courtois suffers in his legalistic idealism, and that we Post-Moderns can relate to both. But even though we remain post–Romantics to some degree—and Thoreau is still read—I'm not sure that is exactly what *The Advocate* is about for us. We can contemplate the fifteenth century's social problems with a certain grim knowingness, and we know enough about the animal in man to appreciate both the truth and the irony of beast fables; about tyranny we are too well informed. But *our* idealism? Do we retain the high-mindedness (both the ethical commitment and the analytic detachment which keeps it from becoming mere emotionalism) necessary to care about yet another (fifteenth-century French) urban dreamer out of his depth in country matters?

The peculiar sensible power of the medieval world in this film helps us to care. For as we surrender to the tangible immediacy of fifteenth-century problems and worries, we can suspend for just a little while our own skepticism regarding politic ideals, and our cynicism about the blurring of the distinction between human and animal nature. We may pass over the skepticism lightly, since the ongoing nostalgia for Camelot demonstrates our hidden hunger for political fables, especially the remote, simplistic and (for us at least) painless ones like the Round Table. But if the human image also embodies an ideal, there seems to be little hunger for it. The blurring of distinctions between human and animal is commonplace. It seem almost a necessary assumption in popular culture, where dogs are assigned to dog psychotherapists, chimpanzees are taught to communicate in sign language (and with i-pads), and killer whales are sentimentalized as playmates for small children (while on the non-fiction Discovery channel it is possible to watch them beating Arctic seals to bloody pulp). Arguably, these examples belong to the beast fable tradition, like Disney cartoons, while stories of humans acting like animals are probably a variety of romance—gothic, for instance, or detective thrillers, or science fiction. I am not giving them much importance. I would argue merely that in popular art, it is common for animals (even great white sharks) to be assigned human motives. Conversely, given titles like *The Killer Ape* or (the movie) *Birdie* or *The Silence of the Lambs*, we are not surprised when humans carry out animal behaviors. Conceivably, the impact of these mingled images may contribute to an increased anxiety over questions of human identity (for example, the moral backlash in rural Kansas against the teaching of evolution), and to our increased interest in scientific advances, like the description of the human genome or the theory of socio-biology, both of which are popularly assumed to have identified a "script" for human form or function.

As moderns, nonetheless, we react to the pig trial with a condescending shrug: we find it childish, contemptible even, that humans and animals were judged as equals under the law. But it is probably more significant that we can still find it touching, and even a little stirring that Richard Courtois, the Advocate of Abbeville, should care so much about it ... that he has *reason* to be concerned. Sharing his darkly thoughtful gaze as we do, however—for the director's eye for coded detail quickly has us searching for social, legal and historical implications—the medieval ideals and conflicts implicit in this serio-comic beast litigation become vivid and emergent for us, and we find ourselves pondering over the law as a mirror of human reason. It is mildly amusing, for example, that the Advocate Courtois summons the rats to bear witness in defense of a woman accused of *maleficium*—of inciting them to bite a neighbor. But when the rats do not obey the summons (issued on posters written clearly in the French language), he quotes Roman law (the *Corpus Iuris Civilis*) to justify their absence: given that their mortal enemies, the dogs and cats of the village, might cause harm to their persons, the rats may rightfully absent themselves—even though summoned by law—because they have the natural right to act in defense of their own safety.[28] Amusing it is, and yet this is precisely the point of law that was invoked to excuse a king's resort to warfare in defense of the public good, even though such an act would otherwise contradict the *ius naturale*, the natural law. Within the context of European history, it was a serious matter, this reasoning about the differences between *ius gentium*, the law of men, and (its putative source) the *ius naturale*, God's reason in Nature. Within the events of the film, it manifests itself as the necessity of human imperfection, and the social and legal attempts made to compensate for it. For us, however, it is ultimately a question of human identity. And so we, too, meditate upon the governance of a lord whose bookkeeping is exact, but whose pleasure is riding to the hunt for human quarry; and we wonder, endlessly, whether there is room for human intentions and choices between the crushing millstones of animal behavior and tyrannical control.

Through Courtois's perplexity, and through the villagers' anxiety, the priest's irony, and the frigid humor of the lord, we enter fifteenth-century France, and we ponder its questions—for a time. But we remain aware that we are in it, not of it. That is the condition of medievalism; but, in any case, the movie will not allow us to forget ourselves. For its fundamental style is to present medieval life as paradoxical: lifelike, yes, and true to its own assumptions, but essentially opposed to our empirical and eclectic frame of mind. And here is where we feel most keenly the film's narrative "slant." The animal trials are such a paradox for us, as is the Inquisition and the matter-of-fact absolutism of the Seigneur d'Auferre. Centrally, and somewhat surprisingly, however, the chief paradox is Courtois himself and the nature of his reasoning. To be sure, he too finds it absurd to have to defend "witches," and even pigs, in a court of law. Yet the law he practices itself rests upon abstract ideals (e.g., the "natural right" to self-defense) which are treated as though they were real entities and provide the basis for real-world decisions, including wars and executions. This law is certainly a disciplined practice of reason, yet reason reduced to formulae and based on premises which often go unexamined. In this connection, Huizinga is again helpful:

> The spirit of casuistry, which was greatly developed in the Middle Ages ... is another effect of the dominant realism. Every question which presents itself must have its ideal solution, which will become apparent as soon as we have ascertained, by the aid of formal rules, the relation of the case in question to the eternal verities. Casuistry reigns in all departments of the mind: alike in morals and in law, and in matters of ceremony, of etiquette, of tournaments and the chase, and, above all, in love.[29]

One might reasonably object that, like medieval people, we have our own abstract ideals and our own casuistry, including the legal kind. Without question. Yet even though we can warm to their courtroom drama, try on their attitudes, and savor their legal wit, their habits of mind are not, cannot be ours. Even Courtois, whose youthful idealism is steadied by solid legal principles, finds his purpose and identity in practicing law whose deepest logic is theologic: God's reason applied to men. And so, while the movie's affect—its elemental images of medieval pride, dirt, loveliness and pain—reaches us directly, just as practically anyone is quickened by Alysoun's friskiness or Nicholas's scorched behind, its instruction, its medieval "sentence" must come to us by analogy, and no doubt it is clearer and more helpful for that very reason. Charmed, then, by *The Advocate*'s historical detail, its color and wry comedy—all of it quite faithful to the period—we are lured into sifting and, at a certain distance, caring about questions of legal, political and moral philosophy that give us back a troubling, ambivalent reflection of our human image. Thus are we drawn to question a little more deeply and truly who we are. That is how a movie can be about the Middle Ages as well as about us, and why, if it is going to be good, it probably needs to be both.

CHAPTER FIVE

Northern Light

Direct, sensitive, profound—Ingmar Bergman's *The Seventh Seal* and Carl Theodor Dreyer's *La Passion de Jeanne d'Arc* have been called these and similar things for nearly a century, and they retain the power to transfix an audience and haunt the memory. These Swedish and Danish landmarks of *auteur* cinema date from a time when directors of proven quality were sometimes relatively free to write, cast, shoot and shape a film. In these two cases, the results were brilliant. But for our purposes, *The Seventh Seal* and *La Passion de Jeanne d'Arc* are less interesting as icons of high modernism than for the powerful ways they exploit the conventions of medievalism. Their settings—plague and war in Sweden and France in the fourteenth and fifteenth centuries—enable in each case an unrelenting focus on spiritual quest that has never seemed so nakedly and humanly genuine as it does in these two films.

The Seventh Seal

The Seventh Seal begins with a brief paragraph on a black screen—a knight, Antonius Block, has returned from years of crusading in the Holy Land to a Sweden ravaged by the Black Plague.[1] Then the first scene opens with a shot of the heavens, the sun forcing its rays through a glowing bank of thin cloud, while a powerful chorus sings the "Kyrie Eleison" (Lord, have mercy) from the *Requiem Mass*, the mass for the dead. Then CUT to an overhead shot of a large bird, wings extended, silhouetted against the sky as it rides the air; and CUT to the stones of the beach, far below, framed on one side by rocky cliffs and on the other by endless sea and sky. A narrator reads from Revelations in a voice powerful for its muted restraint and perhaps humility in uttering last things. The Lamb of the Apocalypse opens the seventh seal of God's commandment. The seven angels prepare to sound their trumpets. Earthly life has come under the judgment.

The time is pre-dawn, the light is gray, and at first nothing moves but the distant lines of surf. The camera angle shifts and we can see two horses standing at the edge of the water and something else lying on the beach. Another shift to a closer point of view—two men are asleep or dead in this stony waste, and CUT to a close-up of the knight awakening, sword in hand. Opening his eyes as the sun clears the horizon he sighs, as though weary of his days. He wears a crusader's cross—it is Antonius Block, journeying homeward with his squire. Since the plague is here, and no one is safe from it, these men will probably die soon. Life as it has been in Sweden is ending. Every man must confront what he has done and who he has become in these final hours.

In this opening scene our gaze has moved from the heavens to the earth, to men so exhausted they slept on the stones where they landed, and this movement has prepared us to understand the film. Until the men wake, we have only the paragraph about the knight and the plague, the Requiem music, the deep sky overhead, the bird, the vast seacoast, yet these have already created a *mise-en-scène* that is unmistakably "medieval." It is the fourteenth century, certainly, but its temporal milieu, the underlying world view that we begin to share, is derived from two realities already present. We see the ragged cliffs, the sea below, the men on the beach, yet we know by now that another reality lies beyond this scene and is already implicit in it. The water and the rocks are real enough, but the plague—nowhere and everywhere—is equally real, and the eternity that waits is surely most real, shadowing every feature of the action and, in the end, of course, inevitable. The chorus sings its dirge in a minor key, and overhead the great bird hangs in the wind. All this, perhaps, is part of God's plan, the bird manifesting the descent of God's word, the song a prayer sent upward. The sleeping men, alone under the sky, will continue their journey, completing their lives between these mundane and transcendent realities; and, without a word spoken, they stand for all of us.

In these ways *The Seventh Seal* moves toward allegory, and that is one of its central strengths.[2] Things mean beyond themselves in this film, as they do in medieval literature and in medieval life generally. Consequently, we do not have to be intrigued with the quaint roughness, the apparent simplicity of medieval life, nor is it enough to be charmed by medieval beauty (Bibi Andersson, who plays Mia, will be quite beautiful) or repelled by medieval cruelty, of which there is much in this film. All of these things, delightful or appalling in themselves, have their artistic and human importance in the ways they represent a life that has entered its last act. Now that there is so little time, and Death sits quietly, playing chess with our representative knight, every word and gesture resonates with the tragic sense of man's short life, but also with its implicit hope and momentary brightness.[3] The weight of these mundane and transcendent realities is ever present, creating the surprising amplitude of the film. Its interpretive reach allows the small doings of these rather ordinary characters to cast long shadows on the human condition[4]; even their small mercies and acts of love have their greatness because we see them *sub specie aeternitatis*—under the eye of eternity. Not every medieval film is able to create this sense of immanence, the indwelling significance of small things, because it requires a world view—an attitude not a scene, a vision rather than a perception of our existence. To share it we must be brought into that world, first through our experience of the film and then by the ways it opens into the fear and despair that stalk us in our own lives, as well as the hope and love we too hold up in defense. In these ways *The Seventh Seal* draws us.

The drama of the film, its conflicted human relationships, begins as the knight (Max von Sydow) stands to face the day. His face is lean, rather long and barren of emotion, the face of a dedicated, driven man. Soon he will walk unsteadily over the stones into the surf to bathe his face, and then he will kneel and pray. The absence of any other word or gesture to qualify these simple acts implies a cleansing, an ascetic life and perhaps a troubled spirit, for prayer does not seem to have brought relief. The scene shifts to the squire (Gunnar Björnstrand). Opening his eyes and seeing the sun still on the horizon, he turns over, and we see the knife that never left his hand while he slept. Shortly the knight will pass, giving the squire a light kick—their journey waits—and the squire will look after him with an ill-natured hiss. These are men united by their service in the Holy Land and by the various dangers that lie before them, but they are obviously quite different, and, as we will learn, they see their world differently.[5]

The knight is one of many who left Europe on crusade, carrying out God's will, as they thought, but yielding finally to death or to increasing disillusionment as the bloody years passed. He is one of the few whose quest has only become more intense. He wishes, or rather craves, knowledge of God—a sign, a word, something to show that life is more than a random series of events, meaningless in their absurd cruelty. In the film we will follow his search. But whether he is confessing its emptiness, which has deadened all feeling within him, or interrogating a girl accused of witchcraft and about to be burned as a witch (she says she has seen the devil, and surely the devil must have some knowledge of God?), only death keeps him company, as death alone seems to offer a kind of certainty. Indeed, this man's time has come; the stark figure of death—whiteface, robed in black—appears to him in the opening scene.

In contrast to Block's austerity, his squire Jöns is constantly in touch with the sensible world—singing, drinking, wenching when the opportunity arises—holding himself aloof from the possibility of heaven but maintaining at the same time an ironic view of his own absurdity, as well as that of other people and of life in general. Block searches for God and plays chess with death, seeking in every event an answer to ultimate questions, but Jöns is always in human company. While going about the knight's business he drinks with a church painter, prevents a rape, brands a thief, consoles the oafish blacksmith (his wife has run off with an actor). With Jöns, we enter the social world of the film, the average people lost in their superstitions, fearing the plague and clinging to what little they know of life. Block and Jöns remind us of Don Quixote and Sancho Panza.[6] They never see the world the same way but support each other as they encounter the mad confusion of everyday life and the profound questions that lie beneath it. Between them they bring the transcendent and mundane realities of life into a dramatic conflict that creates the infrastructure of the film.

Distinct from this conflict between the mediocre and the ideal is the little family of Jof and Mia (Joseph and Mary), and their little son Mikael. They are humble people, traveling players drawn by their horse and wagon from town to town to earn what they can by singing, dancing and playing allegories and farces for small audiences of ignorant folk. Yet the happy innocence of their lives interrupts the narrative of Block's painful quest and lightens the oppressive darkness that hovers over them all. Like the holy family they resemble, Jof, Mia and Mikael are in the world but not entirely of it; their simple humility is heartwarming, but as one scene follows another, it becomes clear that they represent something like an exalted merging of the mundane and transcendent realities that strain against each other in the film. A poor but loving family, no grief seems to touch them. Even the angel of death passes harmlessly overhead at the end of the film, and when bright day breaks, they will journey on together. They are the remnant, the embodiment of our eternal hope for the future.

It is still early morning when Block and Jöns pass Jof's wagon on their way through the land stricken by plague, and from now on the two journeys will be interwoven—Block's return, his questions still unanswered, and Jof and Mia's pursuit of livelihood. Finally they will travel together through the midnight forest, a thunderstorm raging overhead, until at the end of night the knight comes home to death, and Jof and Mia travel on in the summer morning. But when we first encounter them, husband and wife and Skat, the third player, are asleep in the wagon, heads together at the center and feet stretched out in different directions, intimate but chaste. Suddenly, one of the men starts (it is Jof, played by Nils Poppe)—a bug has bitten him. Then he swats another bug, leaving a spot of blood on his forehead. Soon he will get up, stretch, do some tumbling on the grass, greet the horse, have a drink of water, and see an ecstatic vision of the Holy Mother and Child. But already we know him. He is the one to whom visions and bug bites happen—a kind of holy fool and, like the knight, a crucial figure. Without his whimsical antics, which create

Bibi Andersson as Mia, and Nils Poppe as Jof, in Ingmar Bergman's *The Seventh Seal* (1957).

the oddly beatific texture of their way of life,[7] Mia's beauty would seem irrelevant and the film's weight tedious, its darkness appalling. Now a phrase of music—the Holy Mother appears in a sunlit glade, helping her baby learn to walk, and when the blessed sight fades, Jof jumps back into the wagon to tell Mia (*his* Mary), waking her from a sound sleep. She is patient with his visions, because they are innocent (you saw a woman, *what* woman?), and likes the song he sings, because, as with most things (though she falls back to sleep during it), he sings it for her. This morning scene takes its wryly blissful tone from the music of the vision and Jof's song, from the laughing of little Mikael, who wakes up crying but is soon a happy baby, and from these two young parents who seem to love even the little faults we can see in each of them. The warmth of their happiness, the emptiness of Block's quest—this tension in the film, the dialectic of its themes, is another authenticating feature, an aspect of its medievalism.

The agon of life and death is the prime dialectic of the movie, however, and the starkly embodied figure of death is a requirement of that form.[8] Bergman's first version of *The Seventh Seal* was a play, *Wood Painting*, that he wrote for the members of a drama ensemble he was coaching. The play was supposed to recall the wall paintings he had seen as a child in churches where his father was preaching—each panel a scene with its message, and the messages often linked, as they are in the famous dance of death, where Death dances now with the king in his robes, now with the worker in the field, with wives and children, priests and magistrates. Hence the alternating focus in the film—Death visiting the knight at various times during his last day, but also, at times in between, the sweet, silly or ugly lives of others who are soon to die themselves (since, after all, the plague is upon them). Bergman's casting for the figure of death was Bengt Ekerot, who had himself directed a recent performance of *Wood Painting*, and Ekerot plays the dark lord with an understated, lightly ironic menace, relentless indeed but willing to talk about it, to pause for a game of chess, even though he will not, cannot answer Block's questions. Death has no answers.

"Have you come for me?" the knight asks. "I have been at your side for a long time." "I know," says the crusader who has traded in death for a decade, and now perhaps is weary enough to welcome an end to all of it, even his own questions. Yet between the pursuer and his prey a kind of bond exists—not companionship exactly, but a mutual recognition of things, a shared knowing, which is figured by the game of chess. Block is playing for his life, and, later in the film, for the lives of Jof and his family. Still, their game is played in grimly good-natured rivalry ("Yes, in fact I'm a pretty good chess player," says Death), and their talk is mixed with banter and edged wit. In its way, this game is like the dance of death itself, its meaning dire, its end inevitable, but a dance, nonetheless, which shows the distinctiveness of the man and frames his last acts in complementary moves, rendering them less lonely.[9] Death in medieval times could and did evoke horror, but it was a familiar part of life, not a distant responsibility of funeral homes. The chess game and other meetings between the knight and Death are milestones in the film which we recognize and finally come to accept as necessary to the story, just as we accept the logic of Godfather Death's dreaded return visit in folktales. Death and the game of chess create necessity, but also give Block a way of dealing with his final day and a purpose in doing so; in that sense, his last day is preferable to the life he has wasted looking for answers.

Block's search for God, and more generally for meaningfulness in life, is admittedly a modern theme, not a medieval one. Medieval people knew the answers perfectly well; their struggle, for the most part, was to conduct their lives according to truths they had known since childhood, despite the many temptations to do otherwise. Our own tendency to seek meaning in our lives was strong in the 1950s when Bergman made *The Seventh Seal*, and many have said it resembles an existentialist text.[10] As for Block's journey into death, Bergman's own preoccupation with death at that time in his life was probably

Bengt Ekerot as Death, and Max von Sydow as Antonius Block, in Ingmar Bergman's *The Seventh Seal* (1957).

one reason for its prominence in the film. A few critics, less persuasively, have said that the nuclear threat so deeply felt in the 1950s was the modern counterpart to the medieval fear of the plague, and must have had an influence on the film. Inescapably, at any rate, *The Seventh Seal* is a modern movie that is (indirectly) about modern people. The question is how the medieval themes, characters and setting seem to give us back our own deepest concerns and offer a kind of release from them. There is much that appeals to us in each of the principle characters and in the ways they relate to each other—Jof and Mia, for example, or Block and Jöns. Like them, we cringe from the cruelty of burning a young girl (*obviously* she is not a witch!), and, like them, we watch, fascinated and appalled by the procession of flagellants (how can human beings torment themselves so?). But the scene where we are brought closest to them—where our own desires are closest to theirs—is probably at the end of the day when Block has tethered his horse and encounters Mia and Mikael sitting by their wagon.[11]

He recognizes her from the performance she and Jof put on earlier in the day; she says he looks tired, lonely—and doesn't he have someone? He praises the little boy. Will he become an acrobat? Perhaps a knight, she says, and then Jof staggers around the corner of the wagon (at the inn, he was beaten and made to dance over the fire). When Jof recovers, he acts the host, inviting Block to share their simple meal, the berries Mia has picked and the milk they owe to a generous cow. Then Jöns arrives—after helping Jof escape the fire and an even worse beating, he now brings with him the girl he saved from rape and murder that day. They come together at the evening respite and are to each other an aid and comfort, like a family united. In this moment of shared peace, Block is able to say that his isolation, the difficulty of his fruitless quest—all that seems unimportant now as they sit together at the end of the day. He takes up the wide bowl of milk, drinks, and, still holding the milk before him, his face shining in the evening sun, tells them he will always remember this time—Jof with his song, Mia and Michael and everyone at rest—and it will be enough for him. Marc Gervais has written that Block's drinking from the bowl of milk and then giving a kind of benediction is, in effect, a secular celebration of communion, a moment of identity rising from the common meal and the spiritual oneness it signifies.[12] Shortly he will walk down the slope to the left, where his chessboard waits. The shadows of evening are gathering, and all of them must face terrible things that night. But the human bond has been formed; Block will escort Jof and his family through the forest, and his last act at chess before he is checkmated will be to distract Death long enough for them to slip away and save themselves.

    The power of scenes like this one draws upon our feeling for the characters—we care about them by this time, and are aware of the dangers of their journeys—but other features are involved as well. The film is remarkable for its contrasts between bright and dark, innocence and evil, kindness and cruelty. The bowl of milk scene would not work as well if recently we had not seen the so-called witch girl tied like an animal to a stake in front of the church, her cries virtually unbearable. Or Jof, dancing like a bear over the flames of torches, fainting while drunks beat time with their beer mugs. Seeing things like this we are in a sense violated. Our moral boundaries are invaded, and it is impossible not to invest the scene with our own pain and resistance. We are aided in this by Block and Jöns, whose role as knight and squire is, surprisingly, less acting and doing than observing what goes on in the world during their last day. Of the two, Jöns has the more active role, but even when he brands a thief or prevents a rape, his major function is to bear witness to the immorality released by the plague, or, in other cases, the superstition, the cruelty, and the desperate hope. The knight and his squire are not ineffectual. They are capable of acting, and we know by now that despite their hard life they are decent men. But for the most part they can do nothing about the dying and the evil things people do to each other in the time of plague. Because they are forced against their will to witness such things, and we have come to share their perspective, our own reaction is all the stronger.

The strength of the dark and bright in this film, and the effect of its contrasts, derive also from its being shot in black and white, which emphasizes form, light and texture rather than a palette of colors. The sudden appearance of Death in the opening scene, black robes silhouetted against the stones of the beach, would have seemed realistic but probably ridiculous if shot on color film. The bird seen against the dawn sky in the opening frames would also lose its effect in color, as would the striking initial shot of the sun behind clouds. Shapes command more attention when color is absent. Thus symbolic forms tend to resonate more strongly in black and white, so that even though Bergman is careful to avoid clichés, the film continually reminds us that things mean beyond themselves in this medieval world; it shows us the transcendent as it takes form in everyday things. When Block confesses in the church, for example, it is hooded Death who hears his confession, and we are the more aware of its hopelessness because the strong light coming through the window grill is casting the shadow of its grid. And as Block sinks to his knees, we see on the wall beside him the dark pattern of squares—is it like his chessboard, is it the window of his self-imposed imprisonment? The form constitutes a question, and our move toward interpretation becomes habitual as we experience the film. These symbolic contrasts work also at the level of the movie's gross structure. The events of the day, sun-filled and open-ended (even though there is suffering, no one but the comic Skat dies during the day), are answered by the frightening scenes of the night: the girl is indeed burned as a witch, and even the hardened Jöns finds it more than he can stand; the ex-seminarian and would-be rapist writhes, screaming in the forest, dying of the plague; and the knight marches forward, knowing that when their next meeting comes, Death will take him. These are last things, and one of the film's real strengths is that they are final and unrelieved: this medieval world is allowed the dignity of mortal limits.

Yet the end, when Death comes to the knight's castle in the pre-dawn storm, is surprisingly quiet and, in its ritualistic way, reminds us of how medieval people saw themselves. They sit at breakfast, and Karin, the knight's wife, reads to them from Revelations: a mountain of fire falls into the sea, a great star falls to earth and its name is Wormwood. The verse continues from what was narrated at the beginning of the film, and the sense of an ending is strong. As if in answer, the distant door booms, as if beaten by a mailed fist. No one is there, but the hallway glows and Death has come for them. They stand, and one by one, account for themselves—Karin, the smith and his wife, the knight and Jöns, and finally the girl that Jöns saved. Until now she has been a victim, silent through it all, but here it is she who kneels, looks into the light, and says, "It is finished." As in the dance of death, all must die, and Death comes to each according to their estate or occupation. They speak their piece, leave their portrait, as it were, and are gone. In the final scene, Jof sees them on a faraway hill, hand in hand—the human community following Death away from the morning and into the dark lands. But, of course, Mia, his wife, does not see them. Such visions are for saints and dreamers. And so the film preserves its two realities, the mundane and the transcendent, merging them only in the eyes of men such as Jof, and in our own.

La Passion de Jeanne d'Arc

With the title, stark white on black, we enter the world of this film and its awful necessity.[13] This is not the life story of Jeanne d'Arc, nor is it Joan the Woman or even, finally, her trial for heresy; instead this film witnesses the final agony of one who lives in a fallen world but obeys the laws of heaven, a woman for whom the only meaningful choice is to repeat the passion of Christ. The soundtrack for the title and credits is a solo female voice, high and pure, singing the Latin words to what its composer called Exclamavit/Prelude[14]: a voice, a spirit crying out—not in the wilderness, perhaps, but in the waste world—and that is the impression we retain, with increasing force, during the remainder of the film. Spiritual struggle is common in medieval movies, but nowhere else does the debate between body and soul so dominate the narrative; in no other film do we believe we are seeing the profound simplicity of a soul laid bare. To be sure, Dreyer grounds the picture in selected details and behaviors that reference the everyday life of late-medieval France, and it is chiefly the contrast with the mundane courtroom, Joan's prison cell, and even the stake itself that creates Joan's intensity—that of a woman giving testimony in defense of her life, while at the same time listening with all the strength of body and soul to the voice of God.

Dreyer's decision to confine the film to Joan's trial and execution, and to present that process as if it were taking place during the course of one day, foregrounds the procedural events of the trial. After the title, Dreyer's text outlines Joan's situation, but the following scene is not yet the medieval world; instead, a contemporary person's hands turn the pages of the manuscript record of Joan's trial. So her story is fact. The words of those questioning Joan, as well as Joan's answers to them, are taken directly from the trial record, and if we look carefully, the recording monk with his book is quietly present in several scenes. From the beginning, then, we are placed within a particularized temporal reality. Words and events are not merely suggestive of innocence on trial but are the *real* words and (it is easy to believe) the real gestures, grimaces and tears of people who were actually involved. The opening shot is a slow pan left to right across the courtroom. Groups of English soldiers—the guard—stand around talking, and clerics are filling the jury box. Here someone has brought a stool for the accused, there a priest takes his place. Nothing would suggest this is not business as usual, things as we know and expect them to be. Then the priest looks to his left, the camera follows, and suddenly Joan (Renée Falconetti) is there, stiff in her shackles, with wide, terrified eyes. From here on the film is dominated by a continued contrast between the materially known and the spiritual intensity of Joan's face. While Bergman's *The Seventh Seal* gives us man caught between earth and heaven, Dreyer shows us a small, earthly person within whom the strangeness of heaven has come to dwell.

Dreyer's many close-ups show a face which is not beautiful in any conventional way—at first, Falconetti's face seems full, almost round—but renders her emotions with the utmost delicacy. By the latter part of the film, we probably feel that it is quite a beautiful face, since by that time both the depth of Joan's experience and the strength of her self-mastery have come to us through the power and subtlety of her expressions. Possibly we experience not only Joan's thoughts and emotions, but the events of the trial itself through these close-ups of her face. Often it is a face shown from below, in high angle shots that reinforce the connection between this humble martyr and the heavenly mandate that is, for her at least, always present.

Initially, the intensity of Joan's expressions may strike the contemporary audience as overly dramatic, since most of us are accustomed to the understated intimacy of small-screen acting. We tend to associate full expressions with melodrama or broad comedy. Some critics believe the faces in this film bear witness to Dreyer's attraction to the lurid effects of Expressionism, a trend still powerful in the 1920s.[15] In the course of the film, however, the great round eyes that reflect Joan's terror, or astonishment, begin to seem less exaggerated, less an emotional overload, because the dangers that surround her are immediate and pressing. Every question is potentially a pitfall into heresy, the punishment for which is death at the stake; while on the other hand, if she is true to herself, and to God's wishes, she is barred from telling convenient, self-saving lies. And there are nuances in expression. "When you saw the Angel Michael, was he naked?" they ask her. There is almost a smile, a softening of the features: "Did you think God was unable to clothe him?" And then, "Who taught you the Creed?" She hesitates, looks down and to the side, remembering. A tear runs down. "My mother," she finally says, the tender sadness of her face bringing back a time when instead of enemies, love and comfort were all around her. Ultimately, Joan's face provides the emotional and spiritual axis of the film, even though the extensive use of close-ups runs counter to traditionally accepted ways of constructing film narrative.[16]

The close-up of a face, if held for any length of time, and if the extended close ups are repeated, tends to interrupt the narrative flow of events, where one action gives rise to the next. A film may show a brief close-up of a face as part of an action, perhaps to show a character's intention or reaction. But a longer close-up draws the viewer's attention to that character's inner life—his or her feelings at the moment, the memories brought to bear, the implications of what is now happening.[17] During the (actually, fairly short) time of the close-up, and even for a certain time afterwards, the viewer is invited to imagine a world related to the action at hand but different from it in time, space and affect, as though it were a virtual interior monologue or dream sequence. Hence, movies that require a seamless narrative tend to avoid long close-ups, and introspection is at a minimum. But *La Passion de Jeanne d'Arc* is above all an introspective film, a visual accounting of Joan's struggle with herself.[18] Without the close-ups, where we try to feel what she is feeling and attempt to imagine her bond with the ineffable (which we probably cannot feel)—without these many moments of gazing into Joan's face, the movie would flatten out along the axis of events; like so many other films about Joan, it would become merely another (briefer) account of the events of her life.

Joan's frequent close-ups invite us to share (as far as such things are shareable) her spiritual presence at the end of her short life. What anchors her pain and exaltation in the fifteenth-century moment, however, is the constant assault on her testimony and on her sense of self carried on by members of the church who are, in this case, judges. Joan's emotions are timeless, and so is her faith; even her conviction that God has sent her to save France has more to do with her privately experienced voices and visions than it does with the machinations of the Hundred Years War. But under examination by Pierre Cauchon (Eugène Silvain), the wrinkled, grandly crafty chief justice, who directs the proceedings with an iron finesse, she is very much a part of the late-medieval world, a young female peasant who cannot read or write and scarcely knows the year she was born. Cauchon is a Burgundian ally, and it was the Burgundian army which captured Joan at the town of Compiégne and sold her to their allies at that time, the English. The English, who have lost many of their numbers in combat with Joan's army, want her dead. The Burgundians certainly want her out of action; they do not want God to save the French. And while Cauchon and the other priests are duty bound to defend their faith against the heresy that might well be present in a woman who wears men's clothes and claims to hear voices of the saints, they must also make sure that Joan never goes free, lest the alliance with the English be broken.

Cauchon's wise-smiling manipulations owe as much to the political situation and his concern for his office in the church as they do to his personal iniquities, and later in the film we see his pained sadness when he realizes that Joan has chosen to recant her confession and must be burned, rather than going to prison for life. Silvain was the grand old man of the Comedie Française. As Cauchon, he seems to radiate infinite slyness, amusement, warmth, irony, anger, and contempt—his face is virtually never still—and in so doing he creates the sense of historical *mise-en-scène* that Joan's role needs if there is to be a narrative at all. The narrative is also strengthened by the relentless pace of the trial. We come to expect that one question will follow another as these strange old priests, each one a caricature, devise questions to draw Joan into their theological trap. This tangle of church casuistry is aided (or, better, darkened) by Nicholas Loyseleur, Cauchon's second-in-command, a priest who exerts his quiet power behind the scenes to ensure that Joan is not acquitted. Played by the esteemed French actor Maurice Schutz, Loyseleur has hooded eyes that peer from shadowed pits of ancient flesh. Where Cauchon is animated, his face a kaleidoscope of expression, Loyseleur is still and watchful, almost reptilian. So calculatingly cold are those eyes that when he finally smiles, making Joan believe he is trying to help her, the effect is almost Satanic. He is the one who realizes they can break Joan's defenses by forging a letter to her from the King of France, and it is he who finally, with horrible tenderness, guides Joan's hand when this illiterate girl attempts to sign the confession they have prepared for her. It is Joan's trusting honesty and openness, betrayed by the practiced craft of Cauchon and Loyseleur and the politico-religious necessity that drives them, that gives the film its weight of inevitability. Our painful acceptance that Joan will certainly die, however unfairly, is our entry into what seems "medieval" about her experience. She must die; we have, by this time, put ourselves empathetically in her place, and so we too are forced to confront ourselves at the edge of eternity.

Another underlying sense of the medieval derives from the nature of the trial itself. It is, in essence, a debate, a dialectical process that is supposed to wring the truth from this fraught situation. From our own point of view, of course, there is no truth at all to the inquiry. This innocent girl will die in prison or at the stake, and powerful interests will be served thereby. That too is a part of medieval warfare and medieval life. The "truth" that we derive from the interrogation is rather that Joan's innocence has been vindicated: whatever the source of her "voices," her conviction that God sent her to save France is one she will die to defend. In fact, she has the courage of a saint, and her death, however wrenching to watch (Dreyer brings us deep into the smoke and flames), is a moral victory. Like many stories of the saints and martyrs, it makes us proud to be human.

Joan's struggle to be true to herself and her God is another way in which the emotional/spiritual axis of the film crosses, and is enhanced by its contrast with the "horizontal" axis of mundane events, attitudes and schemes that oppose her. This onslaught of worldliness joins her own fears of torture and death, which, for a little while, cloud her understanding of where her life must lead. The reality of these fears has been shown from the beginning by the shots of the spears held by the soldiers as they file in and out of the courtroom, by the chilling array of funnels, hooks, chains, saws, and spiked wheels Joan sees in the torture chamber, and by the stake itself, which confronts her when she is led out into the courtyard. In the torture room she faints and is bled for fever; and in her weakened state, Loyseleur comes with the insidiously compelling proposal that she should try to save her life because the king still has need of her aid. The possibility of life is gripping because Joan has not given up wanting to live.[19] Unlike the Joan in Bresson's *Le Procès de Jeanne d'Arc*, a militant child of God who does not seem to care if she dies, Dreyer's Joan is merely a girl who heard God's voice and has staked her life to help her countrymen; given the choice, she would rather live and continue to help. That is why we identify with her so strongly, and why the certainty of her death is so hard to bear.

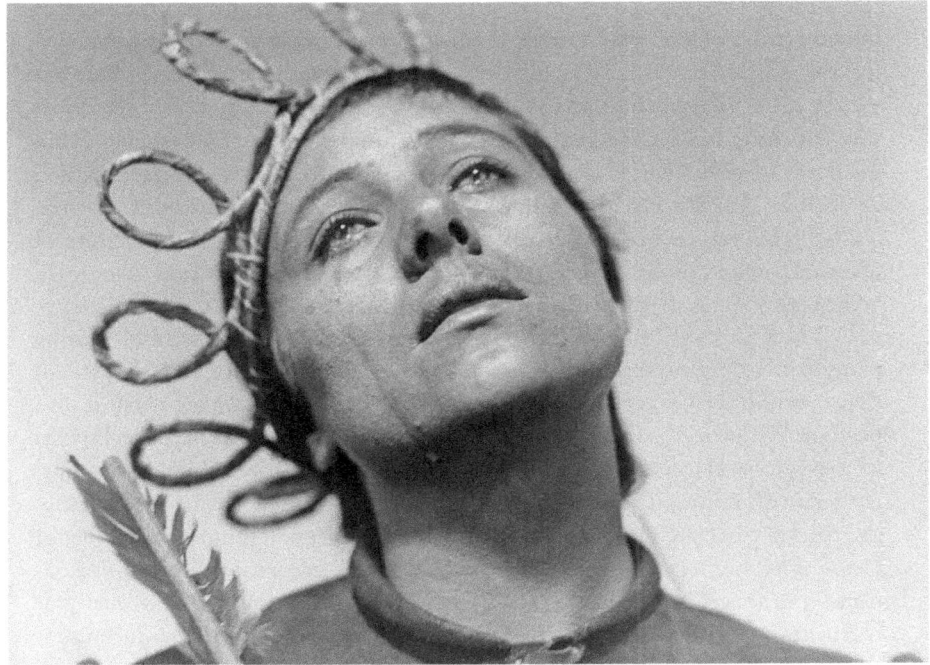

Renée Falconetti as Jeanne d'Arc in Carl Theodor Dreyer's *La Passion de Jeanne d'Arc* (1928; courtesy the Academy of Motion Picture Arts and Sciences).

Joan does sign the statement of confession, and is promptly absolved of excommunication and acquitted of heresy; but for her "great offenses" against the church she is sentenced to life in prison "to eat the bread of pain, and drink the water of anguish." Having signed, she shares faintly in the general relief—the clerics really did not wish her death, only the breaking of her rebellious will—but back in her cell she seems barely conscious, drained by the loss of God's purpose in her life. At this lowest point, she is transfixed by the straw crown she wove in her captivity—the soldiers had mocked her as Christ had been mocked with his crown of thorns. The crown is being swept up, along with the hair shorn close when she was made ready for the stake. Perhaps it is impossible to say what the crown and the hair mean to Joan, but with this shock of insight, it is clear that meaning has returned to her life: she will no longer deny her voices. Jesus died for her, and she will die with his name on her lips.

This turning point leads quickly to the final ritualistic scenes of Joan's approaching death, the most important of them her taking of communion, administered by the young, sympathetic and strikingly handsome priest Massieu, played by Antonin Artaud. At this point the debate has ended and the interior struggle is over. Here at the abyss, paradoxically, is a moment of nurture and love that reaches back to the life of the girl Joan used to be. Accepting the host, she seems filled by a powerful inner light, her eyes closed, her face beatific—the portrait of a soul in exaltation—while crouched at the doorway watching her, as he has so often throughout the film, is Loyseleur. From his point of view, Joan is now safe in union with God; but as he gazes at her, he realizes that she has always been as she is now: simple, obedient, not the willful rebel he worked so hard to convict but indeed a soul in the state of grace. His final gaze at her is extraordinary, the terrible gimlet eyes now open, artless, almost beautiful, filled with pity and what must be a hellish regret.

These gazes of recognition, Joan's and Loyseleur's, are two symbols among many providing the intangible, almost subliminal assurance that despite all that is unfair and even contemptible in Joan's trial, overarching truth is also present. We have experienced the suffering so often present in her face, known its necessity and its isolation, and through this pain the film achieves its apparent sense of medieval reality. But there is also the transcendence of suffering, the reaching through pain and despair toward a deeper strength, and a sort of union with higher laws, as Thoreau called them. Everything in Joan's situation—the sly cruelty of her interrogation, her isolated helplessness, even her frustration—renders her mask of pain convincing, but her quiet endurance of that pain manifests the irreducible truth of spirit that torture cannot kill.[20] This and other implicit symbols of that transcendence leaven Joan's suffering and constitute what has been called Dreyer's "cinema of the soul"[21]—a second way the film creates a reality we tend to accept as "medieval." What are these underlying symbols? First are the many arches built into Dreyer's large, expensive, solidly built set for the film, its walls sheathed with ten centimeters of cement.[22] The arches are echoes of faith, they reach skyward and have a purity about them. Surprisingly, the arches resonate with the caps and tonsures of the priests and monks, their curves larger and more subtle due to our seeing them in close-up.[23] Then there are the crosses—not merely the cross that Joan takes, and is taken from her before she burns, or even the cross that Massieu holds before her eyes as the smoke and heat rise up and she faints into death, but the cross-like shadow cast by the window frame in her cell, and the cross Joan leaves as her mark, after Loyseleur has helped her write the Jehanne-signature that will never be hers. The crown of straw is, of course, a symbol, with its loops and arches, and so perhaps are the elegantly arched letters of the signature of Charles the King, forged indeed, but for Joan a symbol of God's plan for France.

Dreyer's cinema of the soul surrounds us with tacit evidence of a transcendent reality that is somehow present, but, remarkably, it also disorients our perception enough that the emotional and spiritual reality conveyed by Joan's face begins to destabilize the realism of the trial setting.[24] The foundation for this effect is the frequency of high angle shots. We are not accustomed to seeing people from below, and when we see Joan elevated in this way, silhouetted against the white background of the courtroom walls, her face fills the whole screen, her suffering enters us, and for a moment we inhabit a world quite different from the scene of the trial. By contrast, the inquisitor priests, when seen from below, seem merely domineering. They connect with her world only by representing the absence of spirit. Other odd camera angles add to this effect. Priests come into the frame from above, or below, or we see them in a line, one behind the other, unsettling our perception of depth. Lines of sight diverge—that is, someone may look right, but in the reverse shot the person he is speaking to may not look left, so that even though we assume they must see each other, they seem disassociated. Even the construction of the sets gives the impression that we are not in the ordinary world. Two windows are set into the wall of the courtroom, side by side: one is inexplicably set higher in the wall than the other. Houses outside the church have angles that should be ninety degrees but are not. Even the shape of Joan's cell seems odd. And since nothing looks normal in the man-made world of Joan's interrogation, the powerful reality of her suffering, inaccessible to those assailing her, comes to dominate our experience of the film. It is as if we watched the trial through the eyes of someone from another world—a world perhaps where Joan's simple virtue would be the norm, and the carefully drawn symmetries of church and state, warped and chaotic.

Eugène Silvain as Cauchon and Adolphe Rodé as Warwick in Carl Theodor Dreyer's *La Passion de Jeanne d'Arc* (1928; courtesy George Eastman House Motion Picture Department Collection).

As the film comes to a close, the sense of altered reality presses upon us even more heavily. In a charmed circle of peace and comfort, Joan has taken communion from the priest Massieu, but as soon as she is brought out into the courtyard to be burned, the action begins to be intercut with increasingly violent scenes involving the peasants who have come to protest the judgment. Shots of acrobats, contortionists, sword swallowers and other entertainers drawn by the occasion give way to scenes of the crowd beginning to surge against the cordon of soldiers. The moral and legal deformity of Joan's trial is amplified by the bizarre antics of the performers, the unruly anger of the crowd, and the cruelty of the soldiers. As Joan is led to the stake, people are rushing toward the castle, forcing themselves onto narrow bridges and paths of access. The firewood is placed and lit, smoke rises, and maces and other weapons are dropped down from the walls into the waiting hands of the soldiers. The crowd moves against the soldiers, who attack, injuring mothers, grandmothers, little children—and as Joan enters her last agony, enveloped by smoke and seared by the fire, we see the soldiers' arms rising and falling, again and again, wielding their maces and clubs. The camera angles for these last scenes are often extreme. Soldiers run out through the gate of the castle: the camera above the gate follows them until they are directly beneath, then continues to follow until, by the end of the shot, the soldiers are running upside down. In a moral sense, this is indeed a world "up-so-doun," as medieval people liked to say.

Joan dies, and we are not spared a shot of her blackened body slowly being consumed by the flames. Together with the brutal, often deadly suppression of the crowd, her death is an indictment of a fallen world, a world out of tune with and separate from the world toward which Joan has painfully been moving during the entire period of her trial and execution. The film ends in *contemptu mundi*, a familiar medieval contempt for the world which is nevertheless lightened by a flock of white birds that rise from the dome of the church and move through the sky as Joan dies. *La Passion de Jeanne d'Arc* is sometimes hard to watch. As cinema of the soul it is uncompromising, and that is the source of its greatness.

CHAPTER SIX

French Arthuriana

We never tire of Arthur and Guinevere, nor of Lancelot, Gawain and Merlin. Whatever the mood, style or slant of the film, we know them, the ever-familiar spirits that give medievalism its family story. Father, mother, big brother, little brother and great-grandpa: they are at once the intimate presences we have felt since childhood, and the great, dim archetypes—fated, tragic king and queen, strong prince, clever prince, wizard—that loom beyond the Arthurian story, extending its timeless reach. But if the story of Arthur stretches the imagination between youthful dream and ancient myth, what do we make of the *real* Arthur of *Camelot, Excalibur* and *King Arthur*? Opinions differ, naturally, but I think realism has not been kind to the story of Arthur. Somehow it feels as though these well cast, expensively produced films miss the Arthurian point. I would not say that the two very different Arthurian films by Robert Bresson and Erich Rohmer, neither of them examples of realism, are necessarily better than other Arthurian films, but merely that each in its way is compelling and deserves a serious look.

Perceval le gallois

The first time I saw Erich Rohmer's *Perceval* I didn't like it.[1] Expecting to see medieval people whose lives I could identify with and share, I was less than entertained by this stage production where Perceval walked his horse through artificial trees to Blanchefleur's little castle, about fifty feet to the left. The script, I thought, was similarly barren. A chorus of young people in medieval dress played period instruments and sang lines from Chrétien de Troyes' *Perceval*, and the hero himself recited some of the lines that described his progress. What did Rohmer think he was doing? How could anyone call this a medieval movie?! During the discussion at the end of the show, an old

Fabrice Luchini as Perceval in Eric Rohmer's *Perceval le gallois* (1979).

friend of mine commented that whatever the interesting novelties of this version of *Perceval*, as a film it was an absolute disaster.

In many ways, of course, Rohmer's *Perceval* is *not* what we would call a movie, but neither is it a stage play or a musical like *Camelot*. Instead, Rohmer presents a spare, stylized, sometimes ritualized acting out of the main episodes of Chrétien's romance, in a stage setting which denies realism, thereby forcing upon us the authenticity and splendor of the costumes, the courtly grace of the performers (or, in Perceval's case, the lack of it), and, not least, the nuanced ironies of Chrétien's text. Some critics—those on the positive side of this polarized debate—have said that it brings us closer to the Middle Ages than any other film has done. That is an unprovable assertion, but let us explore some ways in which it might possibly be true.

Perceval le gallois opens on two groups of musicians and singers.[2] In the group of young women, one plays a flute, others a viol, a lute or an array of cymbals as they sing lines translated from Chrétien's introduction to *Perceval*. Their hair is long and dark. They are dressed with the simple elegance that would suit well-born, attractive young women of the twelfth century when, as now, they leave their castle walls to enjoy the spring day. They sing of green fields and the songs of the birds. Then the camera moves to the group of young men producing chirps and trills from various whistles and bird calls, not a parody of the song but a lightly ironic response—what birds would sound like if here were birds. But also, naturally, these bird-boys will accompany the girls in any way they can.

These young people are often present in scenes involving Perceval. Like a chorus, they take the place of Chrétien's narrative voice, and, as with any narrator, their description or commentary distances us from the action at the same time that it mediates,[3] creating continuity between events and providing an explanation of what is happening just then on stage. Their commentary is lightly ironic because, like the Chrétien-narrator, it allows us a point of view that is not Perceval's. Like the choruses in Euripides' plays, who might be a group of slave women or Corinthian women perhaps sympathizing with Elektra or Medea but quite separate from those tragic princes, these young people embody the social reality of twelfth-century aristocratic culture which Perceval, in full ignorance, is about to enter. Individually they are nameless, but as a group we know exactly who they are—young, privileged, carefree, beautiful, and, above all, knowing: it is they, not Perceval, who understand the subtleties of *amour courtois*, the terminologies of arms, the etiquette observed at court, the depth of a mother's sorrow. Sometimes they observe a scene or fill out a group, and sometimes they carry the narration; but once provided with the wise innocence of their knowing gaze, we retain it and turn it back on the action, helping to create the arch mixture of amusement and admiration with which we experience this film and its hero, who comes so slowly to wisdom.

Now the camera pans to the left, and here is Perceval, the untutored Welsh ("Gallois") boy raised in the forest, far from the world of chivalry, but javelins in hand. His mother has kept him from knowing he is descended from a line of famous knights, but his chivalric blood makes him an able hunter: taking over the narration from the chorus, he himself describes how "he casts his javelins before, behind," using the third person but miming the action, as though he were a little boy showing us his moves. This behavior has an obvious naïveté, and Patrice Luchini, who is youthful and slight, with wide, expressive eyes and shoulder-length hair, maintains this air of openness—call it innocent confidence—throughout the film. It is true that this Perceval does not look or sound like any knight we have ever seen in a movie. He seems to represent not so much the sturdy youth we encounter in Chrétien or Wolfram von Eschenbach, but rather the *idea* of Perceval's blank innocence and innate goodness, despite the violent things he is apt to do in his eager boyishness. Later in the film we see that Gawain, too, is played by a young man accomplished in every way as Gawain must be, yet in no way overbearing or dominant. We are meant to understand him as a man of endless courtesy, just as Perceval's endless innocence, so often an obstacle for him in the courtly world, will ultimately become a strength in the grail quest, which is really the service of God.

But soon Perceval's hunting is over. Five mounted knights approach through the forest, their armor clashing against the tree limbs (the musicians make clashing and knocking sounds with cymbals and wood blocks). Emerging from the stage trees, which are about 15 feet tall, abstract in form and apparently molded from metal, these knights, high on their horses, seem as beautiful as angels to Perceval, but to us they seem acceptably true to type. The chain mail, steel helmets, shields, the deep voices of command, all the detail seems authentic enough, creating a chivalric reality in the midst of the metal forest and other stage features.[4] We will see similar contrasts in later scenes—when Perceval childishly asks the Red Knight for his armor, for example, and, after being refused, sends a javelin through the man's eye, killing him instantly. Sometimes the realism in this stage production is like this shocking death (some member of the audience always screams at this point, according to one critic), and sometimes it builds a slow charm, like the clothing, the manners, and the clever, smiling faces of the chorus as they observe the action. The story of Perceval is a myth, this film implies, a beautiful old story of the service of man and God. But it is being acted out, narrated and observed by real medieval people in steel armor or lovely dresses who can appreciate the nuances and ironies as well as the sorrow and pain of love, chivalry and the service of God in this story of long ago.[5] That is the realism peculiar to Rohmer's film, and its effect grows stronger with repeated viewings.

Where does this story take us? In search of adventure, of course, but these will be misadventures because Perceval, untutored youth that he is, knows nothing of the world of chivalry, the love of women, the world of the spirit ("What is a church?" he asks his mother), the existence of his family members, or the importance of that lineage. Much of this he learns from the hard hand of experience, and his stumbling efforts to do what his knightly nature commands will continue for as much of the romance as Chrétien was able to write before breaking it off, perhaps in death. Rohmer carefully follows Chrétien's text, recounting Perceval's first kiss, his knighting by King Arthur, his instruction in arms by the kindly Gornemanz de Gohort, and his rescue and winning of the beautiful Blanchefleur; then his failure at the grail castle (one simple question would have healed the Fisher King!), his denunciation (actually, "cursing") by the loathly maiden, and finally the beginning of his spiritual life, when he is brought to the worship of God by his uncle, a famous knight now living as a holy hermit deep in the forest.

As in Chrétien's romance, Perceval's adventures begin to alternate with the adventures of Gawain after they meet at Arthur's court. Rohmer devotes less space to the Gawain material, preserving the ongoing comparison of the two heroes but soon returning to the central theme—Perceval's gradual understanding of who he is and what he must do. Perceval's tongue-tied clumsiness is awkward but often touching in contrast with Gawain's ease and sureness in dealing with men and women, young and old, in increasingly problematic courtly situations. These contrasts project the dual themes of Gawain's courtly service (of women especially) and Perceval's sometimes amusing, sometimes tragically slow progress toward the service of God. They are an additional source of the realism peculiar to this film.

Bodies, for instance, come frankly before our eyes in scenes involving both heroes, as in Perceval's first adventure with the maiden in the tent. In fact, she is a damsel in the protection of the Haughty Knight of the Heath, and she is fast asleep under her colorful silken tent in broad daylight. Most men would ride quietly away from such a place, but Perceval assumes the tent is a church, since churches are very beautiful according to his mother, and he walks in to find the maiden unattended. The camera pauses at the foot of her bed, giving us a foreshortened view of the girl, fast asleep in her long flannel nightgown. She turns over, relaxed and unmindful, and in the moment before she suddenly wakes, her warm physical reality, innocently erotic, dominates the shot. She is young, female, full bodied indeed yet sheltered from our prurient interest by the haven of sleep. And so when Perceval decides he wants a kiss (his mother said he should kiss, but no more) and seizes the wrists of the struggling girl, forcing her down on the bed to kiss her, we are not led to share his desire. Her unconscious presence forcibly recalls the social constraints that allow her to sleep, unmolested, in her nest of silks; and it makes a strong contrast with the childish delusions of Perceval, who is, up to a point, insensible to such constraints.

The scene might have been ugly, and Perceval's rude childishness repellant, if three young women from the chorus, one of them the flute player, had not come to the tent door to peek at what is happening inside. These grinning, "impish" girls, as one critic rather solemnly refers to them,[6] are not at all worried about the damsel—but they are the chorus, after all, and *know* she will not be harmed. Also they are just young girls who want to see the kissing—"He kisses her one, two, three ... seven times!" says one—and all in all we find it easy to enjoy their point of view: not outrage for the maiden, not eagerness to see how far Perceval can go, but an amused knowledge that kisses are a naughty but natural thing for boys and girls like these two, even if the girl's Ami is dangerously nearby, even if the boy is blissfully ignorant of delicacy or the laws of courtly love. In effect, the presence of the chorus controls our response to the scene; like Chrétien's narrative voice, it forces us to see Perceval's simple acts as part of the complex social reality represented by the three young musicians who sing and exclaim and trill the flute while he blunders through his first experience of love.

But Gawain's adventures with women also have their humor, for his sophistication and know-how are sorely tried by chivalry's contrary complexity.

Here too, bodies count. On his way to a mortal combat, where he will contest an accusation of murder, Gawain arrives at the castle of his accuser, but the man is out hunting. He is welcomed by a family member, however, who (unaware of the accusation) tells his sister to treat Gawain as a dear friend. Left alone with this lovely girl, Gawain behaves gallantly, she responds graciously, and soon they are in each other's arms. None of this is surprising if we know Gawain's reputation at court, but the warmth and charm of the episode is produced by simple body language. Gawain gives the young damsel a squeeze, she hugs him back, and her face, turned toward the camera, beams with absolute joy. They are at one, and the physical immediacy of this carefree and seemingly inevitable version of a*mour courtois* banishes any thought that Gawain is now in the castle of his mortal enemy. Very soon, of course, he is recognized by someone in the castle who knows him, and an angry crowd assembles. Gawain and the maiden take refuge in a tower, from which she pelts the crowd with big chess pieces (is it not a game of war?), and he uses the chessboard as a shield. An "inane adventure," as one critic wrote?[7] The lack of recognition (in effect, a disguise), the wooing of an enemy, and the chess/battle (the old ironic motif of a battle in a banquet hall) are standard romance features. What keeps the scene from seeming trivial and contrived is the rapid but ingenuous and heartfelt bonding of this courtly man and woman. That does seem real, and it grants the scene its dignity.

In another pair of episodes, Perceval comes to the aid of his bride to be, Blanchefleur, while Gawain becomes the knight-defender of the Maiden with the Little Sleeves. The contrast could not be greater. Perceval, knighted by Arthur and instructed by Gornemant, is eager but untested, a parody of a knight at arms when he arrives at the grim castle where Blanchefleur and her remaining knights are starving under siege. Yet he is faced with the classic role of defeating the army outside the walls and releasing the *châtelaine* from peril. Gawain, charged with murder, rides toward mortal combat, but a tournament intervenes, and, counter to his best interests, he must compete: a little girl is slapped by her older sister, and when she pleads with Gawain to be "her knight" (surely he can defeat the proud young man who is her sister's love?), Gawain, without hesitation, promises to defend her "honor." For is she not a woman? And if so, how should he refuse her plea?

Thus the absurd knight finds himself in a hero's role, and the seasoned knight meets an absurd challenge. In Chrétien's elegant narrative, both knights acquit themselves nobly, and in both cases, paradoxically, something absurd is ironically turned inside out to reveal the innate greatness of chivalry. Rohmer's treatment of these two sequences demonstrates the surprising emotional strength of this film, despite its stylized, stage-bound mode. We begin with Perceval, as he enters the besieged castle and meets its lady. Most of this sequence is narrated in song, either by the young women and men in the chorus (now playing the roles of Blanchefleur's retainers) or by the lady herself. The action proceeds slowly, as one after another the singers take up the narrative in its French couplets, and we hear of the beauty and goodness of Blanchefleur, the peril she faces, the hunger of the siege. The set is ablaze with colors—purple, gold, red, deep blue with silver fleur-de-lys; Blanchefleur, tall and blonde, is dressed in a rich red gown. These young people are attractive, but as the somber narrative is sung, their faces are somber, and we are allowed time to feel the sadness of the melodic line (adapted from French music of the twelfth and thirteenth centuries). Our gaze lingers on their candle-lit profiles. Drawn into the action by this ritual of song and setting, we are ready for the pathos of Blanchefleur's sung narrative, as, unable to sleep, she rises, hesitates, then in her thin white nightgown makes her way toward the sleeping Perceval. She bends over Perceval's face, shedding tears that wake him. "Belle, what is it you wish—why are you here?" And she continues her song of woe—in the morning she must kill herself!—until finally Perceval promises to lift the siege and famously invites her to lie next to him, and all night long they rest, lips pressed together.

This slow recital of Perceval's love adventure emphasizes the resonant purity of the voices, the solemn restraint of the singers, and not least the touching figure of Blanchefleur, so desirable in her thin gown yet cloistered by her terrible grief. In this castle, Perceval has scarcely known what to say or when to say it, but now, to our enormous relief, he acts as a man should, strong but gentle, comforting, and worthy of trust. In a realistic film, the same scene would have us judging the verisimilitude of the acting, or even the plotting (realism rejects the predictable). There would be no singing, and since the castle had been under siege for months, its people would be starving and dressed in rags. But when the old story is brought to life by present (i.e. twelfth-century) people, we forget realism and instead appreciate the reality of the young faces and figures, their compelling voices, the color and light of the set—all of this given narrative life by the graceful clarity of Chrétien's verse. If we lived in a castle, and our friends had taken the trouble to act out the romance of Perceval, would we not enjoy it in much the same way?

The story of Gawain and the Maiden of the Little Sleeves has a different kind of grace. Gawain has agreed to be this maiden's knight in the tournament, but here is the problem: ladies give their knights a colorful token to wear in the *mêlée*—a sleeve, perhaps, for sleeves hang long and full from the elbow, are sewn to a dress with coarse thread, and can easily be removed. But this little girl only has little sleeves, and how ridiculous would it be, a tiny sleeve streaming from her knight's helmet! The situation is saved by her father. Learning of the spat between his daughters, and satisfied that Gawain can be trusted, he opens his chest and gives the little maiden sufficient cloth to make a fine sleeve—this after taking her in his arms and carrying her home on his horse so that he could hear the whole story. Gawain prevails in the tournament, of course, and afterward, to the maiden's great satisfaction, promises to be her true knight, whithersoever he might go. Rohmer found a suitably petite young woman (Anne-Laure Meury) to play the maid, and her antics as she fights with her sister, pleads with Gawain and (with the help of some girl friends) keeps all this from her father until just the right time, have considerable charm. It is not realism, of course, yet as drama it is realistic: we are touched—especially those who have raised children—and Gawain's kind willingness to serve even this least of all ladies seems in its small way a profound expression of the chivalric ideal. Again, it is the focus and compression lent by Rohmer's stage treatment that provides this episode with the understated irony and emotional depth that it has in Chrétien's text.

Very well, says the part of me that loves realism, and was brought up on it, emotional depth—good. But what about those little stage castles, the aluminum trees? They are laughable, are they not? And Perceval himself: surely Fabrice Luchini does not look like a knight, and when he becomes the narrator, speaking about himself in the third person, where is the drama? The trees, yes. It is said that no one on Rohmer's set was happy with them. Even in stage production, trees are best if somehow they convey the archetype of the waste forest, vast and mysterious. But this little stand, each one with the same rounded arch of branches, seems a deliberate denial of what we know and feel about forests. The castles, of course, are not much bigger than the trees, and in their lack of detail, accord with them stylistically. Perhaps what Rohmer had in mind, as one critic has said, was a set small enough that its trees and castles would be reminders of the world of romance, but would not in any way diminish the stage presence of the actors. Given these proportions, the set might recall the illuminations in medieval manuscripts, where trees, cliffs, and even castles are necessarily scaled down to privilege the ornamental letters or the human and animal figures combined (or intertwined) with them.[8] Illuminations are not portraits but icons, visual seeds which come to full flower in the imagination of the reader. In somewhat the same way, Rohmer's film attempts a dramatic illumination of the "real" story of Perceval as it unfolded in the expansive fictional world devised by Chrétien.[9] And beyond Chrétien's world, the great, timeless shadows of the archetypes—dim forests, ancient seers, pale maidens and the heroes who defend them until the end of time.

In some ways, Luchini's Perceval is, like the trees and castles, a lesser stage version of a larger fictive life, for it is impossible to imagine him as the invincible Red Knight. We are distanced even more when he describes his own actions in the third person. Yet this boyish actor with large innocent eyes in

A knight riding through the forest in Eric Rohmer's *Perceval le gallois* (1979).

a sensitive face delivers a powerful sense of Perceval's *inner* development. Watching him, we understand the naïve resolution that drives his entry into chivalry, and we find it easy to accept his slow progress toward practical, then emotional, and finally spiritual wisdom, which he finally begins to achieve after five years of random and fruitless chivalric encounters. During this lengthy maturation, made to seem even longer by interspersed adventures of Gawain, Perceval is a sensibility in process of becoming. Gawain is always the same, despite the circumstances—truly he is a man for all seasons—but the essence of Perceval's character is slow change, and we are simultaneously conscious of the boy he was, the (incomplete) grail knight he is at present, and the ideal, projected into the future, of what he will be, the perfected grail king. The boy or man we see is both himself and a promise of the reality that must come, and to know that is to be distanced from what he now is. That is why Perceval can slip in and out of character as he narrates in the third person without disrupting the dramatic moment or the flow of the narrative.

In the final episode of the film, Rohmer radically increases the distancing of Perceval's character. In Chrétien's text, Perceval encounters a group of pilgrims on a Good Friday and, admonished by them for riding in full armor on such a day, begins to realize his spiritual desolation. They have come from visiting a holy hermit in the forest, and he goes there to offer his confession. The hermit is actually Perceval's uncle, the brother of his mother and of the Fisher King, who lives in the castle of the grail. It is the uncle who identifies Perceval's early sin of leaving his mother without a thought (she fainted and then died of grief). This sin in turn caused his failure to ask questions of the Fisher King that would have healed his ancient wound, healed the family. In the romance, Perceval and his uncle pray and keep company until Perceval, now enlightened, sets off once more on his grail quest. In Rohmer's film, Perceval's confession and his uncle's revelation of his sins are followed by—the passion of Christ! Luchini, now bearded, plays Jesus captured by the soldiers, scourged, crowned with thorns and crucified. Then finally, as Christ's side is pierced—that is, at Christ's death—Rohmer cuts to a scene of Perceval riding away through the trees, as he has done so many times before, and the credits begin to roll. Some critics have attributed this final passion scene to Rohmer's devout Catholic faith, but surely an additional reason for it was that Chrétien left his romance unfinished, with Perceval still a young knight questing for the grail. Showing Luchini/Perceval as Christ in his emblematic sacrificial episode implies that Perceval's remaining life will be, if not sacrificial, then in some sense an imitation of Christ. In effect, having embodied the guidance given him by the hermit, Perceval has put off the old Adam and put on the new man, who will be a true knight of Christ, a *miles Christi*.[10]

Like Gawain, Perceval in this film is never ambiguous—always he is the questing knight—but finally we realize that his character is multiplex: different versions of him manifest themselves as he develops.[11] Gawain is the achieved chevalier, the sun of chivalry as he is called, while Perceval is forever the *potential* grail king, so that whatever he might be at a given narrative point, we sense further depths. They are both symbolic characters, referencing a complexity of cultural ideals—their "medieval" quality stems from that—but for Perceval, the references continue to multiply so that finally he is everyman, and as the final glimpse of him tells us, he is underway on an eternal journey of becoming.

We see this polyvalent (medieval) quality most strongly in the winter scene at Christmastide when Perceval has wandered close to Arthur's tents but has paused in the midst of a great snowfield to meditate over three drops of blood, stark red against the white.[12] The blood is from a goose wounded by a hawk, nothing more, but as it melts into the snow it recalls for him the lovely lips and cheeks of Blanchefleur, left far behind across the months or years. Sagremore, then Kay ride out to challenge this solitary knight—who will not answer the challenge but absent-mindedly knocks them from their horses as he dreams of his heart's desire. Rohmer's set for this scene is spare and beautiful, the metal trees dusted with white and grouped far upstage on an expanse of pure snow, whose whiteness recedes toward a distant horizon tinged with greens and blues. Where is Perceval in this white waste? He is here, but also, and more importantly, elsewhere, a strong young man whose heart is far away in search of beauty, wisdom, and the abundant spiritual fulfillment of the grail. It is a lonely scene but all the richer for that. Perhaps one could say the same about this film, which provides little of the live action customary in medieval movies, but because it is a stage drama, can, with its stage intensity, bring life to Chrétien's twelfth century in ways unavailable to realistic film. Where are the hawks, where are the hounds, where are those laughing eyes? If anywhere, they are here.

Lancelot du Lac

With no forewarning, *Lancelot du Lac* opens on the deep shade of a forest where two heavily armored men are trying to kill each other.[13] Now the light catches a sword as it drops to the ground, then another sword as it moves upward in a powerful slanting stroke and cuts a helmeted head from its body. The headless corpse, dimly seen, falls in a clatter of armor, and we hear a sound like the spilling of water as blood streams from its neck.[14] Soon a script, blood-red, will begin to crawl up the screen, and the credits will roll to the accompaniment of military bagpipes and drums, but first we see four additional scenes—murky clips—displaying the blind brutality that is the context of this film: a (dying?) knight sits helpless as another knight dispatches him with a full swing of his sword; blood sprays from the sliced helmet. Two armored skeletons hang from trees (we hear calls from the birds that feed on them); bodies lie in or near the blazing ruins of a peasant's hut; a knight rides into a chapel and, with one stroke, sweeps from the altar the chalice, candles and other holy things. Each scene ends with a sudden roar of hooves, and a file of armored knights riding into view and disappearing, finally, into the dark trees.

Who were these men? We cannot know, but the recurrent shots of knight riders tell us that slaughter and mayhem are common in this moral darkness, and the fact that no word has been spoken, beyond the agonized gasp of a man stabbed below the navel, makes the anonymous violence seem even more inhuman. Obviously, this is not the merrie olde England of *Camelot* or even *Excalibur*. When the red text begins, we learn that Merlin swore Arthur's Round Table to a quest for the grail—the chalice Joseph of Arimathea used to catch Christ's blood at the foot of the cross—and made Perceval its leader, Perceval the pure. But soon after they set forth, Perceval vanished and was never seen again. Many of them died, and now, two years later, the remnants are returning to Arthur's court with empty hands. Even Lancelot has failed. We wonder if Arthur's knights were the ones we saw in the horrible opening scenes, and as we see them become increasingly divided, their aggression turning inward, we begin to realize that the chivalric dream of Arthurian equity and order has given way to a nightmare reality where ignorant armies clash by night, as Arnold put it. This regression, and the cyclic atrocities that must accompany it, is conveyed by the tight, tripartite structure of the film. Beginning with the killing scenes in the forest, it leads to a tournament in the open grounds of neighboring Escalot, but in the end returns to the forest, where Mordred's archers are perched in the trees and Arthur will die with his remaining knights heaped about him—a round scatter of motionless armored bodies under a silent sky. Forest scenes and motifs are frequent in this film. Gradually the forest comes to represent both the fear and savagery that stalks these men from within, and the doom that awaits them—in effect, the end of the Arthurian age.

Yet there is more to this rich forest metaphor than savagery and fear. From the beginning there is prophecy.[15] The film's main action opens again in a forest where an old woman stands listening, while nearby a man and little girl gather firewood. "He whose footsteps precede him will die within a year," she says. "Even if it is the footsteps of his horse?" the girl asks. "Even if it is his horse." And at that moment, Lancelot, high on his horse, appears in the foreground.[16] Returning from the grail quest, he has lost his way in the forest of Escalot. The woman offers to show him his road—we wonder vaguely how she knows where he is going, and whether that road will, in fact, lead to his death—but we also feel the positive force of her offer to guide Lancelot, the legendary hero and focal character of the film, who is displaying an uncharacteristic weakness. Lancelot, lost? Later in the film, when he returns through this forest from the tournament, he will fall from his horse, fainting from his wounds, and we will discover him recuperating in this woman's cottage. She saves his life but tells him that if he leaves his bed he will die (he does leave, of course, being Lancelot). In a structural sense, the woman is an information post, pointing the way the plot must take us (like the old woman on the way to Dracula's castle), casting a sense of dread over the events to come. But in the film's symbolic economy, she is also a maternal archetype of nurturing and death, a surrogate for the promise and threat of nature itself.

For the question posed by Bresson in this film is fundamentally that of man's nature, the power of nature in man, and his questionable ability to transcend it. If Arthur's Round Table stands for unity, equality and civil order in the face of moral chaos, what does it mean when Arthur's knights become savages even as they search for the grail, a symbol of spiritual perfection? What are we to think of Mordred, Arthur's son, who plots against his father and ultimately has him killed? And closest to the Arthurian heart, what about the love that unites Lancelot and Guinivere but separates Arthur from the two people he loves the most, his two centers of strength, and fuels the dissent among his knights? Here, as in Malory, the Arthurian story is tragic, another tale of man caught in the net of his own being; but in this film, the man who struggles and for whom we care the most is not Arthur but Lancelot. He failed in his quest for the grail, he tells Guinivere, because of his sinful love for her. He is the natural, inevitable leader of Arthur's knights, but already they are divided by Mordred's ambition, and their suspicion that Lancelot loves the queen renders impossible his efforts to bring them together. He could simply leave her to Arthur, devote himself entirely to chivalry, yet in the aimless and apparently meaningless life that followed in the wake of the failed quest, she becomes his only purpose; loving and defending her creates a sense of identity, so that without her there really is no Lancelot. Thus Guinivere is oddly parallel to the old woman in the forest, both a refuge and a reminder that this way lies death. And Lancelot, so entrapped, is himself a microcosm of the knights of the Round Table, who also lack purpose but attempt to find it in the pursuit of arms—"chivalry"—which leads directly from the tournament to war and death in the savage forest.

We enter the world of Lancelot (Luc Simon) and the lesser, younger knights as he returns from his quest. Night has come, and as he walks his horse over the drawbridge to Arthur's castle, the hoofbeats on the wooden trestle are like hammer blows. Gawain (Humbert Balsan) hears a knight riding in, sees that his visor is down and comes to challenge him: "C'est tu, Lancelot?" he asks, and Lancelot, raising the visor, "C'est tu, Gauvin?" Seeing each other, they are guardedly relieved—their friendship is close, as in all Arthurian tales—but it is night: why does Lancelot ride into his home base with his visor down, so that Gawain must challenge him, and he (being Lancelot) return the challenge? Why do those hoofbeats strike so sharply? Bresson gives scrupulous attention to this fine detail, and through it is able to convey the haunting sense of threat that is normative in this film.[17] Knights do not usually travel alone at night, and visors are useless if not protecting the face in battle. Challenges guard against incursion by an enemy. And the steel-shod hooves announce the approach of a massive machine of war, a swift, powerful horse and rider carrying an array of deadly weapons. Lancelot dismounts, but almost immediately we hear two horn blasts from off-screen—odd, resonating sounds at which Gawain turns and others come running. A small group of knights has entered the walls, some of them seriously wounded and wrapped in bloody bandages. Lancelot, Gawain and others raise them from their litters and help them limp away. This horn sounds again at various points in the film, and even though it is seldom apparent that it announces anything, we remember the wounded and again feel that the grail quest was a painful disaster, and that the suffering continues.

Within the walls of Arthur's castle, what kind of life do we see? The knights are living in tents. Logically it makes sense that the castle keep—a defensive structure with limited space for habitation—would be reserved for the higher-ups, while the many knights would be quartered outside the castle but within the walls. That is not how medieval movies imagine it (movie knights have always lived in the castle). But in Bresson's film, the Arthurian veterans come home to military-style peaked tents that glow with lantern light, tents pitched on the ground, their walls providing little protection from other men or from the elements. On the evening before the great storm, as knights sally forth to look for Lancelot (he lies wounded in the forest), men are driving the tent pegs deeper; and on the following morning, Lancelot's pennant will dangle from his tent pole in strips, shredded by the wind. These men seem vulnerable in their tents, and that effect is only increased by the armor they wear in virtually every scene.[18]

This plate armor is not what men wore in the (timeless) time of Arthur, or even in the twelfth century, when Chrétien de Troyes was writing "The Knight of the Cart," the first romance featuring Lancelot. Bresson did not concern himself with historical accuracy; as he explained later, he avoided such easy "costume drama" identifications because they interfered with the cinematographic effects he desired. The effect of the armor is manifold, a powerful undercurrent of image and sound.[19] Since the men are almost always armored, we come to think of them not as tin soldiers, but as men who have normal bodies and minds yet can never shed the metal skin that defines their perilous lives. Rather than making them seem monumental and impervious, the plates strapped to their torsos, arms and legs remind us of the tender flesh that lies beneath, and the streaming blood which keys the palette of this color film. Finally, the armor is an undersong, the raw clank and clatter of metal plates as they ride, but especially as they walk: how many times do we see Gawain turn from Arthur, Lancelot or Guinivere and walk away, the camera holding on him so that we have to see the unprotected backs of his legs in their pink hose, crossed by the straps of shin, knee and thigh armor, while the prolonged jangling of the plates reminds us that this beautiful young man, Arthur's nephew, and (if anyone can be) the soul of Arthurian chivalry, lives bonded to the risk of death.

The armor announces these men-at-arms, but it also conceals them, rendering them anonymous beneath the hard military shell. Their individual identity, the blazon of their chivalric pride, is expressed by the blues, greens or reds of their hose, and by the colorful designs of the pennants that fly from their tent poles and are run up the flagpole when they joust at the tournament. These colors are so closely identified with the man that after the storm, when Lancelot's pennant hangs limply from the tent pole, torn by the winds, they assume that he is dead. We might expect such a heavily defended sense of self

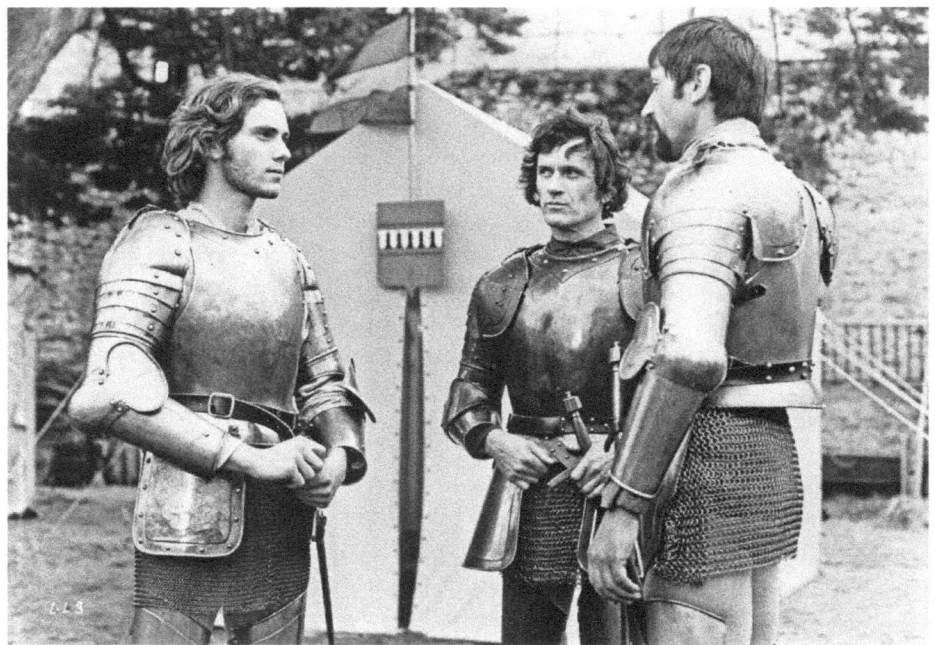

Humbert Balsan as Gawain, Luc Simon as Lancelot and Vladimir Antolek as Arthur in Robert Bresson's *Lancelot du Lac* **(1974).**

to express itself in conduct, and it is typical of Bresson's meticulously constructed version of chivalric culture that the social relationships of Arthur's court are interlocking rituals of pride. Lancelot comes to Mordred's tent, offering his hand in friendship / Mordred stands motionless / Lancelot leaves. Gawain confronts Mordred at the chessboard, challenging his remarks about the queen / Mordred rises and moves forward / Gawain jerks a foot of his sword from the scabbard / Mordred moves back, turns and walks away. In a continuous ballet of social manners, they approach and distance themselves from each other, greeting, kneeling, turning, gazing, eyeing askance or piercing with a glance. In these small, almost invisible ways, we apprehend the sensibilities of their lives.

The deepest feelings, fears so pervasive and nameless no word can convey them—these too have their place in Bresson's film and are fundamental to its distinctive strangeness. The current of existential dread that flows through the film is voiced by no one, yet from the opening frames it is there, embodied in the presence of the horses.[20] By the opening scenes of murder and desecration, we are repulsed, but their terrible power derives from the thunder of hoofbeats as five armored knights ride between the crime scenes: these men are unstoppable, implacable—in a wordless, visceral way, we know this. In a little while, Lancelot arrives at Arthur's castle. His ride through the night forest is not mentioned, but we know what it means because we see a brief close-up of the eye of Lancelot's horse, wide and terrified, searching for a source of threat. Now for the first time we hear the shrill, piercing cry of a horse, not the comfortable whinny of farmyards but a cry of fear impossible to ignore. Then a shot of horses in Arthur's stables, and more cries of horses, the same unnerving sound repeated several times. Horses enable the movement of knights throughout the film. In the tournament, Bresson does not show knights jousting but keeps the camera low on their horses, legs thrusting, running full out, then churning the soft earth as they pull up; we hear them panting deeply at the end of the course. Finally we experience the joust through the horses as much as through the knights that Lancelot hurls to the ground. The end of the film begins as Lancelot and his horse lie wounded in the forest. We expect a close-up of Lancelot, but see instead a close-up of his horse's head, its eye wide, beautiful, and, as we must imagine, full of pain. An arrow thuds into its head behind the eye, and as Lancelot pulls free, we hear the ragged breathing of the dying horse. As Lancelot staggers away, his sword falling from his dying hand, it is the horse's pain that allows us to feel the solemn agony of the man's death. Perhaps the cries of the horses, recurrent in the film, give his dying word its resonance of longing and despair: "*Guenièvre!*"

At the center of Arthurian chivalry, naturally, is the king, who contributes substantially to our sense of the human condition in this film. Arthur (Vladimir Antolek) is a well set up, dark haired man with a strong profile, not as tall as Lancelot and less handsome, but appropriate to his role. Like Lancelot, Gawain, Guinivere and indeed all of the characters, Arthur is played by a man who had never acted in a film. Bresson insisted on casting not actors, with their ingrained theatrical habits of expression, but untrained "models," men and women who were carefully chosen for their looks and, more important, for what he sensed they had within them—qualities which would express themselves unconsciously, thus genuinely, when they had practiced their parts so often that voices, expressions and even gestures became automatic subroutines, flattened out perhaps, yet without false pretense and true to the underlying person in minute ways that Bresson believed the camera would capture. This directorial method results in characters who at first viewing seem cold and affectless, as if they were reading their lines instead of speaking them, as one critic said. Yet with repeated viewings, one begins to notice that in the absence of characters *acting* their parts, the impact of the cinematography— the way images inflect one another, the effects of lighting and sound, repeating motifs and the patterning of scenes—becomes more apparent and memorable. And because the characters project less, paradoxically one tends to focus on them all the more closely, as if to ask, what is this person feeling; behind this expressionless face, this lowered (or raised) glance, what understanding must have occurred?[21]

Arthur, then, is such a *modèle*; yet a theatrical king, a man of sorrow and fury might have seemed out of place here. This Arthur says little as he receives the few knights who have returned to him, and his silence contributes to the overwhelming sense of their loss. The day after Lancelot's arrival, Arthur leads him and Gawain into the room where the Round Table sat. He intends to close it permanently. As critics have noted, we never see a full shot of the table itself, only a slice of it entering the frame as Arthur walks around it, naming the knights who once sat in each empty chair—"Ici Urien, ... ici Perceval, lá Claudas, et lá, lá, et lá."[22] Gawain has been saying they must reform the Round Table, recruit new knights, regain strength. Arthur: "No, we have suffered a terrible blow. No, no, we must wait." In this room that echoes with defeat and loss, Lancelot and Gawain want to know what is to be done *now*, what should they try to achieve? Tonelessly and without expression, Arthur turns toward the door: "Exercez vous, perfectionnez vous"—improve yourselves in body and mind. Then, "Remain under arms, remain united, heal your separations from one another." This inner-directed regimen might have been prescribed by the spiritual director of an abbey. Ironically, it is the only advice that might have been useful in the grail quest and the self-transcendent spirituality it represented, yet the quest failed: Arthur's knights were capable only of conquering others, not of mastering themselves. Arthur's advice seems a gray voice from the past, spoken by a sad, disappointed king with no mission or hope of any kind to give them, only the tired, monkish admonition, "Priez Gauvin," only pray. Gawain shrugs. What is prayer to this man in a metal skin?

Now having greeted Gawain and consulted with Arthur, Lancelot turns to Guinevere—for is he not the queen's knight, entrusted with protecting her? Guinevere—her name, *Guenièvre*, so beautiful in French—is a slender brunette, a quiet and, as we come to understand, thoughtful young woman played by Laura Duke Condominas. The first meeting of Lancelot and Guinevere takes place in secret, in what critics have variously called a lodge, grange or barn—in any case, a small outbuilding with a hayloft, surrounded by trees. It is the forest again, but this time the forest of the heart. Over the years they have come here many times, we imagine, casting aside their official roles in their need for solace. During this first of their three meetings, Bresson includes a shot through the window of the loft: a bird sits in a low bush, and we hear its call, a strident burst that will recur, like the horn signal back at the castle. But this time Nature is calling, and we want Lancelot to hear and comply.

He does not. The distance between one knight and another, and between the king and his knights, has reappeared in this, the closest human relationship in the film. In each of their meetings, Lancelot and Guinevere are shown in profile, facing each other, so that their conversation does not proceed in shot/reverse shot (which would imply a connection), but in alternate shots as the camera moves from side to side, each time measuring, thus emphasizing the interval between them. Lancelot has returned from his quest a repentant man. He did see the grail, in a ruined chapel, but a voice sounded in his ears revealing his "treachery" with the queen and forbidding him the holy chalice. He vowed he would no longer seek her love but devote himself entirely to chivalry, like a soldier-saint, as Gawain says. Guinevere, of course, wants something different: first a declaration of love, then his hand—the left hand, that bore her ring!—and then the man himself. But this proud, confident man was another casualty of the failed quest; now he desires only to be released from his vow.

Frankly, this is a disturbing scene. It lacks most of the conventions we associate with love-encounters, joyful or sad. Guinevere is young, intelligent, queenly in her robes, yet her glance is frozen, her face impassive. She has a good voice, clear and resonant but toneless, as if the life had gone out of it long ago. Lancelot is Arthur's premier knight ("For Lancelot," Gawain will say, "to decide is to strike"), but here he seems aimless and uncertain. He has determined what he must do, yet we sense his deeper indecision. He speaks to Guinevere, sits beside her, gets up and stands apart, then returns to her side. They trade words back and forth without expression. Both seem to bear an enormous weight that drains their vitality and strength, not the weight of social or even official sanction but something larger and harder to grasp—the devout might call it moral law, others an existential burden. It is more than a question of doing the right thing. No matter what they do they will suffer, and if the grail quest tells us anything, it is that these knights have come home to die, despite the efforts of Lancelot or the loyalty of the queen. The issue, really, is identity: who is this man, this woman, and how might they simply be true to what they are?

Lancelot and Guinevere meet twice in the loft, and nothing is decided—neither will yield. But in their third meeting Guinevere mentions that the time before she left a scarf here and now it is gone; someone has taken it—they are discovered. At that moment Lancelot begins to take off his sword and armor and let it fall into a pile on the floor. Then he steps forward and takes her in his arms. What has changed? Now that they are revealed, he might as well enjoy her love? More likely, and truer to Lancelot, is that when challenged he always attacks. She hears sounds in the woods outside—Mordred and his men approaching, waiting to kill Arthur's champion and discredit his wife. Lancelot only embraces her more closely—this is the warmest they will ever be with each other—and says his arms will always keep her safe. At his core he is a warrior, and through that a lover, and a man loyal to his king. Luc Simon is a convincing Lancelot, a tall, strong man with good eyes in a craggy, sensitive face, and it is easy to imagine medieval knights who were like him, or tried to be. We too identify with Lancelot, but this paragon of knights who tries so hard to keep his king, his queen, and the Round Table safe, is a man for whom war is the fundamental reality. Very likely, in Bresson's vision, he is us.

This Arthurian film about war and despair was made in 1974, after France had suffered defeat at Dien Bien Phu, and in the U.S. the long war in Vietnam was coming to its own bad end.[23] For many, the early seventies was a time of disillusion which eroded authority of all kinds and made us wonder whether the military-industrial complex had made the Kennedy Camelot impossible in any form. There was a refreshing energy, especially in the young, but traditions were dying. In *Lancelot du Lac*, we enjoy a brief glance at military dominance in the tournament which forms the centerpiece of the film. Arthur accepts the challenge from neighboring Escalot—it will give the knights something to do—and, in fact, they begin to prepare themselves with exhilaration. "Look at them," Gawain says to Lancelot, as they watch the jousting and broadsword practice, "they are happy." He leaves unspoken the pointlessness of the upcoming chivalric contest. They have failed in the grail quest and simultaneously failed in war: "All is lost to us in Brittany," Lancelot tells Guinevere. The tournament is a distraction, a game that pretends at war while they wait, restlessly, for death.

Pretend they do, however, and Lancelot is, as always, their champion. He promises to visit Guinevere when the other knights have gone to the competition, but at the last moment he too leaves for Escalot. In disguise he defeats every man at the tournament, demonstrating his superiority to those who spread rumors about him. Once challenged, Lancelot must attack before seeking the woman who nurtures the other, inner part of his being.

Still, it is just as well he went: Mordred's men had stayed behind, waiting with naked daggers, and his deeds at the tournament make a fine spectacle, the best medieval jousting sequence ever filmed, some have said, and a celebration of chivalry's central icon, the man on horseback. Indeed, the horse was vital to medieval war. On his big horse, an armored man had the even greater advantages of speed, weight, height and enormous strength. In the time before long bows and cannon, nothing could stand against him. We remember this ancient strength in Bresson's filming of the joust, where the camera stays low on the straining of the horses' powerful hindquarters and the speed of their legs as they gallop down the lists toward the explosion of impact. Horses are rearing, fidgeting, snorting hard as the bagpipes announce nine different jousts, each one a victory for Lancelot. But we also hear the off-screen whinnying of a horse, the same terrible piercing cry we have heard at intervals throughout the film. It sounds when the disguised Lancelot enters the tournament gate, and again when he leaves with a lance point in his waist. The pipes we recall from the nightmarish opening sequence, and we will hear them at the end of the film as Mordred's forces march off and Lancelot dies in the forest with Arthur and the remaining knights. Now he leaves the tournament as mysteriously as he had come (a common romance motif) but soon drops to the forest floor, blood trickling from under his mail. Gawain and Arthur smile, having recognized his prowess: he has defended their pride in this surrogate battle, and for the moment the tradition lives. Yet nothing has really changed, and from this point on, the film descends quickly into tragedy.

Bresson signals the oncoming disaster by the storm scenes that follow— night shots of wind and rain blasting the tents, and knights returning after a fruitless search for Lancelot. "Did you see him?" "No, but the forest is a devil." Our point of view becomes that of Guinevere, who lies awake weeping, fearing for Lancelot and wondering as the wind rattles her door if he has fled the impossible dilemma she represents for him. As the search continues, she waits, and from here on it is Guinevere's strength that counters and makes meaningful the coming Arthurian doom.

Our way to understanding Guinevere is through images of doors, walls and windows—a series of enclosures. "She is our only woman," Gawain says, gazing up at her window high on the featureless stone wall of the castle, "she is our sun."[24] Guinevere is the only woman knights can desire in this courtly film (her maids, and the old woman and young girl in the forest of Escalot, are, after all, peasants), and, following romance tradition, she is a priceless possession. She meets Lancelot in the little barn off in the woods, and her first impulse is to climb into the secret, protected loft (outside their window the bird sings in its bush, the natural freedom they have only in hiding). In the castle, we are conscious of the door to Guinevere's room: Gawain passes in and out, keeping her informed. Mordred has his men in the next room, poised to stab Lancelot if he touches the door latch, but only the anonymous maids in their long dark skirts come in or out with water for her bath. When Guinevere confesses her love for Lancelot, she will be confined, but Lancelot will burst through that locked door and take her away to an empty castle, where Arthur's siege will confine her once again. These enclosed spaces lead to the dramatic long shot in which Guinevere and Lancelot walk out through the castle gate toward Arthur, standing beside his tent across the meadow, waiting for her. Staring woodenly into space, she lifts her hand from Lancelot's arm and begins walking back to Arthur, freed by her decision to end the war but freed to a marriage she loathes. She enters the tent and is not seen again.

Within her confinements, Guinevere struggles for freedom, and if freedom is impossible, then something to justify the sacrifice of her life. Waiting for Lancelot's return, she is afraid, then despairing, and finally beyond fear: he *must* come for her; she can only love Lancelot and is ready to die for that. Gawain is appalled (the punishment for adultery is burning), and when Lancelot does rescue her he kills Gawain's brother Agravain, creating a blood feud. In the abandoned castle where they are besieged, big as a cow barn and more rustic than even the hayloft in earlier scenes, Guinevere lies wretchedly on a pile of straw, surrounded by knights in bloody bandages. She hears that Arthur will take her back—no evidence to judge her, he concedes—but Lancelot must leave.

The climactic event in this graceless place is Guinevere's reversal. In the previous three scenes with Lancelot, she used every argument to preserve their love, worth more to her than life. Lancelot, torn between loving her and serving his king, was reduced to speechlessness. But as he once said, "Without you there is no Lancelot," and she promised "to go into the dark void" with him. In effect, she gave him the existential purpose—indeed, the identity—that Arthur was unable to provide. Now she has reversed her argument: she must return to Arthur. But here in this barren castle, Guinevere does not regress into fear and despair, nor are her queenly sensibilities overwhelmed. This very young, sheltered and (is she not?) willful queen has moved toward responsibility and a larger sense of self. Perhaps nothing can prevent more misery, but she will do what she can to end the war, which means living with her heart in bloody shreds. Lancelot: "What is left for me?"—an echo of her former craving. "I won't let you out of my hands," he says—another sort of confinement. Mastering herself, she tries to prevent more deaths, and Lancelot, led by her strength, lets her go.

Guinevere's decision is central to other reversals, each in its way selfless. Lancelot refused to be Guinevere's lover, vowing to become more perfect, but he yields to love, then nobly gives her up again and dies defending the king. Arthur, after endless rumor about Guinevere, prepares to execute her, but heeds Gawain's dying words and takes her back again. Gawain's reversal is probably the most affecting. Gawain is loyalty personified, loyal to Arthur his uncle and loyal to Guinevere, despite her love for Lancelot, which probably leaves him with mixed feelings. Most of all he is loyal to Lancelot, who is like an older brother. But Lancelot kills Agravain, so Gawain must attack him. In a whisper, with a huge blood-soaked bandage around his middle, his dying man's words prevent Arthur's revenge.

Gawain is indispensable in this film, as he is in every Arthurian story, a handsome go-between who represents loyalty and good fellowship, service to women, strength in arms—in short, he is every virtuous thing that chivalry imagined (even his love adventures, mentioned by Guinevere with a grin, seem somehow admirable). We get used to him riding, greeting, maintaining the

Arthurian status quo as well as anyone can in this twilight of the Round Table. Especially, we remember the pink hose—as he walks away from his many encounters, we see that distinctive color, vulnerable as flesh, worn by a man who lives for honor and tradition, and, Christ-like, tries to save others as his life ebbs away. Opinion differs on *Lancelot du Lac*, some saying it could easily be understood from an Atheist point of view.[25] At the very least, Gawain's morality, linked with Guinevere's, Lancelot's and Arthur's, sounds a note of chivalric virtue that makes bearable the death of Bresson's Arthurian age.

CHAPTER SEVEN

The Name of the Rose

More than almost any other film, *The Name of the Rose* drew its being from a book, Umberto Eco's *Il nome della rosa* (1980), which achieved rapid success in Europe and was followed in 1983 by an English translation that was read all over the world.[1] Other novelists writing about the Middle Ages had drawn at least a modest readership—Barry Unsworth and Sigrid Unset come to mind—and since the 1950s, Tolkien's fantasies had so prepared the ground that many kinds of medievalist fiction easily took root. But *The Name of the Rose* brought medieval times closer than before. To read this novel was to enter an intimate imaginary, the bookish, blissful, sometimes luridly fearful habits of mind of an average, young, early fourteenth-century Benedictine monk. This Adso of Melk, a sixteen-year-old Rheinlander, confronts the traditions of an Italian Benedictine monastery, with its 700-year-old liturgical rhythms, customs, and taboos. He is distracted by the changes, the social pressures and new ideas that excite or terrify the monks at this watershed of European history; and like almost everyone within these ancient walls, he wonders why the monks are dying. Is the Evil One waiting for them in the darkness after compline? In this advanced age of the wicked world, in these ominous signs, do we recognize the coming of the Anti-Christ?

And that is merely the setting. Further complexities unfold as we realize that young Adso's mentor is not a Benedictine. He is William of Baskerville, a wry, fiftyish Franciscan, a former student of Roger Bacon and friend to William of Ockham, who were, respectively, an early scientist and a "new" logician, both Oxford-trained and neither of them much to the taste of the conservative Benedictines. William has been sent to the monastery by the emperor-elect, Louis IV of Bavaria. With Adso in his charge, he will attend a debate between representatives of the Franciscan order and a papal legate sent from Avignon by Pope John XXII. The subject is the poverty of the Franciscans and, by extension, of the church itself. If the spiritual wing of the Franciscan order has vowed to live like Christ and his apostles, owning nothing and subsisting on people's donations (the Franciscans were a mendicant, or begging, order), and if *not* to live that way would break their vow (a deadly sin), is it then a deadly sin for the rest of the Franciscan order to have possessions? And if the spirituals will not obey Pope John's directive to own what they use, as the main, or conventual body of Franciscans owns convents, lands and foodstuffs? Punishment could include burning at the stake, as happened to four spiritual Franciscans in 1318. But, of course, Louis IV, the new emperor, opposes the Pope's authority. And the Benedictine abbot sides with the emperor, hoping to preserve a balance of power in which he, the aristocratic abbot of a wealthy abbey, might, like other abbots in previous centuries, have an influence on European politics.

In this fraught atmosphere, the abbot of the monastery asks William to investigate the death of a youthful monk, a famous, innovative illustrator of manuscripts, found broken and lifeless at the foot of the monastery tower walls shortly before William and Adso arrive. William, like the incomparable Holmes, loves a mystery and is a man who misses no clue on the way to solving it. So William and Adso begin to muster their—mainly William's—powers of empirical observation and logic, while Adso manages to retard the action, filling pages with semi-learned but highly colored reflections as he falls in love with a peasant girl and registers for us the passionate spirituality and personal eccentricities of these monks who have died to the world, yet find that in this Year of the Lord 1327 it lives in them.

Eco's novel is plotted like a detective thriller, but like all good thrillers it is really about the world of its setting, the state of Europe at the beginning of the "calamitous" fourteenth century, as Tuchman put it.[2] Not only Benedictines, but also the new orders, the Franciscans and Dominicans, were having to engage the new money economy, answer laymen's needs for a deeper spiritual life, and weigh the demands of emperors and kings that the Pope assume a separate or even a subordinate political authority. The peasants are increasingly hungry (winters have been cold, the summers wet) and seeking greater independence from church regulations. Adso, disciplined yet in a deeper sense inspired by Brother William of Baskerville, is doing his best to grow up. Eco conveys all this in about 500 pages. That, surely, is a great deal to pack into a movie, which perhaps explains the epigram that appears just before its title: "A palimpsest of Umberto Eco's novel." A palimpsest (from Greek *palin,* again; *psestos,* scraped) is a manuscript which has been scraped clean to make room for another text. Jean-Jacques Annaud, the director, has said he exhausted four different writers in the course of producing the final screenplay. Much has been scraped away. What remains is a fairly straightforward detective plot which some critics have thought shallow, but the images, the casting, the shadowing forth of historical nuances by some remarkable acting—in these different ways the film shows us what it was like to be Adso in 1327.

The Name of the Rose opens in darkness, nothing but the black screen and a high ringing of chimes—perhaps the ones the altar boy holds during the mass—and then an old monk's weary voice recounting things that happened a lifetime ago. It is Adso voicing the narrative he writes as a farewell to the world. Terrible things occurred at the abbey, whose name he finds it "prudent, even now, to omit" (the soundtrack begins an ominous low-frequency roar), and, curious, we turn to his *Bildungsroman* of a narrative which will tell us as much about leaving boyhood as it does about Europe's painful emergence from its feudal past. In both respects, this old man's story has a yearning quality, a sweet, sad look backward toward the world when it was a little younger. The lovely theme music, two triplets, largo, moving down the scale, is another sort of farewell, sounding throughout this film about the fading Benedictine age of patience and prayer, of copying the precious works of ancient men and living the works of the ante–Nicene fathers. Of these things, *rosa pristina*, yesterday's rose, becomes the symbol. Like the peasant girl, much is lost as life changes and history moves on.

In keeping with that retrospective mood, the first shot of the film withdraws slowly up the vast bowl of a mountain valley, zooming out until we can see snowflecked peaks along the horizon (they are the Abruzzi, northeast of Rome), and far below, toiling up the cart path toward the monastery behind us, the tiny figures of William and Adso on their mules. These winter peaks and valleys appear several times in the film, marking the dawn or sunset, and establishing the rhythm of the monks' liturgical day with its services, prayers, work, supper and sleep. In any light, early and late, misted or clear, the mountains are beautiful, cold and grand (the foley artist adds a whisper of wind for these shots). We are looking at the world from which monks everywhere have been retreating, coming in from the cold for more than a thousand years. Here within this abbey's walls they find the warmth of community and the private commitment of faith, the useful work preserving and commenting on ancient texts, the daily struggle—even and especially for monks—with temptation, and the endless desire for God.[3]

We join William and Adso as they crest a rise and for the first time see the monastery on its hilltop. The old tower, once a fortress, rears massively into the sky, and as the film progresses, its height gradually becomes a kind of metaphor, an echo of the abbot's obsessive control of access to the library high up in the tower, and, more generally, the attitude of the Benedictines, over centuries, toward the gross ignorance, violence and spiritual vacuity of secular life in the Italian cities—indeed, the cities of the world. We follow William and Adso, coming beneath the abbey that rises from the top of the cliff. But traversing the cliff base we pass a crude wooden hut with a smoking chimney, and on the soundtrack faint voices are speaking an Italian dialect. The hut is quickly out of sight, but the people it represents—the Italian peasantry—are crucial to the film. The abbey is a little world in itself, a paradise of the mind and spirit where the monks, like Christ and his apostles, own nothing but dwell as though in the city of God. The Italians, naturally, represent the city of man. Dirt poor, hungry to the point of rooting among the garbage dumped from the abbey walls, these are miserable people who live with their animals and in some ways resemble them. Yet the monks, too, are men, not angels, and Augustine's great concept of the two cities depended for its vitality on the tension between them, a dialectic to be ceaselessly worked as men come gradually to understand themselves in relation to their hope of heaven.[4] The Benedictines, over time, have become a wealthy order, superior to the baseness, greed and desire of worldly men. But Adso will fall in love with a peasant girl as she fights for pieces of the monks' kitchen refuse, and in the plains and valleys of Italy and France, poor men and women have for a century been turning their backs on their former lives to embrace a perhaps heretical but desperately heartfelt imitation of the life of Christ.[5]

William and Adso enter the gates of the abbey, and, framed by the entry, we can see the abbey church. Behind it looms the mass of the great tower, the *aedificium*. Annaud, in his commentary on the film, says he had to build both the church and tower—nowhere could he find a monastery where gate, church and tower enabled this significant opening shot. In Latin, *aedificium* means "building, edifice, structure," but in the film it is *the* building, a *mise en abyme* where the ground floor houses the kitchens and refectory; the scriptorium above is where the monks do their characteristic reading, writing and copying; and above that is one of the greatest libraries in Christendom, the forbidden source for their labors and in many ways the basis for their life. In short, the *aedificium* is their temporal world, just as the church represents the other world of the spirit. The question that haunts the film is never "where are the books?"—*of course* they have to be in the tower!—but why has the world of knowledge contained in those books (another *mise en abyme*) been concealed from the monks for centuries? Only the librarian and his assistant can go there; the other monks can only consult the handwritten catalogue. Knowledge is power, and it is treasure, walled up in this and other monasteries by men who have kept the flame of civilization alive since the fall of Rome. The abbots and their monks have painstakingly built this collection. They are dedicated to conserving it through copying and illustrating. Those who are able write commentaries on the Bible and other texts, illuminating the wisdom they contain, resolving its contradictions, and revealing the inner truth hidden by difficult languages, arcane symbolism, or apparent simplicity. Preserve and protect: that is the sacred trust. Do not sell, lose, destroy or change this precious, closely held gift.

Sean Connery as Brother William of Baskerville, and Christian Slater as Adso of Melk in Jean-Jacques Annaud's *The Name of the Rose* (1986).

The man entering these ponderous gates with their outsize locks and iron portcullis is not a Benedictine, however. Brother William of Baskerville is a Franciscan, a member of the Friars Minor, the little brothers of St. Francis.[6] Like many others in his order during the past hundred years, he entered university life as a young man, studying logic, theology, astronomy, and what we would call general science. He has an inquiring mind, the better to know the world, which he sees as the book of God's secrets, open to him who can read it. His is a preaching order, so he has also studied rhetoric, the art of persuasion, and dialectic, the logic of debate (he enjoys a good argument). He is a holy but not a superstitious man, and as we come to understand, his years as an inquisitor for the church have left him with an understanding of heresy that finally will not allow him to persecute it. William is a priest in an order that ministers to the world, and in his worldly knowledge he is something of an anthropologist, a theologian, a philosopher, a logician, and a psychologist. Sometimes he reminds us of a high school science teacher. His young apprentice, Adso (Christian Slater in his first film), is trying to learn who his master is and, to the extent possible, what he knows. In Eco's novel, Adso is a young Benedictine monk, which gives him a sensibility that is usefully different from William's. In the film, Annaud makes him a young Franciscan, but that brings him closer to William's experience, and we easily accept that the mentoring he receives throughout the film has an avuncular, even fatherly warmth. But William, played by the crusty Scot Sean Connery, is not an easy man, and his distance from the monastic world is the distance necessary for us to take its measure.

The world of the monks seems a rather strange one, thanks in part to Annaud's casting. His previous film had been *Quest for Fire*, an epic tour de force about a small tribe several hundred thousand years ago—cave men, in fact—whose shaggy hair and crude, sensitive faces compensate for their comparative lack of language. Ron Perlman (of whom more later) is the only actor Annaud brought from the earlier film, but with his massive jaw and close-set eyes he typifies the exaggerated features we find among the monks. As Annaud has said, virtually the whole cast are men, and all wear the same brown woolen habits, so their faces need to be distinctive. Each man's head is shaved in the center—the tonsure (Latin *tonsūra*, "shearing") of all monks and friars—making his features stand out even more. What a splendid variety of noses! William and Adso move toward their dormitory, passing the herbalist who looks up, bows to the newcomers and bends again to his plants but continues to watch them. We see the large fleshy nose and lips before we notice the clever, careful eyes of this man who keeps the infirmary. Up in the dormitory the abbot has been talking with his librarian about William. "Shall we tell him?" "No." The abbot (Michael Lonsdale) has a minimal fringe of hair, severely shaved (disciplined, one might think). His words are slow and sibilant, his movements calculated. A heavy jeweled gold cross hangs prominently from his neck, and he fingers it as he thinks, displaying a ring with its great red stone, which Adso will be invited to kiss. The abbey is old, and the treasures of its crypt would be the envy of kings. This man is the defender of the abbey.

its possessions and its ancient peace. He has a complacent, guarded look, and when surprised, his eyes are frightened.

The librarian is the defender of the books. Tall, stern, emaciated, with an enormous beak of a nose and bald except for a ring of wispy hair that stands out from his head like a halo, he has the look of a large, predatory bird. As we might expect, his characteristic word is "no." Played by Volker Prechtel, Malachia seems, and is, Germanic, and is thus quite typical. This Italian monastery houses monks from every region of Europe. In effect, it is a microcosm of the western world, a representative slice like the ship of fools or the Canterbury pilgrims. It would be tedious to keep repeating *mise en abyme*, but, like the novel, the film insistently folds the world in upon itself so that even though its drama never leaves the monastery walls, we are constantly reminded that every person, every act has its counterpart in the larger events of the day, whether social movements, religious imperatives, or the spiritual and erotic affairs of the heart, like those that Adso continually suffers. Yet surely there can be a kind of peace, a pan–European harmony among the self-chosen who dwell in this paradise of the faithful, which from a different point of view might be called a self-contained religious republic?

Adso is not at peace, and, increasingly, neither is anyone else in this film that rushes toward crisis—*apocalypse*, as the monks like to call it. Do the terrible events of the time (and in the monastery) not suggest that the end of the world might be at hand? Standing against this tide of emotion is William of Baskerville, in most ways a thoroughly rational man. Up in their dormitory room he notices that Adso is dancing in place, and tells him where to find the latrines. But both of us are new here, says Adso-Watson, how did you know? William has an observant eye, and believes that the material world proceeds by cause and effect. Down in the quadrangle he saw where a monk went in such a hurry, and how he emerged "with an air of contentment." When the abbot comes to visit—an apparent social call, *pro forma*—William has already looked out the window and, having seen a fresh grave mound, can ask a question that releases a burst of perplexity and frustration. Poor Adelmo, how could he have fallen if the scriptorium windows were nailed shut? The monks fear the Devil has been hurling beautiful boys out of windows. Perhaps worse, the Inquisition will attend the upcoming debate: the monks fear the Evil One, but a witch hunt would poison relations with the Church.

Not to worry. William and Adso are soon climbing down beneath the walls, and the steepness of the path makes it obvious that Adelmo must have jumped from a different place farther along the wall, struck the rocky path and rolled down, coming to rest where the bloodstains are, below the tower with its closed windows: "My dear Adso, it's … elementary" (Annaud should have resisted this line, but it's hard not to like). If William is like Holmes, just as Holmes is like the incomparable Jeeves, they share a common scientific root. William is supposed to be a sometime student of Roger Bacon, a driven, brilliant, late-twelfth-century scientist who joined the Franciscans, perhaps because he felt it would protect him from the superstitious fears of those who could not think clearly about flying machines, speedy land vehicles, large seagoing vessels and especially the science of optics.[7] Bacon was a man before his time, but he was not unique in being interested in material reality. William of Ockham, another Oxford man, would have been a contemporary of William of Baskerville. The next year, in fact, he left Avignon in the company of Michael of Cesena (head of the Franciscan order, and present at the debate), traveling to the safer German (Munich) court of William's patron, Louis IV ("King of the Romans"), the King of Germany who had also been crowned King of Italy on May 31, 1327, and would have himself crowned Holy Roman Emperor on January 17, 1328.[8] In the film, William of Ockham is supposed to have been a friend of William of Baskerville.

William of Ockham was, in fact, a scholastic logician and philosopher, one of the new men in late medieval thought.[9] His importance to scholasticism was his ability to argue that reality inhered in one's experience of individual entities, empirically observed, and not in universal concepts. In other words, reality inheres in a chair, but not in chairness, which would be a universal concept derived from the individual entity chair, and necessary to human discourse, but not an existent entity in itself. A universal entity, Ockham argued, was like whiteness without anything being white—thus an unobservable and unreal category.[10] Ockham helped to establish the empiricist habit of mind that would eventually lead to the scientific advances of the seventeenth century. His relevance here is that William of Baskerville is another careful observer. Neither of these men was a materialist—both of them were religiously orthodox, and made a clear distinction between matters of faith and temporal matters—but both of them lived by their ability to make logical distinctions based on a clear perception of what we would call the facts. And so while the monks assume that the illustrator Adelmo was a victim of Satan, or perhaps of Satan's evil, William of Baskerville seeks the material cause of death (i.e., suicide by jumping from a different part of the abbey). Moreover, instead of assuming the Devil tempted the boy to jump, William finds out who saw Adelmo before his death; who worked with him at the library; what evidence remains of their communications; and what could have frightened the boy so much that death seemed a refuge. In other words, he constructs a chain of the possible material and psychological causes of death, and seeks the truth by eliminating those that are less likely (he would typically say that the fewer causal assumptions we have to make, the more likely we are to find the truth—a habit of mind that later came to be called "Ockham's razor").

William easily isolates the material cause of Adelmo's death, but he has discovered enough to know that possessing something from the library led to the boy's suicide. More investigation is necessary, while the debate approaches, the Inquisition waits, and heresy spreads through the mountains of north Italy like a dark sea.

William and Adso's first night at the monastery unfolds in a sequence of brief, anecdotal scenes that help us care about what follows. A shot of the mountains in the failing light and CUT to the refectory, where the abbot says the recent death involved no supernatural elements. CUT to the monks sitting to dinner and the lector reading from the Benedictine Rule, a passage on silence: talk and laughter belong to fools. Here is the venerable Jorge, his blind eyes glaring (he likes this passage); Venantius the Greek translator, watchful; Adso, eyed by the plump assistant librarian, Berengar, Adelmo's friend; William, taking in all of this. CUT to the moon gleaming on the abbey's purple-dark stones, cats yowling in the night and CUT to William and Adso's dormitory room. Adso can't sleep. What were those "onerous duties" the abbot mentioned to William at dinner? "Even monks have a past, Adso." William is sighting his astrolabe at the moon and would rather not recall that old pain. CUT to Venantius the translator, the only light in the scriptorium—reading, he starts at the squeak of a mouse—and CUT to the cell next door to William, where fat, naked Berengar lashes himself, every stroke with its little scream of pain, then CUT to Adso, who clutches William's arm in his sleep, and William who stands comforting him, holding the lamp, waiting for dawn.

From this eventful night we know that old Jorge favors silence (i.e. secrets); Berengar the librarian is bound to Adelmo by love and death; Venantius the Greek translator has read something he should not have; Adso's curiosities and fears need fathering; and William would rather study nature than revisit his inquisitorial past. In the morning Venantius will be found head down in a vat of pig's blood, the news breaking on the monks in chapel at about prime (7:30 a.m., according to Eco's novel), as they sing the morning service. William's investigation must continue, then, but its deeper significance for him, for Adso and for the film lies in what happened to him eighteen years ago. This leads us to his own father surrogate, the Franciscan spiritual polemicist Ubertino da Casale, whom they had found earlier, praying alone in the church.

Once a man respected at the papal court, Ubertino has fallen increasingly out of favor with Pope John XXII. He fled from Avignon in 1325 and has now been in seclusion at the abbey for several weeks. In earlier years he supported the losing cause of the spirituals against the less austere conventual Franciscans; now at the debate he will join Michael of Cesena, the minister general of the order, arguing against the Pope for the right of all Franciscans to absolute evangelical poverty, or, as they called it at that point, *simplex usus facti*.[11] "Simple use" meant the consumption of goods without possession of them, which they based on the historical fact of the absolute possessionlessness of Christ and the Apostles.[12] But in his bull *Quia quorumdam mentes* (November 10, 1324), John XXII denied that the rule adopted by the Franciscan order could be interpreted literally as Christ's gospel ("[M]any things are contained in the rule which Christ neither taught nor confirmed by his example").[13] In an earlier bull he had rejected the doctrine of Christ's absolute poverty. John XXII was concerned for the authority of the church and for his own authority. In order to command the obedience of the Franciscans, he "destroyed not only the basis of Franciscan poverty but the order's special claim to sanctity."[14] Ubertino's fame derived in part from his *Arbor vitae crucifixae Jesu* (*Tree of the Crucified Life of Jesus*), "a sustained paean in praise of Christ and the Virgin," written in 1304. The next year he added a fifth book that Michael Leff has called an "almost complete Franciscanizing of the Apocalypse"—in short, the coming of the Anti-Christ (a Pope, perhaps?) and "the coming of St. Francis to convert the infidels."[15] This is the man William and Adso find alone in the church, spread-eagled in front of the altar, arms thrown wide in imitation of the crucified Christ.

As they approach, William comments that some would call Ubertino a saint, others a heretic, given his writings, and during this scene the remarkable William Hickey causes us to wonder. Desiccated, skeletal and almost hairless in his great age, Ubertino has lost none of his force. His voice is a subtle weapon, a kind of purr to caress an old friend ("William ... my son ..."), or a bark of warning ("Franciscans, you must leave this place at ONCE!"), but then an invitation, kind yet insinuating when he draws the adolescent Adso to a nearby chapel to adore the statue of the Virgin ("She is beautiful, is she not ... hmmm ... ?"). We are almost afraid for Adso's virtue, yet Ubertino is not dangerous; it is what he knows and has experienced, for better or worse, during his long impassioned life. His warm relationships with the mystics Angela of Foligno, then, later, Clare of Montefalco, both of them (eventually) sainted, both of them spiritual mothers or sisters to him, were the core of what we would have to call his emotional and spiritual existence. Of course he was tempted: God commanded it. Yes, he brought his well-known rhetorical powers to bear in defense of the spiritual Franciscans, praising the "poverty, humility and charity," the "purity of faith" of St. Francis, while launching an all-out attack on "the laxity and corruption in the church."[16] With his urging, some heretics were burned. He knows, and feels, the razor's edge that divides lust from spiritual love, religious conviction from heresy. The perpetual struggle burns in him, a purgatorial fire, and in this sense he embodies the war between heretic and orthodox forces which surges through Italy and France. When Adso is swept away by love for a girl who lives in the squalor beneath the abbey walls ("It does present certain problems for a monk," William says), we have seen this also in the fervid complexities of Ubertino.

We see Ubertino again the next day when Venantius's body, streaming with pig's blood, lies at the feet of the horrified monks. The abbot despairs, William tries to explain, but a powerful voice rises above the crowd:

> After the hailstorm, with the second trumpet,
> The sea became blood ... and behold, *here is blood* ...

It is Ubertino, and these apocalyptic lines from "The Revelation of St. John the Divine" appeared in the fifth book of his passionate *Arbor Vitae*, prophesying the end of the world, brought on by the sins of men and the laxity of the Franciscans. The monks are credulous and otherworldly, perhaps, but everywhere times are hard—hard winters, sickness, hunger, hopelessness that breeds heresy—and when strange signs appear, it is easy to believe that the last days are at hand. Ubertino was an effective preacher in his time, and in this scene we have a glimpse of what popular religion was like for the many who thronged about him.

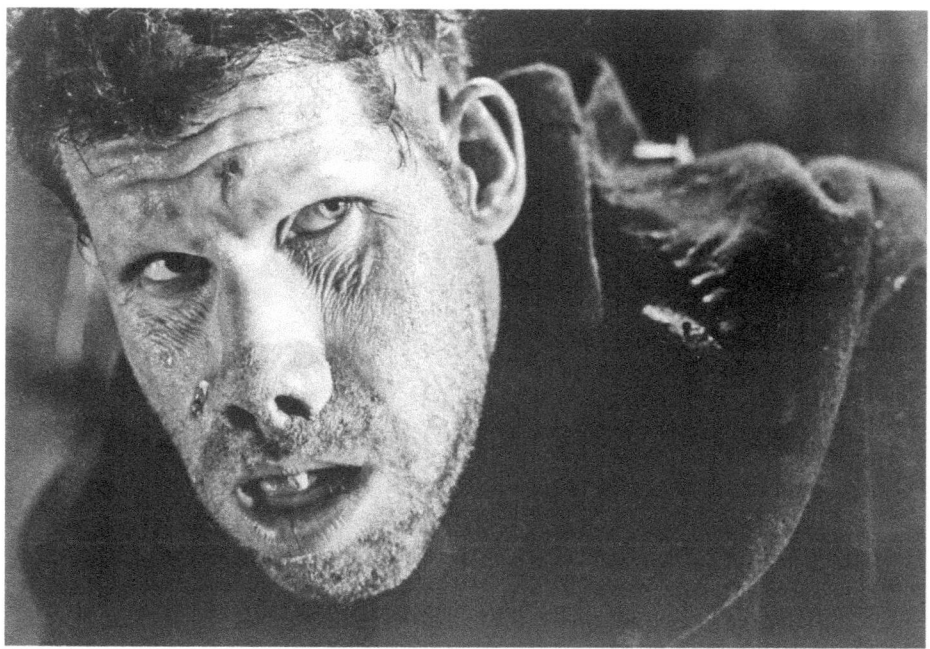

Ron Perlman as Salvatore in Jean-Jacques Annaud's *The Name of the Rose* (1986).

Ubertino is part of Adso's education as a monk and as a man, but there are other influences. We find him pausing before the tympanum over the big west door of the church—Annaud had it copied from the French cathedral at Moissac. Here is the huge, stern image of Christ, in judgment over the souls who will be saved and those bound for hell. Along the walls and on the pillars of the recessed entrance are carvings of demons, fantastic creatures, grotesques of all kinds; and staring up at them, Adso (who is brave enough but a sensitive boy) begins to see the distorted faces moving, grinning at him, and that is when we meet Salvatore, another monstrous, deformed figure in the darkness: "Penitenziagite! Watch out for the draco who cometh in futurum to gnaw on your anima! La morte is super nos. Tu contemplar l'apocalypsum, eh? La bas, nous avant il diabolo, ugly comme Salvatore, ... eh, eh? [He grabs Adso, swings him around roughly.] Ah, my little brother ... Penitenziagite!" Salvatore lurches, he is a hunchback, his scalp displays scrofulous naked patches between tufts of hair, and his face scarcely seems human, with its great underhung jaw, broad nose and hooded eyes peering out beneath the narrow brow.

At that point William intervenes, but who is this frightening creature? And what language is he speaking, as Adso later asks? "All languages, and none," William says. Salvatore, brilliantly played by Ron Perlman, is a strange but oddly compelling medley of the several countries, languages and religions through which this man—the poorest of the poor—has passed before finding employment and a kind of refuge as a lay brother among these secluded Benedictines. "Penitenziagite" (as Eco tells us) "was the uneducated man's way of saying 'Penitentiam agite, appropinquabit enim regnum coelorum'"—"Repent! For truly the kingdom of heaven draws nigh."[17] It was the cry of Gherardo Segarelli, a thirteenth-century enthusiast who walked the roads with his crowd of believers, whom he called his Apostles, living like them on donations and calling every man to repent and live simply, as Christ had lived. He let his hair grow long and wore white clothing, and many thought him a saint. But he was refused entry into the Friars Minor and gradually sank into heresy, proceeding to robbery and saying that the bonds of marriage were meaningless. He was finally burned as a heretic. But his cause was taken up by a certain Fra Dolcino, leader of the Dolcinites of northern Italy, who also lived simply but imposed their austerity on the wealthy, murdering "fat bishops and wealthy priests," as William says, to bring the kingdom of heaven closer. "Brother" Dolcino and his beautiful consort, Margaret, also came to a bad end, tortured and burned at the stake.[18]

If Salvatore is a linguistic microcosm of the vulgar tongues, the vernaculars of the poor throughout southern Europe, he is equally a mixture of loyalties and beliefs, having joined whatever households or bands of faithful he could find that offered food and safety. Surely he was at one time a Dolcinite, perhaps a member of the no less murderous Fraticelli in north Italy,[19] or even a follower of the spiritual Franciscans, before coming to rest with the Benedictines. Now he serves Remigio de Voragine, the abbey's cellarer, bargaining with the villagers for fresh meat and produce but also passing some food back to them in exchange for sexual favors and other things not to be found within the walls. The importance of Salvatore and his peculiar appeal is that despite his odd appearance and his animal hunger for food, sex and the shelter of community, his intent is not evil. His voice and expressions have a kind of simple-hearted warmth. He will be caught trying to summon demonic powers to charm (Adso's) village girl, and he nearly kills William with a big stone he drops from the walls, but the monks tolerate him and William spares him, for like the rest of the miserable poor, he merely craves relief, and moves desperately toward anything that offers hope, wherever that might take him.

Who is a heretic, who is merely poor? Where, if anywhere, does the love of God flow together with the love of woman? Adso's perplexities are those of the novel and, if we look closely, of the film. To their credit, neither Eco nor Annaud tries to provide answers. Rather, as the film nears mid–point, heresy stems from endless behaviors linked to social pressure, economic need, and hunger for identity; and love seems too large for any label. Adso, who is swifter afoot than William, is chasing Berengar the librarian as he flees with the Greek book the monks have been dying to possess. He enters the huge, shadowy kitchen to relight his lamp, hides from Remigio, and there behind the wine jars and sacks of grain, also hiding, is the bedraggled and radiantly lovely girl (Valentina Vargas) from the village. They have seen each other before. William and Adso were looking for bloodstains, she was scavenging, and one glance was enough. Now they will make love: she needs this beautiful boy to forget, for a while, her hopeless poverty, and he is a teenaged monk starving for affection that old books cannot give. It is an innocent scene, erotic, necessary and sad. He is a German baron's son, she an Italian peasant, so their love is wordless. At length William comes in and she runs away, leaving behind Remigio's trade offer: the enormous, bleeding heart of an ox. It would feed a family for a week. And it is Adso's heart.

Of the two great engines that drive human acts—love and war—love is perhaps the stronger, as it promises a future. The film is Adso's love story, but when asked, "Master, have you ever been ... in love?" William readily answers, "Yes, of course—Aristotle, Ovid, Virgil ..." So William's passion is a consuming love of books, and of knowledge about men and the world they live in, God's world, which (along with revelation) is a system of signs pointing the way to God. The abbot defends the infinitely precious library, the treasures and relics in the crypt and the timeless Benedictine peace, for these are God's gifts, to be loved and held close, as they too lead toward God. For the Franciscans, who are now about to reach the abbey after their long journey (on foot, naturally), it is the love of poverty, the blessed condition of Christ's life, thus the core of Franciscan being. And for Bernardo Gui, the inquisitor sent by John XXII to accompany his papal legate, love is the fiery zeal of purity: purity of doctrine, of orthodox ritual, and even purity of Christian intent, which can be ascertained by incisive or insinuating questions, and, failing that, by white hot iron or the stake. He is searching for evidence of heresy, of course, yet surely it is not heresy that he loves. In each case, the man's love is frightening—a terrible power, as the Romans said—because it is far greater than he is; it masters him, though, like William and Adso and Ubertino and some others, he may struggle for clarity and balance.

About the same time the Franciscans and the papal legate (an Italian cardinal) enter the monastery, William and Adso find their way into the many-chambered library, with its infinite wealth of books, the preserved sacred and secular wisdom of the Greeks, the Hebrews, the Arabs, and the entire reach of Latin Christendom over many centuries. William is ecstatic, whooping like a boy, the Greek book forgotten just now because, given this vast plenty, all things potentially can be known. He moves from room to room, discovering old and new friends, books unknown, forgotten, recovered from the deeps of time. Adso pauses, they are separated, voices echoing among the stairwells. Where is William? Soon they locate each other, and because Adso (like Ariadne) has picked a thread from his habit, unraveling as he walks, they find their way out again. But the point has been made: the library is a labyrinth, and so are its myriad books, and the forest of their knowledge. At its center, the windowless locked room in the south tower, they will eventually find Aristotle's forbidden *Poetics* of comedy, with its poisoned pages that the doomed monks licked their fingers to turn. Holding the book, waiting for William, will be old Jorge, the former librarian, for whom the idea of laughter is a turning of one's back on the fear of God. Like the Minotaur, this blind librarian is a metamorphic monster, an oxymoron: what librarian would preserve knowledge only to bury it unread? And what is buried knowledge if not a decaying relic, like the necrotic bones and fingers of the saints.

Having sensed the jubilation and the darkness that dwell together in the love of knowledge, we move toward the debate. The Franciscans are worried about the presence of the Inquisition, but their own love of poverty entangles them in disputation with the legate's supporters that is hopelessly loud and chaotic. It will gain them nothing, for obviously the Pope has already decided to force them into submission. In the meantime, the real poor live on as best they can. Salvatore has promised the girl a rooster in trade, but, sadly, he also wants her love, and so he is conjuring in the dark stables, with the little dead rooster and a black cat (she is petting the cat) and two boiled eggs, which require the sputum of a virgin (she spits in his eye—"Thank You," he says neatly, words found somewhere in a lifetime of wandering). He can't resist touching her, she lashes out, and his oil lamp flies into a pile of straw. The instant blaze terrifies the horses, who scream and bolt, bringing the monks, along with Remigio, the abbot, William and Adso, and, of course, the satanic inquisitor Bernardo Gui. Here indeed they find poverty and love—it couldn't be plainer—love as the basic calculus of need: begrimed, absurd, and, in a way, touching. The Franciscans would do well to reflect on this reflection of their own ideal of *usus pauper*—"poor use"—for is poverty not a labyrinth in its own right, and especially for those unable to find it blessed? But Bernardo is not touched, he is triumphant: "The black cock and the black cat!" he cries, piercing the confusion. To him these are familiar signs. Here, in fact, is the work of Satan. Heretics have burned for less, and this heretic and his little witch will burn as well.

It will surprise no one at this point that Bernardo is himself a labyrinthine figure, a monstrous priest who tortures to reveal the truth and kills to preserve the body of the faithful. The labyrinth, in this case, is the subtle, practiced interrogation of the inquisitor, raised by him to a high art, which (in real life)

F. Murray Abraham as Bernardo Gui in Jean-Jacques Annaud's *The Name of the Rose* (1986).

he described in his detailed and comprehensive manual for inquisitors, *Practica Inquisitionis Heretice Pravitatis*, finished in 1322.[20] This art is demonstrated by Bernardo the next day. Salvatore faces torture—a heap of red coals and glowing irons is there to remind him, and us, of what that means. By dawn the pain has reduced him to a vacant animal state, but he is ready to testify against Remigio (another former Dolcinite) rather than suffer even greater pain. Bernardo's voice is a caress. "Salvatore, do you remember what you were going to tell me today?" Or it cuts like a whip: "Remigio de Voragine, do you remember that you wantonly *looted* and *burned* the property of the CHURCH?" In his black Dominican's habit, thrown open to reveal a gleaming white cassock, F. Murray Abraham is somehow able to make Bernardo a living reality, sadistic arrogance made incandescent by an absolute assurance that he is driving home the sword of truth. The victims of this process are Salvatore, Remigio and the girl, but Adso as well, who in the stables looks on in horror and later asks William why he said nothing. The girl is not, after all, a witch.

William said nothing because there was nothing to be said: "She is already burnt flesh, Adso. Bernardo Gui has spoken." And it follows that anyone who questions the verdict will himself be accused of heresy. "How do you know these things, master? Are they part of your past?" At last, in weariness and self-disgust, William gives up what has been for Adso the secret of his identity. "Oh, yes." For he too was an inquisitor once, in the early days, when the Inquisition was meant to guide, not punish. He knows how heretics think, their devices, their innocent-sounding patter. But at length he realized, as he once told Adso, that "the step between ecstatic vision and sinful frenzy is all too brief," and he could no longer tell what was heresy and what was the need, born of hunger and hopelessness, to believe in the promise of better things, even if it were an insane call to poverty and freedom, or an apocalyptic myth preached to them by a renegade priest. Unfortunately, before he could leave he was assigned the case of a man whose only heretical offense had been the translation of a Greek book that conflicted with holy scripture. He acquitted the man, and Bernardo Gui immediately accused *him* of heresy. He appealed to the Pope, was imprisoned, tortured ... "and I recanted." The man was burned at the stake, "and I am still alive." Even William's stern morality and powerful, logical mind fell victim to what we would have to call Bernardo's moral chaos. After that, William returned to the university and studied "nature," which we may take to be a time of convalescence (he too was burned, in a way) and a retreat from the affairs of the church.

The final act of *The Name of the Rose* is a gathering of forces and a rush toward the final fires which will consume Salvatore, Remigio and Jorge, along with every book in the abbey library. The books come from every country in the civilized world, so their destruction seems an apocalyptic end to the various arguments over the meaning and use of knowledge. The fate of the victims, on the other hand, is a stark reminder of what they loved and why they died for it.

It is proper to begin with William, since he is central to both plots. Waiting among the monks the next day while Bernardo completes his indictment of Salvatore and Remigio, William hears himself named, with the abbot, as a judge. Knowing his past and his stubborn pride, the Franciscans groan silently. Indeed, when predictably the abbot endorses the verdict, William embraces the dangerous truth: "Yes, [Remigio] is guilty ... guilty of having confused the love of poverty with the blind destruction of wealth and property ... [Michael of Cesena, the Franciscan conventual, nods agreement, while Adso despairs] ... Yet he is *innocent* of the crimes that have bathed your abbey in blood!" For the crimes stem from the reading of a Greek book, and Remigio knows no Greek. Disaster! No one is listening but Adso. The trial ends, William is seized by the legate's soldiers, and Michael of Cesena trails the legate out of court in a pointless, contemptible plea to continue their debate. But the Franciscan cause is lost, and William, convicted of heresy a second time, will burn.

CUT to the evening service, where the oldest monk in the abbey, the former librarian, has been chosen to restore community with a sermon. Jorge of Burgos is a small man and practically toothless, yet his wasted face, with its whited eyes, is powerful, a magisterial presence. This terrifying old man is played by Feodor Chaliapin, Jr., son of the great Russian basso, and he too has a deep, resonant voice:

> Let us return to what was and ever should be the office of this abbey, the preservation of knowledge.... "*Preservation*," I say! Not "search for." Because there is no progress in the history of knowledge ... merely a *continuous and sublime recapitulation*."

But while Jorge sets forth his perversion of the Benedictine love of learning, Malachia, the once-formidable chief librarian, has been fainting among the monks in the choir, slumping in agony to the stone floor as blind Jorge confirms their "return to peace." Malachia, too, has read the poisoned book. Jorge hears what happened: "When will it ever end? Malachia ... !" But in the confusion, William and Adso flee the church and climb the many stairs to the library. The Greek book would be evidence of the truth.

Shrouded in darkness, Jorge is waiting for them. "What a magnificent librarian you would have been, William," says the old man. "Here is your well-earned reward. Read it ... you have won." What a beautiful moment it might have been, William with his surrogate son and surrogate father, and all about them the age-old wisdom, the enduring voices of the *auctores*. But, of course, the book is deadly; Jorge wants both of them to die from it, and many have already died because of this old man's tyrannical pride. He is a grim embodiment, the dead hand of traditions that kept learning alive during the centuries of blood and fire but grew hard and repressive with repetition and time, until learning lay entombed and nothing remained but to defend a shell full of moldering parchment and paper. The world around this monastery has changed—William and Adso, Roger Bacon, William of Ockham and even Ubertino are evidence of that—but the abbey is part of the old world, and here, at least, that world is ending in fire.

For as soon as Jorge knows William is wearing gloves, he darts away, spilling burning oil from the lamp, and as they search he tears out pages of Aristotle's book and swallows them: "Can we laugh at God? The world would relapse into chaos. Therefore I seal that which was not to be said in the tomb that I become." Soon all the books will burn and Jorge with them, but below the *aedificium* the monks prepare to burn the heretics, long lines of them with torches, singing the *Dies Irae* (Day of Wrath) as they move out toward the stakes.

The girl has fainted, bound to her stake. Remigio is unrepentant, and Salvatore is singing parts of an Italian love song in a sweet falsetto—"... en la vita non é l'amor" (in life there is no love)—isn't this what the girl was singing as she held the cat? Tortured and helpless, he is the martyred innocent, jesting with death. The fires are slow to light, and he grins and puffs at them. The smoke and fire billow up—"Salva me!"—the salvator calling for salvation. When the flames envelop him, his last cry is "Remigio"—the man who kept him safe and fed him, his heretic master, friend and father.

Meanwhile, the library burns, flames roaring from the old fortress windows and roof, and as the monks run back in a hopeless attempt to save it, the villagers move in to save the girl. William sends Adso out of the tower as burning stairwells crash down into what is now a vast fiery pit. He lingers, hands on the few books he could gather, while hope drains from him and he bows his head in despair. Bernardo Gui's carriage hurtles out the gate, slides, hangs over the abyss, then falls, pushed by rioting villagers, and Bernardo is horribly impaled on the cruel tines of the rack he carries with him everywhere. Outside the tower, Adso waits, but there at the door, blackened by soot and smoke and surrounded by the library's smoke-addled rats, is William, who drops his armloads of books and hugs the only son he will ever have.

As these few scenes demonstrate, *The Name of the Rose* is a movie with a heart, while Eco wrote a book which is mainly about thinking. Their audiences, materials, and methods are different. Still, Annaud is able to leave us with a balanced view. Like Adso, we love the girl and grieve for her poverty (as the Franciscans grieve for human poverty, adopting it as sacred), yet we are required to remember the gulf that separates her from Adso—not simply language (love is its own language) but family, tradition, profession, and, at the bottom of it all, culture. On one of the excursions that move him toward independence, Adso walks down to the peasants' hut and, peering in, sees the girl amidst members of her family, picking lice from an older woman's hair and eating them. In *Quest for Fire*, people in the tribe groomed each other in similar ways, bonding and maintaining their place in the group, as hominids (and other primates) have done for many, many years. An old woman is lying under the chicken roost (outside they might be stolen), and a dropping has plopped into her eye: the family screams with laughter, and again we remember Annaud's earlier film where cave people discover laughing (it is when minor accidents happen to somebody else). And didn't William of Baskerville argue that laughter is peculiar to humans? Adso moves away from the hut as one of the older boys (a boyfriend?) throws something at him. Obviously he does not belong here, and though he would move heaven and earth to make her happy and save her from her poverty, the world and its necessities lie between them, deep as oceans.

Nevertheless, it is sad—no, it is practically unbearable—when William and Adso ride slowly down the path under branches shining from a recent snowfall, away from the burned abbey and away from the girl, who waits beside the path and reaches for Adso's hand. He has been looking around for her as he rides, and now she is kissing his hand, laying it against her. A tear is making its way down Adso's cheek, and as the love theme returns (cellos, this time), we probably feel the same way. But William has ridden on into the mist, and Adso leaves, wordlessly taking back his hand but turning his donkey to see her one last time. "Of all the faces that appear to me out of the past," old Adso narrates, "the one I see most clearly is that of the girl.... She was the only earthly love of my life, yet I never knew, nor ever learned ... her name." Let us finally steal something from the book: *Rosa pristina stat nomine, nomina nuda tenemus.* Yesterday's rose has become a name, only the names remain. *Ubi sunt?*—where are they now? This is old Adso's goodbye to the girl, to William, to the world. What remains but the memory, the trace of how he loved her. Perhaps that is all we bring with us out of the past. Perhaps, in the end, that is enough.

CHAPTER EIGHT

The Return of Martin Guerre

The Return of Martin Guerre (1982)[1] takes place in the mid–sixteenth century in the south of France. So it is not, strictly speaking, a medieval film; yet as we enter the little country village of Artigat, with its muddy streets and crude, weathered houses, pigs rooting in the puddles, and women cooking over open fires, we realize that not much has changed here since the fourteenth, perhaps even the twelfth century. The peasants here—for this film is squarely about people of the third estate—sweat daily to wring a living from the land, planting more wheat now than barley, perhaps, but breaking the earth with their oxen, casting seed, chopping weeds, scything, then threshing and winnowing the grain in just the way it has been done for centuries on the plains of Languedoc, between the Pyrénées and the bigger town of Toulouse to the north. The film will be about farming, then, and what it is like to live in a tiny town where there can be no secrets, where marriage consolidates land, and there is no life apart from one's extended family. Tradition here is an absolute law. Ancient methods are not questioned, proverbs account for every conceivable situation, and the head of the family clan makes decisions that are final.

But changes have begun in France that will be felt even in Artigat. The famines, plagues and wars of the fourteenth and fifteenth centuries had reduced the population roughly by half, raising wages and making available more land and food for those who survived. Consequently, by the 1480s the population began to rebound, gradually forcing wages down and restricting the amount of land each man could hold.[2] Each son inherited a piece of the father's land, so the relatively large tracts of the previous century became progressively sub-divided, and the smaller one's fields, the more difficult it was to make a living from them. Families responded to these stressful conditions by combining their labor and sharing their resources, which led to sons and their wives living under their father's roof, subject to his authority—an old custom revived in a time of need.

The conservative Basque family led by Pierre Guerre had to come together in this way, but they are holding their own, a prominent family in Artigat.³ Our story concerns Pierre's nephew Martin, the son of his brother Mathurin Guerre, who chafed under the perpetual load of farm work and the hard hand of his father. Martin also disliked the tradition-bound life in Artigat, and one night when all were asleep he left his father's house, left his young wife and baby son, and went away to fight in the King's wars. He had been gone for about eight years when, in 1557, someone calling himself Martin Guerre walked into Artigat, was recognized by friends and family (and by Martin's wife Bertrande), and took up the life that Martin had left. In fact, he was Arnaud du Tilh, another war veteran from a village two days' ride to the northwest. The drama of his self-fashioning as Martin Guerre, his gradual unmasking, his trial in 1560 (the real Martin Guerre, like a fairytale hero, returns at the final moment), and his execution is the main storyline of the film.

Remarkably, it is a true story. After the trial in Toulouse, the member (*conseilleur*) of the Parlement of Toulouse who conducted the investigation and wrote the report on the case published an extended account of the affair, to which he added a series of learned annotations. This was the brilliant Jean de Coras, appointed to the Parlement in 1553 but already a regent of the University of Toulouse and famous for his lectures on civil law.⁴ He had written "Latin commentaries on the Roman law, on subjects ranging from marriage and contracts to judicial actions and the constitution of the state."⁵ But Coras wrote his 117-page book about the *Arrest Memorable* in the French vernacular, and after its publication in 1561 it was reprinted in 1565 (three times), 1572, 1579, 1596, 1605 and 1618.⁶ This haunting, popular tale of a man who led another man's life for three years, and in many ways improved it, was passed down to the twentieth century, inspiring a novel in 1941 (Janet Lewis, *The Wife of Martin Guerre*) and catching the attention of director Daniel Vigne and scenarist Jean-Claude Carrière in the early 1980s. Having begun work on the screenplay for *The Return of Martin Guerre*, they were joined by the historian Natalie Zemon Davis, who served as consultant to the film and subsequently wrote an historical study which supplemented and to some extent corrected the movie's compressed version. The film appeared in 1982, winning a French Academy Award (César)for Costumes and Scenery.⁷ Yet despite the country realism of the sets and costumes, this is no costume drama but, of all medieval movies, the keenest in its understanding of how French peasants coped with their life, and how, by 1560, it was beginning to change.

The film opens onto a stretch of shallow brook—the Lèze, flowing south from the Pyrénées. Riding up the brook bed toward us is a man in a dark formal cape, a portable desk strapped behind his saddle, urging the horse along and taking this shortcut because he is late for an appointment. Jehan Pegalá, notary of the nearby village of Le Fossat, has come to Artigat to write up a marriage contract for Martin Guerre, son of Mathurin Guerre, and Bertrande de Rols, he 14 and she perhaps nearly that. The notary jogs down the lane toward town, passing a small flock of sheep, and, where it turns into a narrow, muddy street, enters the cluster of roughly built houses, picking his way among wagons, livestock, children, and a stewpot, waving to old friends. He is known here, part of a familiar routine. The boy and girl are being married at the earliest possible time to create a tie between two prominent families, an alliance based on shared land, some of which comes with the bride as her dowry. Why not wait a few years? Sickness might strike, preventing the marriage, or a change of heart come about in either family—and youth is unstable, with its injuries and pregnancies. No, better to cement the agreement now, and the children can grow up together under his father's roof.

The following scene brings us to a slightly later time, the marriage ceremony in Artigat, where the local Curé fits the wedding ring onto Martin's thumb, then the first and middle fingers—"In Nomine Patri, Filii et Spiritu Sancti"—and hears their vows. He is a man of the village, has known them all their lives. Their marriage is blessed by the church and approved—arranged!—by the parents of both families, and is immediately part of the social fabric of the town. Its communal nature seems even stronger as we CUT to the house of Mathurin Guerre, a weathered, fine-featured man who is about to sign the marriage contract, surrounded by the rosy, beaming faces of family and friends, the priest, the notary. For his signature, this wealthy peasant draws a little picture of a chicken (a cock?), for, like 90 percent of the people in small villages, he can neither read nor write. The notary takes back the contract—"It's a good match," he says, "well arranged"—when abruptly the door slams open and in bursts one of the neighbors with his bagpipes, blowing a loud, slightly off-key salute, and the room erupts with laughter and catcalls. It *is* a good match—for the families, for the town—and everybody knows this. But we remember the marriage ceremony, when Bertrande kept peering sidelong at Martin, and he did not return her glances. Now CUT to a bedroom (a luxury—most peasant houses had only one room) where boy and girl, sitting naked under the covers in Bertrande's big dowry bed, are blessed by the priest, kissed by sisters, teased by the maid. Then everyone goes to feast and dance, and they are left alone. He turns away. She touches his shoulder, "Martin?" He will not answer.

This marriage, its joy and sadness, was in an earlier time the next scene tells us. Now, even though the village looks the same (will Artigat ever change?)—its women in headcloths and long skirts, the men in breeches, much as they are in Brueghel's paintings—we are almost twenty years in the future. Jean de Coras the conseilleur from Toulouse has just arrived, thronged by excited people. Coras has come to adjudicate the claim of Pierre Guerre that

Martin Guerre is trying to steal from him and, worse, is not really his nephew. The trial story anchors the film, allowing for extended flashbacks of Bertrande's life with her apparent husband. It also provides us with a point of view—that of Coras, to be sure, for he is the detective in this legal tale, but increasingly we are drawn by the covert, clenched determination of Bertrande to save her children and her husband, even if she sacrifices herself to do it. What does Bertrande really know about the strangely familiar man who three years ago claimed—the whole village agreed!—he was her husband? What is her strategy in this game of identities, her *mentalité*? What is it like to be this beautiful, reserved peasant wife in the County of Foix in 1560?

Let us begin with Roger Planchon as Jean de Coras, tall and distinguished in his black robes of court, who dismounts and is immediately in command of the situation, sending his page boy for the folding chairs, steadying the horse with a clap of his hand, and then, head held high but with a discerning eye on the crowd, proceeding with the other judge to his interview with Bertrande at the house of Pierre Guerre. For Martin is in prison awaiting trial, and Bertrande has moved in with his uncle Pierre, Martin's accuser but also her mother's second husband. Under these constraints, the 30-year-old Bertrande who greets the judge is quiet and reticent, but one would hesitate to say timid. Nathalie Baye's Bertrande has a restrained force that implies her fear for Martin and their marriage, the danger of Coras' legal authority, the press of village opinion (both for and against her husband), but also her own willfulness and a modest but apparent sexuality. In real life, Bertrande de Rols was considered beautiful, and that is what we see here, though the attraction is subtle. If anything, her headcloth enhances the serious, watchful eyes, and the (somehow) demure cleavage in nearly every scene until she is in mourning reminds us that this careful woman who seems a presence apart from anyone other than her husband is, in fact, a proud, passionate being, *une bonne epouse*—a good wife in every sense of the word. In some scenes Baye has the intimate, innocent charm of Vermeer's *Girl with a Pearl Earring* (the likeness is remarkable). In others she is unmistakably a leader among the village women, a mother with the strength to stand by her husband after he left and again when he returned, someone who could use both custom and the King's law to her own advantage.

"*C'est Bertrande de Rols*," says the second judge, and here she is in Pierre's house, full face in a medium close-up, alone in the frame—we see her through the eyes of Coras. The second judge is Firmin Vayssière, an older colleague and, like Coras, a Protestant sympathizer. In 1572, both of them will be hanged in their official robes outside the chambers of the Parlement of Toulouse by an angry Catholic mob, another grim event in the St. Bartholomew's Day massacre.[8] The older man begins the questioning, and Bertrande, obviously ill at ease, answers as briefly as possible. So Martin was not able to consummate the marriage? *Oui.* And others knew of this? *Oui, tous le village* (a hint of a bitter smile). Why? They put a spell on both of us. And suddenly we CUT back to the past, where young Martin has been forced to take part in a Charivari organized for his public ridicule. It is an ancient, widespread custom in western Europe, a carnivalized masking that reasserts the integrity of village customs and mores through rituals, such as having the cuckold, or someone abused by his wife, ridden through town backward on an ass (sometimes his next door neighbor rode the ass).[9] This particular case involves non-consummation. Martin has been forced to put on a bearskin and chase men dressed as women of the town (headcloths, skirts, enormous false breasts pinned to their shirts), while other men wearing face paint and outlandish ragged costumes ("the town warriors") wait to chase the bear, throw him to the ground and "castrate" the big stuffed balls and long beef bone tied to his costume. Whose business is it if the wife is unfaithful (unfaithful husbands are disregarded), if a young widow marries an older man (or vice-versa!), if a man's wife has no children? Everyone's, according to village tradition, which is reinforced by gossip, distrust of strangeness, and the anxiety produced by a constant threat of hard times. We have always lived this way, says the Charivari, who are you to be different?

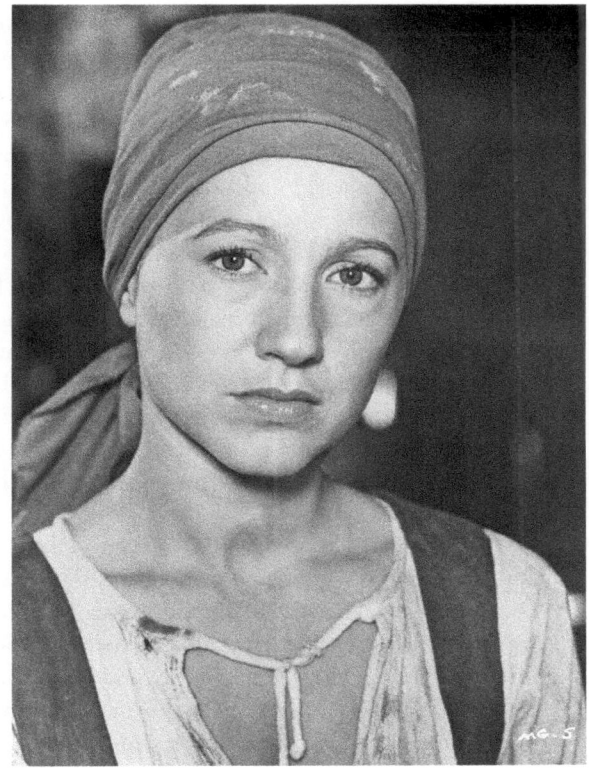

Nathalie Baye as Bertrande de Rols in Daniel Vigne's *The Return of Martin Guerre* (1982), George Eastman House Motion Picture Department Collection.

The Charivari ends up at Martin's house, hooting and calling out insults ("Bertrande, if you want to have children, change husbands!") before his father throws them a small purse and, as custom decrees, they disperse. Martin has fled to his house but, angry and hurt, takes shelter in the barn, the bear lying down exhausted among the sheep while his family endures the public laughter. But traditional life can also heal. It has to, given the current and growing fear of the *aiguillette*, the Satanic castration spell cast by a witch (who secretly makes a knot in a piece of string during the marriage ceremony), rendering the marriage "unhappy, sterile, and adulterous." As Ladurie says, "The complex of castration by ligature was inseparable from the obsession of impotence on the husband's part and, in certain cases, of frigidity on the part of the wife."[10] The following two scenes show Martin's healing, first by the wise woman Jacmette, who sprinkles grain down his body to his codpiece ("Blessed flesh, I conjure you, *REPOUSSE!*"—*spring up*, that is, like a plant). Then one of the exquisite brief shots of Artigat that Vigne uses to establish time of day (evening has come to this fertile green village) and a night scene in the barn where Martin and Bertrande stand naked, tied face to face on either side of a roof pillar while the priest scourges them (her more lightly than him) and recites an exorcism in Latin.

"It worked—that very day," Bertrande says. We are back in the present, and the mood has changed. Coras leans back. *"Bertrande, n'avez pas peur"*— Don't be afraid, he says in a calm, soothing voice, then leans forward: I am Jean de Coras, *conseilleur* of the Parlement of Toulouse, I am in charge of this investigation, I want you to tell me everything that happened, *even if the priest told you not to.* Vayssiére, startled, begins a warning (*"Je ..."*) and raises his hand as if to intervene. For it is better, safer, that no one knows they have little respect for the politically involved village priest or the powerful church that sustains him. Coras hesitates, his smile disappearing, and looks down at the papers before him. Then JUMP CUT to the middle of further testimony by Bertrande, and we are left feeling an awkwardness, as if protocol had been breached. These decent, careful men of law have betrayed a subtle bias, and, alerted by their attitude, we begin to see Bertrande as an individual separate from the combined authority of family, village and church.

The impression grows stronger as Bertrande begins to tell about her life with Martin: they had a son, Sanxi, but Martin wouldn't even look at him ... as the intimate details emerge the camera gradually moves closer and she seems softer, more accessible, but also deeper and more complex. Again we are seeing her through the eyes of Coras, and, implicit in the questions and her introspective answers, we sense a potential understanding, a faint suggestion not of collaboration but a degree of like-mindedness between the investigator and his best informed witness. For if anyone knows the truth about the return of Martin Guerre, it is this woman. She is merely a wife, with practically no legal standing, but it will become obvious that the marriage and the trial's outcome are as much her doing as Martin's.

Martin kept to himself in the village, she says. He didn't like farming and quarreled with his father. These answers send us back again to an earlier spring, planting time, where Uncle Pierre and his oxen are plowing up great clumps of brown dirt, a horse drags a harrow, father Mathurin sows grain, and Martin is late with the drinking water. He staggers in under a yoke with its two pails, his mother scolds (Bertrande brings him an apple), and Mathurin discovers that two sacks of grain are missing. Who loaded them ... Martin! The teenaged Martin is certainly no farmer and apparently doesn't care that Basque families never steal. Soon he will be gone, but the scene remains with us, anchoring the identity of these people in their labor, their utter dependence on the land. All the family is here, after all, women beating the apple branches and gathering the fruit in baskets, and chopping up the garden plot with big hoes. Flies are everywhere (remarkable in a film)—you can see them in the air and crawling on peoples' shirts (the foley artist creates some buzzing). It's hot, these people are thirsty, working hard; and throughout the second half of the film, during the long trial sequences, we will remember this life: they are peasants, narrow and prejudiced but close to the earth and standing for a kind of hard truth.

When Martin leaves his family, stealing away in the night, the second part of Bertrande's life is complete. As Davis says: she was a child for perhaps twelve years, married to Martin for the following nine, and a (widowed?) mother for nine more. By this time in the film she has become the focal character, testifying to Coras and Vayssiére as the flashbacks come and go. In the following scenes, Martin/Arnaud strides into the village with an irresistible vitality and, for better or worse, becomes the focus of every situation. But the well-established character of Bertrande is not displaced. Rather, she provides the basis for how we respond to this compelling, elusive, and perhaps dangerous man.

Martin Guerre left home to escape the narrow life in his father's house, the farm work he disliked, the burden of a wife and son, and not least the villagers (who by that time had some rather negative ideas about him). But he was not unique in taking to the road: many people of his time were doing the same—sailors, artisans, students (and masters), peasants, soldiers, vagabonds and even a few educated tourists (like Montaigne) with some money and leisure time. As many as 6,000 French protestants, almost all of them men, fled persecution to Geneva between 1549 and 1560,[11] and pilgrims still went to far off shrines as they had done in the days of Chaucer. Merchants commonly traveled to other cities in search of trade, and the poor not infrequently wandered the country trying to fend off starvation. The wanderlust that drove so many of these nomads has been called "one of the great social features of the time," a European phenomenon that has something in common with the early modern exploration of the skies and seas.¹² Martin did escape, in any case, and, like many Frenchmen, joined the King's armies, seeking new horizons, excitement, the possibility of glorious deeds in battle, and perhaps even a new identity.

Arnaud du Tilh did something very similar. He too had felt suffocated by his native village (Sajas, not Tilh as in the film), although in his case it was not introversion but an excess of rowdy cleverness that created the friction. He joined the French troops, saw Paris and even soldiered in Spain for a time, until military life threw him together with Martin Guerre, who remembered his life in Artigat with bitterness and made clear his desire never to return. Arnaud listened, and it probably occurred to him that a soldier's life is a risky one, while Martin's position in a well-to-do peasant family was better than his own. One could do worse, having survived the wars, than settle down in such a place to farm and raise a family. Martin and Arnaud were similar looking, and even though some would remember that Martin had been more slender, darker, and a bit stooped, an old friend appeared who mistook Arnaud for Martin, and at that point the new Martin Guerre was born. He left the army and made his way gradually to Artigat, learning what he could about Martin and the Guerre family from people along the way who had known or done business with them.¹³

So now the self-fashioned Martin Guerre nears Artigat at about midday, striding along energetically, crossing a hedgerow—Ho!—two men in a village field look up and watch him approach. We are behind him, looking over his shoulder, and as matters progress we probably continue to share his view, wanting people to accept him. They meet, "*Qui est tu*?" But he only smiles and thrusts out his chin to be recognized. They are looking, the tension begins to rise … "Aren't you the son of Mathurin Guerre, Martin, is it you?" And now Martin *agrees* with what is already an observed fact, not a claim. "But Martin, you were never so big and strong!" Here is the first hesitation, a plea to remove their doubts. So he hooks an arm around each of their necks—"*C'est la guerre*!" he growls, and they all laugh, for really they want him to be Martin, to restore the past. A boy of about twelve comes out from the village and hears them talking. "Martin?" he says, then turns and runs back, all legs and arms, calling out to anyone within earshot that Martin Guerre has returned.

Coming into town they stop at the house of Pierre Guerre where Martin recognizes his tall older sister Jeanne (it has to be her!), his little sister Guillemette, and his own son Sanxi, now about nine years old. In a moment he will confront Uncle Pierre, who is rather severe at first but warms when Martin says he has heard about the death of his parents (he prayed for them); and isn't this Pierre's wife, who is Bertrande's mother, thus Martin's mother-in-law ("*Ma belle mère*")? Soon Cathérine arrives carrying a load of sticks (she is the family servant who took care of Martin as a baby), and her overflowing joy and anger (he was away so long!) creates a round of laughter that moves through what is now a crowd of villagers, and they all go off, led by Martin, in search of Bertrande at the village wash house. This has been a remarkable long scene, building by stages and moving delicately past its series of hesitations and doubts to reach a crescendo with the bursting forth of Cathérine's emotions, which releases the tension, creating general laughter and acceptance that Martin has come back. But has it been too easy? Why do they recognize Martin so quickly after nine long years?

These are real questions, and to the film's credit, it contains answers. Primarily, the villagers and especially the family see Martin in this man because they want to believe he has come back. How could he leave them when he had so much here, where he is needed? Conversely, why would anyone think him an imposter? Cases of impersonation did occur, some of them even in southern France,[14] but was it likely that anyone would try something so risky? Perhaps this Martin does not look exactly like the Martin they remember, but in a time without photographs or even (for peasants) paintings, nothing exists to reinforce or contradict a memory, and surely everyone remembers him a little differently. It has even been argued that while vision is the dominant sense in our own times, it wasn't in 1560, when even poets favored descriptions of colors, not shapes, and these were bright, primary colors—the ones used in livery or in heraldry—whose main significance was a symbolic one.[15] The senses, especially hearing, taste and smell, "weighed heavily in favour of the emotional rather than the rational," and were considered as "leading to error and falsehood"—they were "given to us for the preservation of the body, as instruments of our instincts, 'and not to learn the truth.'"[16] And then there is Martin's extraordinary memory, the way he could call it forth with a silver tongue. He remembered people and the stories about them which are so much a part of village life, but also the little things, like the white hose Bertrande made for him before he left (she made them too big), then put away in the linen chest that was part of her dowry. No small part of Gérard Depardieu's extraordinary performance in this film is his ability to render Martin's nearly supernatural readiness to engage any doubts, master every situation, while simultaneously betraying the act by giving us subliminal glimpses of the calculation that we know must be going on behind that sensitive, smiling face.

But there he goes at the head of the ecstatic crowd, as if it were another village ritual (they do practically everything in groups), making for the wash house where Bertrande has remained, waiting for him. When married to Martin she was a child in a strange house, then a young, highly visible, chaste widow after he left. Now she faces yet another life-altering change, and she is wary. She always wanted him to return, but he had not been a warm, understanding husband, and widowhood gave her an honored place in the village as well as certain legal advantages, despite being back in her mother's house. He appears at the entrance, and they stare at each other. Natalie Zemon Davis finds it hard to believe that Bertrande would not have realized the new Martin was not her husband. Nathalie Baye, who played Bertrande, couldn't believe it either, and perhaps any woman would feel the same. If they are right, what we are seeing is a guarded recognition for both man and wife. Martin sees that she is watchful and somewhat resistant, as well as beautiful, but Bertrande has to consider within seconds whether she should try to make a life with this strong-looking, expressive man who pauses at the entrance—"*Bonjour Bertrande*"—then steps into the shed, stopping again to take off his hat—"*C'est moi, Martin.*" A smile flits across his face and the beginning of a laugh, but instantly he is silent, watching her.

Why the laugh? He might simply be nervous, yet from what we have seen he is far too practiced for that. Perhaps he is already aware of her disbelief, and the laugh is for this little joke they both understand. But surely at this point we simply want these compelling people to be together—the shrewd insight we will save for another time. So let us believe that it is a humble little laugh—just me, Martin, believe it or not—and that it comes partly from Martin's suddenly realizing that he likes this woman and would like her to think well of him. Bertrande's answering gaze in what is arguably the key scene in the film is equally ambivalent. He has come nearer, but her face betrays nothing, and in her eyes we might read hope but also distrust, judgment, fear and pain, as well as the pride of small-town French widowhood at its moment of surrender. In this awful moment she decides, however, and, according to custom, kneels before her husband, welcoming him back with humility and grace.

Martin raises her to her feet, and bending a bit to see her face from the side, "*Mon Dieu, comme ma femme est belle*" (for indeed she is beautiful, though breathless and taut). With that, the tension in her seems to break, and she sinks against his shoulder with a burst of—is it tears or laughter? They are a couple now, for better or worse, and as they leave the wash house, Sanxi leaps into the arms of someone he now can fully believe is his father, and Martin hugs a smiling Bertrande. The crowd cheers joyfully and surges around them, the sound track swells and quickens, and the three of them move off through the people of their village toward home. We are relieved, of course, but so is everyone, since the village fabric is woven from solid, predictable marriages of familiar men and women like this, who work hard, produce children and constitute the only life any of them has ever known.

We are also aware that this new Martin has manipulated all of them. The easy laughter, the open, engaging face with its hundred expressions, the ways he draws people to him, literally reaching out, a hand on the shoulder, a hug

Nathalie Baye as Bertrande de Rols, and Gerard Depardieu as Arnaud du Tilh, in Daniel Vigne's *The Return of Martin Guerre* (1982; courtesy George Eastman House Motion Picture Department Collection).

(he kisses Pierre's hand to ask forgiveness), and even the way he approaches Bertrande, bending down to imply her equal partnership in whatever they both decide—we see all this, and yet we *like* this man who virtually radiates vitality and the ability to handle every situation. He is like the promise of the future for us, for the village, and especially for Bertrande, who has chosen to be his wife in what will surely be a different marriage than before.

In the following sequences we see Martin in Pierre's house—warm browns and reds, the glow of candle light—as he tells stories, bonding with various members of the family but also revealing parts of himself they don't recognize. Bertrande's mother asks What were you doing all that time? A grimace—I was in the war, (to Bertrande) I came back to be with all of you. What was Spain like? (a brother-in-law). He slams down his cup—It's dry. Did you see Paris? (this is sister Jeanne). *Oui*! And now the stories begin to flow, and they are fascinated, since most have never been out of the village. He unpacks some Flanders cloth (the sisters love it), then a book. You've learned to read! (Pierre). Yes, and to write too. Of course, few in the village can do either. But the Protestants in Basel read their Bibles, and by now (1557) there are people in the towns near Artigat who quietly follow this new religion—a troubling development! But Bertrande takes the book from Pierre (it looks like a religious text), paging through it curiously, as though she might like the idea of reading. Some drinking follows, a few jokes (the tone brightens), the women start dancing, and for the first time we hear viols, shouts, the vigorous country dance theme, Brueghel come to life. Now it's bedtime, and Martin has asked Bertrande to bring the white hose she made for him so long ago—they're in your linen chest, upstairs (he remembered!). The old Martin said they were too big and threw them at her ... she moves to the stairs, starts up, then looks back, smiles, and, reaching out, catches his hand and draws him close, looking into his eyes. They go up together.

During this long, carefully modulated scene, Martin and Bertrande gradually come nearer to each other, so that we begin with the bonding of an extended family group but end with two people who for various reasons share a separate union. They like and are learning to trust each other. Both, given their experience, are independent minded and will probably take equal responsibility for the children, the marriage, their possessions. The inevitable strains of a peer relationship will be compensated by the ties of mutual love and respect. Such a pairing might seem a modern anachronism but in fact it represents a different kind of marriage which developed among merchants, artisans and even yeomen (e.g., well-to-do peasant freeholders) in larger towns during the European Renaissance.

George Duby writes that as early as the twelfth century, extended aristocratic kin groups were giving way to the "ménage," a "small conjugal unit defined by the male head of household and connected to a patriarchally defined line." Displacing a lateral network of marriages in which "hierarchies of generational and gender authority were multiple and mobile," the ménage was a narrow, vertical hierarchy: marriage that (with the aid of primogeniture) consolidated and conserved land holdings.[17] But by the sixteenth century, as Lawrence Stone points out, the *mentalité* had changed. The gentry, but also professionals and "privileged commoners," talked of "romantic love in courtship and betrothal, of conjugal partnership and friendship, of the pleasures of domesticity, and of the satisfactions to be had in parenting." This sort of "companionate marriage," he argues, generated "affective individualism," the "psychological and sociological mark of modernity."[18] Merchants and their wives managing their business together, lawyers, goldsmiths, money lenders … even yeoman who, like Martin, bought and sold land and grain, these too made the new marriages. What accounted for the change? Many things, perhaps including, as Martha Howell believes, a shift of emphasis from conservative land owning to the buying and selling of all kinds of "movables," which created a more fluid, less stable environment for individuals and their marriages. The stability of inherited land had once held couples (and lineages) together, but when fungible commodities (and even land) were so easily gained *and lost*, she argues, marriages found the stability they needed from another source: through mutual love, trust, and a "companionate" mode of life.[19]

From the beginning, in any case, Martin and Bertrande represent something new in Artigat, the idea of a marriage where man and wife are something like equals. He has found her—won her away from her widow's position in the village, in effect—and she has accepted him. They have equal responsibility for the fiction that he is Martin Guerre, that their marriage is what everyone assumes it to be. Yet while such equality may have existed in towns, it was not the norm in small villages in the south of France in 1560. A different evening: Martin is telling another story, this time about the natives in Brazil he has heard about—their finery is feathers, not silk, they eat the hearts of their enemies, they share their women, and the women decide everything! Uncle Pierre, the Basque patriarch, takes this in. "The day women rule here," he says, "it will be the end of the world." Everyone laughs, especially the women, who know this game very well. In villages like this, the extended family was predominant over the nuclear family, a father's permission was necessary for children to marry, and, as Mandrou puts it, "no-one seemed to expect from marriage anything more than an association where the wife, 'discrete, polite, unflinching in her loyalty'… was subservient to her husband."[20] It is true that the church sanctioned the equality of the woman, but only in connection with the "conjugal debt" (*debitum conjugale*) based on I Corinthians 7.4: "The wife hath not power of her own body, but the husband: and likewise also the husband hath not the power of his own body, but the wife." This meant that "either of them could 'demand' payment of the conjugal [intercourse] debt and oblige the other to 'pay' it"[21]; but the demand was fully legitimate only if made for the purpose of procreation (thus not for pleasure). How did laymen see it? Here is Montaigne (I:XXX): "These shameless caresses which our first excitement suggests to us in this game [of love] are not only indecent but also injurious when indulged in with our wives .... They are always aroused enough for our needs."[22] Like the clerics, the laymen are concerned that husbands and wives may "burn with such ardour" that they "entirely forget the service of God."[23]

Artigat is a traditional rural Catholic southern village immensely set in its ways, and, in addition, this new Martin has a past. The complication of the film's narrative involves several scenes of villagers turning against him, as inevitably they must. Vagabonds sleeping in the barn identify him as Pansette ("The Belly")—"I knew him in the army, in Picardy." Villagers dressed as wood demons (capes and hoods of reeds and long grass) harass the couple (we remember the Charivari held for the old Martin). Perhaps the cruelest attack is by the village priest Dominique Caylar, who approaches Bertrande as she prays before the altar, head covered and eyes closed, quietly at peace like the Virgin in late medieval paintings. The priest wants to know if she, too, has doubts about her husband. Is she living in mortal sin? If so she will follow him into the depths of hell. Her flesh will burn, her eyes fall out, she will scream but no one will hear. Isn't she afraid to lie to God? Why has she not confessed? ... Bertrande silently leaves the church, and we are left wondering: has she not confessed because the priest would break his vows and tell others while condemning the marriage as adulterous? Or is it also because she has acquired a Protestant sensibility, and has lost faith in various Catholic rituals, including the confession?

These doubts climax when Martin, the hard worker and successful farmer, finally goes to Pierre and asks for his lawful share of the gains from his land while he was fighting in the war. As we might expect, the older man is furious: You dare ask me for this? I, who raised your son, protected your wife all those years? As Bertrande and Sanxi stop working to listen, and other in-laws move in from the field, Martin and Pierre circle each other, crouching a little, hands ready—it looks like a duel, or a dog fight (their peasant's hoods are suddenly helmets framing the grim faces). "Well, Martin, or *not* Martin, I might have expected this from you." "What did you call me? *Répétez le*?!" And then they are fighting on the ground, and the in-laws pile on to stop them. Yes, it had to happen, this and the following scenes, where Pierre pretends he will pay the money after all—just wait until no one is around, early tomorrow morning, up in the hayloft—you'll get what I owe you! Martin has said he needs the money—he intends to sell his father's field and buy Pujol's to plant barley—and that makes things even worse. If Pierre is not simply being tight-fisted and greedy, he is righteously appalled: a Basque never sells family land. And who would plant barley when the cash crop is wheat? Something feels wrong here, but the wrongness is fundamentally that Martin is not Basque, did not grow up in Artigat, has learned the (relatively new) art of buying and selling ("marketing") land; worst of all, he would rather stand on his legal rights than rely on the largely unwritten local and family customs.

So Martin meets Pierre in the hayloft, where Pierre's sons are ready with threshing flails, beating him to the ground where Pierre is about to kill him with a brutal two-bladed field hoe. But Bertrande leaps out of bed and comes quickly enough to throw herself between the descending weapon and Martin's body. "You would have died for him?" Coras asks, laying a kind, fatherly (or is it "husbandly") hand on her shoulder (she notices the hand). But if so, why did she not protest earlier when Martin was arrested? Well, she had doubts—suppose he had tricked them all, she would be an adulterer, her children bastards, she would go to hell! But now, "Yes, he is my husband." What is Coras to suppose—that Bertrande's woman's weakness led her to doubt, but now love and fear have strengthened her resolve? Instead he seems to guess, and if we can put ourselves in her place, we too suspect that she had to go along with village opinion or risk alienation and even death if Martin lost his case. But if he wins, a woman's doubts are soon forgotten. In effect, she is trying to save her family, just as any peasant patriarch would cling to his land.

Coras prepares to decide the case in a village parody of the Last Judgment: To my right side those who believe this man is *véritablement* Martin Guerre, to my left those who do not, and in the middle those with no opinion. What about the priest, doesn't he have an opinion? Dominique hesitates—"*Je suis le curé de tous*," the priest for everyone—but the (Protestant) judges wear their deeply knowing smiles, and, of course, this native villager and churchman joins those on the left. In the event, neither side is in the majority, and finding no clear reason to believe this is not Martin Guerre, the judge too decides to preserve the family, riding triumphantly out of town while Martin and his family simply walk home.

The film enters its final act with domestic scenes, Martin awakening (he was badly beaten, then jailed), Bertrande washing his feet (we think of Mary Magdalene), Cathérine closing the bedroom door, as she did for the young couple so many years ago. Some prints of the film contain brief footage of them making love—Bertrande on top, which seems normal enough but implies again that they are equals: he is tired and sore and she will help with this.[24]

CUT to a profound, Edenic view of Artigat in early morning, shadows among the village trees, mist rising from the valley below, dark greens and lavenders fading off hazily to the blue ridges of the hills; and centered in this lovely composition are two slim French cedars side by side, flame like, as in the paintings of Van Gogh. It is Bertrande and Martin, of course, in the last moment of peace they will ever know.

They are indeed side by side, sleeping, when Pierre bangs the door open for his sons, their friends, the priest, most of them with weapons pointed at Martin. "What?" he asks, but it is obvious that during the night Pierre has found another way. Bertrande has signed an accusation (there is her X!), and Martin will return to trial, this time in Toulouse. The courtroom drama of this second trial is a feast of rhetoric, as one person after another defends Martin or accuses him. Martin and the judge begin to seem more like colleagues searching for what each calls the truth, and Bertrande continues to have the last word. And really, they do not leave Artigat. For Martin demands to have his family, friends—all the village!—as witnesses, so they too must go to the big city, with their country bearing and peasant values intact. One of the most telling scenes in the film is the villagers entering Toulouse in their slow, canvas-covered ox carts, creeping over the bridge and into town where they crane their necks at three-story buildings, people watching them from balconies, the great church adjoining the Parlement. They have never known anything like this and seem awestruck, suspicious and ill at ease. Martin Guerre, fluent and adaptable, is much more at home here than they can be.

CUT to the trial, where the priest claims Martin does not have the moles and scars he once had, or not in the same places. But Cathérine tended him as a baby, she saw him naked more often than the priest (laughter in the court)—look, these are his broken back teeth, like always (she holds his mouth open)—this is Martin Guerre, as sure as night follows day. We begin to see a pattern forming: the priest and others with a place in the village hierarchy side with Pierre Guerre and the males related to him by blood, while the women, and especially those in Martin's lineal family, side with him. The case has divided the Guerres, and it has revealed the ancient division between the political (and legal) force of the men, and the women's power, based on intimacy with the elemental mysteries of birth, growth, suffering and death. Here is Bertrande in the chapel (she is sequestered in a convent for her safety), praying to the Virgin—she feels so lonely. Here Jacmette, the wise woman of the village, who was old even when she cured the young Martin's impotence. "Come, Jacmette, your fingers remember ... tell the truth." The hands tremble and the blind eyes stare, but at the edge of death the voice is firm: "You are Martin, *Tu es Martin Guerre*!"

This division emerges again in the mini-climax where Martin and Pierre each try to invoke authority for their claim. Cathérine has just upstaged the priest, and Martin asks permission to speak. "*Parle*," says the judge with a faint smile, and Martin makes his appeal: "I've seen death. I've heard the roar of cannon and the screams of the wounded (*les cris horribles de la bataille*). You wish me ill, uncle, but I've lived through worse. But must that be a man's fate for wanting to live a little before returning to his family to work the land God gave us?" He has passed through death, now he wants simply to have a wife and children, to work the earth and live from it—isn't that the deepest law? But Pierre speaks as a Basque patriarch: "This imposter ... all he wanted was my nephew's property. I don't want to take it, I'm *defending* it! He's not my nephew!"

But, scene by scene, Martin chips away at Pierre's position, calling witnesses—sister Jeanne, her husband, the village half-wit Dominge Pailhés (apparently he is the bastard half-brother of Martin!)—each in their way affirming that Pierre did threaten to throw Bertrande out of his house, that he warned Martin he was going to harm him, and even offered Dominge money to kill his half-brother. But didn't Bertrande sign the new accusation saying that Martin was not her husband? "No, I did not sign! I would have written my name." Pierre grins, "But she doesn't know how to write." Raimonde (his wife and Bertrande's mother) also has a superior look—they have won, and hadn't she always said that great mischief comes from reading and writing? Bertrande merely asks for pen and paper, and as the judges look on, writes BERTRANDE in beautiful large letters, even better (she has practiced) than how Martin showed her the night she was upset about all the evil gossip. She was proud to learn her written name, and now her determination to sign, to signal her individual will, seems an understated defiance. Martin has an amused, quizzical expression, the expression men have when their wives outrageously save the day. She did it, what can he say? But his eyes slide to the right—he set this up a long time ago, and for just a moment we see the calculation that works beneath his every move.

Later Martin gives Bertrande a chance to swear again. "Swear that I'm not your husband. Swear it on the Holy Gospel." She will not swear to such a thing, but not because she cares little for religion. Several times in the film we see her praying, or fearful of evil spirits, or curious about those Brazilian savages ("Do they have souls, Martin?"—she marks a cross on her new baby's forehead). But why (in the bookless town of Artigat) would she be interested in reading, if not to read the New Testament? So it is somewhat likely that this devout but independent woman cares deeply about the Holy Gospel, her individual access to the word of God. Had Martin asked her to swear that he *was* her husband, she might have hesitated long. But she has no trouble *refusing* to swear on the holy book (though even citing it carries some authority), and here again Martin's cleverness peers out at us.

By the end of the trial, Martin's appeal has answered every evidential objection but one: how could he remember so much? Is it natural to call up the past in such detail, naming names, revealing what had been long forgotten and charming people thereby, as though they had no control of themselves? Does he command demonic powers; is he, in fact, possessed by the devil? Martin sits quietly, innocently, while a woman who danced with abandon at his homecoming says she could not help herself—flames swept through her when he spoke. But her fears were shared by many. Between 1560, the year of the trial, and 1600 an epidemic of witch trials reflected a fundamental instability in the world as people saw it. As Mandrou says, "Even the most balanced of men, those who were most endowed with the famous, evenly-distributed 'common sense,' lived daily in a phantasmagoria, in a universe inhabited by spirits and semi-divine or para-divine demons .... According to Ronsard, the air is peopled by 'demons,' just as the 'depths of the waves' are by fish, the heavens by angels and the earth by men."[25] The judges (although not Coras) are seriously concerned by this new direction, which might conceivably involve extra-legal authorities. They call upon Martin to answer this charge, if he can. He responds that if he were a demon and could work magic, he would be at home with his wife. "I certainly wouldn't be here before all of you." They look to Coras, but he says the man has answered well. And with no real evidence to the contrary, perhaps they can dismiss the charge of deviltry.

The trial ends, the elegant aristocrats and their ladies, along with other spectators (Montaigne was one), are leaving early, and the judges in their red robes assemble on the platform to hear the decision. In his best orator's voice, Coras is proceeding with this when an attendant runs up—another witness desires to be heard. And it is Martin Guerre, the man himself. Legless, like Captain Ahab, he arrives by chance at the last possible moment. He too has been to the wars (he lost the leg at the battle of St. Quentin), he knows Pansette, and most of the family instantly recognize him. It is over.

Naturally, the man we have been calling Martin—let him now be Arnaud—does not give up so easily. "Do not forsake me," he pleads to the family and friends who believed in him, and, despite the imposture, something about him seems vaguely Christlike. He challenges this man whom he has never seen (no doubt hired by Uncle Pierre!) to answer questions to which he, the true Martin Guerre, will know the answer. In a time when fingerprints and photos are unknown, and hearsay (as now) unreliable, the judges allow this dialectical game. Martin answers some, misses one, and then, as we might expect, fails to remember the white hose which Bertrande made for him, then saved in her linen chest when he would not wear them. Apparently she means as little to him now as she did before. Arnaud is triumphant (in his imagination he has changed places with Martin, overcoming, thus *becoming*, him)—I told you about them and you forgot, he cries. But Coras holds up his hand: You said you had never met this man, he says; and, watching from the crowd, Bertrande closes her eyes and bows her head.

Of course Bertrande is summoned to make the final identification. Facing the two men who claim to be her husband, she looks to Arnaud, and he smiles at her gently, kindly—for truly he is the husband he claims to be, if not the man—and drops his eyes. She hesitates and then, as she must, kneels before Martin and asks his forgiveness. When Arnaud is dead and Bertrande has been pardoned for being taken in, as women so often are by clever scoundrels (another legal fiction to preserve the mother and her family), Coras visits Bertrande in Pierre's house and asks her why she did not choose Arnaud instead. He is puzzled, and the case will not let him go (soon he will write his account of it). They had planned to live on with their family, she says, but this time she saw in his eyes what he wanted. He knew that now it was impossible.

In real life, the widowed Jean de Coras had a second wife whom he loved inordinately,[26] and in the film, his interviews with Bertrande are the backbone of the narrative. Questioning her, he has been professional but patient. He seems to understand what she must conceal or reveal, as if walking with her where she needs to go. At her crucial testimony in the second trial, and here with Arnaud dead, he hovers behind her or to her side as though he were a mental or even a spiritual presence, a safe confidant for the secrets she has kept so long. In this he is a surrogate husband or father (her own father is long dead) acting in place of Arnaud—another intelligent, independent person with whom Coras clearly feels some connection. "*Vous n'êtes pas bête*" (You're not stupid), he said after Arnaud had made an especially good, legally useful response. We suspect he would say the same of Bertrande.

What does it mean, this bond between the woman and her husband, and with the man who in a legal way aids her as a husband would? We return to I Corinthians 7.4—the wife and husband with power over each other's bodies. As glossed by clerics, this verse allowed the husband to demand the conjugal debt whenever it pleased him, allowing the same to the wife, except that because of women's natural reticence, it was assumed that the wife would have more difficulty making her wishes known. Therefore it was the husband's duty to know when his wife wanted him, and to comply with her implicit demands.[27] We remember Bertrande's final testimony at the second trial: she reaffirms that she is sure Arnaud is her husband—her real husband—but the Parlement requires more evidence, and Coras urges her to describe what no one else could possibly know, their intimate life. "*Quels détails*?" he urges, for Arnaud's life, and hers, depend on this. "He knew when I wanted him," she says, "and knew what to say before, during, and afterward." Laughter in the crowd, and Cathérine is grinning (the women won that round!). But here is the parallel: he (like a good husband) knew when she wanted him; but she, like a good wife and true companion, knew when he wanted her to confess, to give up on a brutal, perhaps suicidal conflict with the village, and instead give the children a life. Facing death, they are equal in marriage, perhaps even in the sight of God, and Coras the Protestant judge and author is their witness.

The ending is sad, with Arnaud, a noose about his neck, carrying the tall candle (his life) and pausing at intervals to ask forgiveness of the village, the family and God. He climbs the ladder, looks back for the last time at Bertrande, Sanxi and his little girl (we remember him looking back at Sanxi, who watched him leaving for Toulouse on a donkey, hands tied), and, without confessing, hurls himself to his death. Then comes Coras' final interview with Bertrande, and now he too rides away toward Toulouse, where the noose awaits him. Finally it is his story as well as Martin's and Bertrande's. They are the new people, kindred spirits and free thinkers, each in their way, and although they do not change the world, they burn very brightly while they live.

CHAPTER NINE

Kingdom of Heaven

Kingdom of Heaven was released in 2004, when war in the middle East seemed unlikely to end soon, and in the West, opinions about the war differed widely.[1] A film about the Saracen reconquest of Jerusalem in the late twelfth century promised to be topical at the very least, but some feared it would arouse further hatred on both sides of the present conflict. After the film's director Ridley Scott issued copies of the early script to historians and others whose opinions might carry weight with the public, it became apparent that the crusades themselves, let alone the Iraq war, had not ended. Jonathan Riley-Smith, the preeminent historian of the crusades, trumpeted his disapproval. How did he like the script? "It sounds absolute balls," began his oft-reprinted statement, which panned the prospective film for its lack of historical accuracy, indeed its betrayal of Riley-Smith's own carefully constructed and dearly held historical point of view.[2] Another substantially negative response came from Thomas F. Madden, an historian at the (Catholic) University of Saint Louis. Madden also found the film inaccurate, and thought it cast too much blame on the crusading Europeans. After all, Jerusalem had belonged to Europe for a century— it was holy ground, it was theirs, they were defending it against the Saracens.[3]

Remarks by those selected to represent the Muslim community tended to be wary and somewhat more temperate. After Scott cut out parts of scenes showing the cruelty or brutality of Muslims—or worse, the rape and murder of Muslim victims—most responses were carefully and mildly positive. For in this film the Christians are finally driven out of Jerusalem, the Church of the Holy Sepulcher becomes a mosque, and Balian (the male lead, played by Orlando Bloom) shakes the hand of his Muslim counterpart (the cavalry officer Imad) before returning to France where he claims to be, once more, a blacksmith. "Cruelty," as one Middle Eastern respondent wrote, "was not on one side but on all."[4] But since the Muslims were on the winning side in the piece of history represented by the film, the Muslim readers of the script seemed able to accept the thematic of a hard-fought peace (however temporary), and were more apt to praise the noble generosity of Balian and the Muslim general Saladin than those writing from a western point of view.

So *Kingdom of Heaven* was first seen as a film about holy war, and those who read the script found it difficult, even impossible, not to be drawn into that ancient struggle. And yet, as Bill Monahan, the script writer, says in one of the featurettes that accompany the full-length director's cut, the film isn't really about the crusades at all. Certainly we follow Balian to the Holy Land, where he fights desperately in what many believe is a war that manifests God's (their God's) will, but from the beginning he remains apart from that calling, a man struggling with his own isolation and loss, and what he feels to be the absence of God. In effect, Balian is a mediator between us and the medieval past. As someone who has lost his wife, murdered his brother and fled from his village, he is an orphaned sensibility, seeking redemption in the city where Christ died. But God does not speak to him, he feels, and his experiences in the East fuel an increasing skepticism. We follow him in his earnest progress toward the Jerusalem his father, Godfrey the Baron of Ibelin, saw as a "kingdom of conscience," and as it dissolves in factions, betrayal and despair, we wonder what is left for him—and for us—to be. For the film's hold upon us is that even more than in 2004, we are still seeking our own kingdom of conscience, a position that we as individuals—east or west—can accept and defend with pride, despite the realities of torture, death, betrayal, and unending war.

Kingdom of Heaven opens at a crossroads outside a small village somewhere in France in the year 1194. It is a bitter winter afternoon, and scattered snowflakes drift in the wind. The failing light falls blue and bleak on two grave diggers, a priest, the stone cross that stands over them, and the shrouded corpse of the woman to be buried there (she was Balian's wife). In another season the slopes of the distant mountains would be lovely, but here is no warmth or life, only the noise of the spade and the mean, dispirited dialogue of the men. One has a notch in his ear: he is a thief. He asks why a woman—a suicide who denied the cross—should be buried at a crossroads; where is the logic in that? "Shut up, you dig," the priest replies. He splits open an apple, and the camera zooms in to show a worm before he throws it away. The scene suggests a tormented hopelessness: no rest for the dead woman (decapitated at burial, she will wander headless in hell, they believe, while passers-by tread ceaselessly over her grave); no future for the branded thief; and for the soulless priest, no joy in God or man. This emotional stasis will recur in the film, as Balian, the princess he comes to love, the noble leper-king Baldwin IV, and, later, all of besieged Jerusalem confront the emptiness of blank despair. It is the first of many signals that the human condition in this film is less a difficulty to be transcended than an unrelenting burden, borne by a few with courage and a kind of weary grace.

Then comes a hail from the road that leads up the valley. Horses are coming, men in armor—"Crusaders," the thief says. The men peer up at the knight and his entourage as they pass toward the village; the knight's gaze falls on the dead woman, and after a few moments his squire returns with a coin, a mass for her soul. Now the muted score of the first scene makes sense: it is a road song, the rhythmic plod of horses over many miles. These men, marked by a distant war, are tired but tough, led by a man who misses nothing and is not incapable of pity. With their arrival, the film announces its peculiar idealism—tarnished, like the knight who will turn out to be Balian's father, yet normative, and in its filmic way, relentless. Balian, like Beowulf and the heroes of so many early narratives, is first measured by his father's high example. He seeks the Holy Land in search of absolution for his sins, and for those of his wife. Instead, he is faced with temptations to compromise his principles and, in defense of love, pride, power or safety, to become someone he is not. As we might expect, Balian remains steadfast, but his quiet acceptance of hard necessities makes him accessible, a thoughtful man whose essentially pragmatic view we can assume with little forcing.

Balian enters the action on a spring morning (he is dreaming) when his young, very pregnant wife has planted a tiny fruit tree. She straightens and eases her back as pregnant women do, then notices him up on the balcony of their house. They smile happily at each other—at which point the winter light returns, his tan grows pale and we realize that Balian is sitting in jail (his wife's suicide renders him suspect). The plot of *Kingdom of Heaven* now begins its great circle as Balian is released to build the Bishop's church, kills his brother (who mutilated his dead wife's body), joins his father on the way to Messina,

Before the ambush. David Thewlis as the Hospitaler, Orlando Bloom as Balian, Jouko Ahola as Odo and Liam Neeson as Godfrey of Ibelin in Ridley Scott's *Kingdom of Heaven* (2005).

then loses him in an ambush before taking ship. After being shipwrecked, he finally rides into Jerusalem, seasoned by his journey but still naïve in the ways of the East. Soon he is living in a great house that belonged to his father, and is himself the "new" baron of Ibelin, treated with respect by his father's retainers and fussed over by a household staff of Arab men and women who view his Frankish lack of polish with something like amused tenderness. In this lull between the demands of East and West, he is examining a horse's foot (in France we saw him at his forge) when, like a sudden desert wind, Sibylla sweeps into the courtyard, wheels her horse and asks for his master. Played by the striking Eva Green, Sibylla is everything we need to know of the arrogant wealth, power and oriental flair the Franks had acquired during the hundred years they held Jerusalem. Her polite request for a drink of water drips with condescending irony. Sure of her power, she eyes him from above, thanking him for the drink as she casually seizes his heart and—"Haya binna!"—is through the gates and gone.[5]

As yet, Balian knows nothing of Sibylla or her brother King Baldwin IV of Jerusalem—how could he?—but what we desire is now ordained: that Balian will love this princess, fight for her and keep her somehow, despite the insupportable Frankish pride to which she was born, a pride that provokes the Saracens to a war that will crush Jerusalem. For indeed, Saladin's prolonged, awe-inspiring siege of the city, the film's climax (and the main selling point of Fox's shorter mass market version of the film), is brought on by the boundless envies and ambitions within the Frankish court. King Baldwin is dying of leprosy, and the extravagantly nasty Guy of Lusignan (Marton Csokas), who is Sibylla's semi-estranged husband, wants the throne. When Baldwin is gone and Sibylla's little son by a former marriage is king, she becomes regent, knowing the boy's reign will be "bloody and short" without Guy's superior force of Knights Templars, the most feared warriors in the East. She therefore gives herself to Guy in exchange for the knights, and Balian goes to the desert to brood. Can Sibylla not be true? "One hundred years ago my ancestors took this city in blood, and I will keep it any way I can," she tells him. Some time before, Baldwin offered Balian the opportunity to marry Sibylla and take over the defense of Jerusalem once Guy was executed by the hard-handed, fiercely loyal Tiberias, Marshal of Jerusalem (Jeremy Irons). But Balian believes in a kingdom of conscience—more than one character has told him "you really are your father's son"—and would not assent to the murder.

Film does not admit stasis, however, and the catastrophic turn to war comes abruptly with the death of the child-king. Tragically, this charming five-year-old is also a leper, and when Sibylla discovers it, she lets him go, gently, with a poison given in sleep rather than letting him rot away under a mask like his uncle. Sibylla is now queen, but Guy's knights are still necessary for the

Nine. Kingdom of Heaven

Eva Green as Sibylla in Ridley Scott's *Kingdom of Heaven* (2005).

defense of the kingdom, and so she makes him king, this man who would do anything to wage war on Saladin. After yet another truce-breaking raid on an Arab caravan by the Knights Templars (led by Guy's crony, the incorrigible Reynald of Châtillon), there is no alternative to war, Saladin's sister having been raped and murdered by Reynald himself during the raid. And so the army of Jerusalem moves ponderously into the dust and heat of the desert to meet Saladin—a three-day march, as history tells us, long enough that when these powerful Franks finally entered battle they were parched and exhausted, and so were cut to pieces by a better general who gave no quarter. Guy is spared by Saladin (as in chess, "A king does not kill a king"), but Reynald is beheaded by Saladin himself, and virtually all the men in the army of Jerusalem perish, leaving the city without a fighting force.

But Balian was not with the army. Having survived an assassination attempt by three of Guy's knights, he stumbles back from the desert in time to see the army march off to its death; and like his historical counterpart, he undertakes the defense of the city with such forces as remain there—shopkeepers, servants, laborers, few of them properly armed and not one a knight. "The city is defenseless," Sibylla tells him. "Save us from the terrible thing that I have done." "I will," he replies, and he does, knighting his ragged troops in a mass ritual—they were nothing, but now they can call themselves free men, and they will die for him. When the walls burst and crumble under the great stones hurled by Saladin's catapults, he leads these men in a desperate attempt to save the lives of the people of the city. Many are killed on both sides. Yet the Saracen incursion is halted, and, faced with the prospect of even more casualties, Saladin offers safe conduct to the seacoast for all citizens in exchange for the surrender of the city.

It is a bitter triumph for all concerned—for Saladin because he has lost many men and much time taking a city of symbolic, not strategic, importance; for Balian because the kingdom of conscience—Baldwin's kingdom, whose trade route he and his father defended—has disappeared along with the city that gave it place; and for Sibylla because this queen must now walk in the dust of a refugee caravan. The film's merit is that this somber ending seems truthful and ethically satisfying. The last appearance of Saladin, the proudly pragmatic warrior, comes when he enters the mosque that was the Church of the Holy Sepulcher and loses himself in prayer. Sibylla turns aside, and there in the dust, Balian is walking beside her; she takes his hand—she will now become a real wife, if not a queen. And Balian. We last see him back in his French village on another morning in early spring. This is no dream, but there is the little fruit tree, now grown taller, with its buds just beginning to flower. He looks up from the tree, and Sibylla has come out on the balcony in a rich fur-lined cloak; she smiles warmly down at him. Balian looks up at her with a ghost of a smile. He is paler than he was in the desert, and we can see the scar left by his would-be assassins.

Now, as in the parallel scene at the beginning of the film, Balian is beset with difficulties. Can he really be a blacksmith in this ignorant, superstitious little village where his brother's death is hardly forgotten? Equally important, how long will his aristocratic wife be able to stand living in a place like this? After all that has happened, neither of them really belongs here. Will they return to the Holy Land? The last scene shows Balian and Sibylla checking their horses at the crossroads where the film began and then galloping furiously up the road, her furred cloak flying and the gemmed handle of his father's big two-handed sword prominent at his waist. The crusaders had come down this road, but the way to Messina leaves from the other end of the village. So Balian and his wife are riding away from the crusades. Now, or perhaps later, they will go farther north to where the French king has his court, and Sibylla will have her aristocratic relatives, a title, and a meaningful life. Balian has his experience and he knows his worth—he was, after all, the man who defended Jerusalem, and kings value such things—but he is also a man who never surrendered the kingdom of conscience that lies within him, and for this earnest, thoughtful man, that is kingdom enough.

Summarizing the film tells us what happened, but not why or what it meant. For that we must follow the social and political traces that Ridley Scott has abundantly supplied. In a film titled *Kingdom of Heaven*, we might expect to encounter the common medieval yearning toward the great good place where the world's wrongs give way to blessed harmony, and indeed there is much wrong in the world of the film. Balian, for one, seeks something better. But he will not find it in the church, in converse with God, or in holy war. The historians who reviewed the early script complained of the lack of crucifixes in a movie about the crusades. They felt that the church, a central medieval institution, was not well represented in the film either by its ministers, its faithful, or even its physical structures.[6] With the advantage of actually seeing the movie in its fully developed three-hour director's cut, it seems more accurate to say that the church is a powerful presence throughout most of the film, yet as the historians no doubt perceived, its influence is not altogether positive. Early on we are aware of what religion ought to provide for those like Balian who are in desperate need of it, but always he is thrown back on his own resources; he remains to the end a man with questions.

The virtue of Scott's insistence on showing the church as a mundane corporate body is that the reality of Christian politics emerges clearly for us and in detail. Balian's brother, for instance, is the village priest. Balian was the eldest son, their father died recently, and this younger brother wants the land he has inherited. When Balian's wife commits suicide in despair over their stillborn child, the brother uses his influence to have Balian imprisoned, in preparation for an inquisitorial "examination" in search of heretical ideas that surely led to the death of his spouse. The greed of this priest-brother is overt, almost palpable, thanks to some brilliant acting by Michael Sheen: he accepts bribes with a fierce, visceral joy, and his exit from any scene is a kind of demonic scuttling, head down, hands clutching the booty, the black priest's habit fluttering about him. The bishop, however, wants Balian out of jail: the new church can't be built without the iron braces only a blacksmith can make. So he sends the priest (with another bribe) to release Balian, saying he hopes the woman's body was not mutilated? We know, of course, that her headless corpse was buried at the crossroads. Probably the bishop knows it too. Such beheadings are apparently not an unknown practice here, but mentioning to the priest his disapproval of such things ("I ask myself, would Christ have done this?") might, along with the bribe, get Balian back to his forge a little bit sooner.

Low-level corruption seems atmospheric, almost a normal condition in the village. At day's end, out at the crossroads, Balian is on his knees, digging his fingers into the snow where, he imagines, his wife is buried, when the priest appears to torment him ("You think that you are without sin? *That* is a sin!"). Two or three burdened figures move by them in the gathering darkness—"Go on," says the priest, waving them by. Who are they? What is this covert operation—smuggling, perhaps? But if Balian is not himself corrupt, he is no holy innocent. As we learn the next day, he has been to war as a cavalryman and as an enginer, a builder of fortifications and siege engines. Moreover, when Godfrey approaches him at the forge, asking forgiveness for seducing his mother the blacksmith's wife, all those years ago, an innocent might have recoiled. Yet offered passage to the Holy Land and a new identity as the son of a baron, Balian only moves away ("Whoever you are, my lord, my place is here").

As we can see, Balian the soldier-blacksmith is a proud, self-reliant young man. He possesses emersonian qualities that appeal to many audiences here and abroad, but his isolation does not last long. In a remarkable night scene at the smithy, Balian receives another psychic wound, a mortal sin that will exile him from the village and send him down the road of penitence to the Holy Land. In the hot glow of the forge he is hammering out the braces for the church, with a sword or two heating on the coals, when the priest appears, pressing him once more to leave the village and his land: the crusade is a chance to leave "all this"; the villagers will never trust him; in Jerusalem he can find absolution for his sins—and for those of his wife. Cloaked in black, his eyes gleaming in the light of the forge, the priest hovers, Judas-like, probing for a weakness: "She is in hell, your wife, though what she does there without a head...." At that moment Balian sees the gold cross at the priest's throat—it is his own handiwork, it came from his wife's body—and in one motion he drives a white-hot sword through his brother, hurling him into the fire and ripping away the cross as he erupts from the forge and dies on the floor in a mass of flames.

When we see Balian galloping down the road his father took toward the sea, his hand bandaged, burned by the fiery cross, the arc of his narrative has defined itself. Leaving his winter village and moral winter, he seeks warmth and forgiveness in the Holy Land; fleeing mortal sin and hellfire, he hopes to find grace and the freshness of a new life. It would weaken this story to make it an allegory of what some in 2004 were calling America's disastrous policy in the Middle East, and Scott has avoided doing so. Yet Balian's deep sense of guilt, and his need somehow to recover himself in Jerusalem, must have resonated with the feelings of many here and abroad that crushing Baghdad was not a good thing, that rebuilding Iraq was necessary, both for military reasons and for the sake of our international standing. The great surge of interest and popular support that rose in response to Greg Mortenson's building schools in Pakistan and Afghanistan during the past decade and a half may have been another indication of an indistinct but powerful desire for renewal, for a fresh and hopeful new beginning.[7]

As the horizons of the film continue to broaden, the thrust of the church behind the crusade reveals itself ever more clearly. Pausing on the way to Messina, Balian and his now-dying father encounter a young monk with a crazed, beatific expression addressing the endless files of people marching to the sea: "The Pope has said, 'To kill an infidel is not a sin. It is the gateway to heaven.'" The film's credits list him as "Angelic Priest," but his words bear historical truth: he is merely rephrasing the climax of Pope Urban II's famous call for the first crusade at Clermont one hundred years before, a campaign that ended in the bloody conquest of Jerusalem in 1099 and the slaughter of virtually all the Muslims in the city: "Undertake this journey eagerly for the remission of your sins, with the assurance of the reward of imperishable glory in the kingdom of heaven."[8] Later, when Balian first enters Jerusalem he climbs to the top of the mount of Calvary with his wife's cross (in the movie, if not in the actual Jerusalem, it is a high hill signifying the completion of Balian's pilgrimage), but on his way up another pilgrim greets him with "Salaam Aleichoum," and when he carries out his all-night vigil, he feels that God does not speak to him. This night he spends on Calvary is a solemn interval, and Balian's desire to believe is obviously sincere, but in the film the scene works to desacralize the holy ground, letting us know that whatever our religious sentiments about Jerusalem might be, this story proceeds to different ends.

When Balian is settled in the city he is called to visit the Marshal of Jerusalem. On his way there, he has to pause more than once as men are hanged from the battlements that stand over the interior courtyard of the castle. These are Knights Templars, he is told, and they killed Muslims. We find later that Reynald of Châtillon led the raid on a caravan; these are some of his men. The Marshal has hanged them to uphold the law, but, just as important, also to keep the fragile peace with Saladin. Like all Templars, the hanged men wear surcoats marked front and back with large red crosses. They are, in effect, the warriors of Christ, and at that time in history they were one of the best equipped and strongest Christian fighting forces in the near East. But the Templars are not holy warriors in this film. As they prepare to raid a Muslim caravan, they cry "God wills it, God wills it." Again we recall the words of Urban II to the Franks in 1095: "When an armed attack is made upon the enemy, let this one cry be raised by all the soldiers of God: 'It is the will of God! It is the will of God!'"[9] *Deus vult!* In many ways, *Kingdom of Heaven* turns a secular eye upon the church and the unpleasant evidence of its politics and its fanaticism.[10] Yet if the movie's slant verges on irreligious, it is not immoral. Faith, goodness, right action—these too are privileged in the film, and the man who displays them most prominently is actually a Christian.

The crusader who rides with Godfrey of Ibelin, fighting at his side, advising him and practicing medicine at need, is a Knight Hospitaler, a member of a religious/military order founded in the Kingdom of Jerusalem in 1113.

following the First Crusade.[11] At first the order had cared for pilgrims at their infirmary in Jerusalem near the Church of the Holy Sepulchre, but soon they began providing pilgrims with armed escorts, and, like the Templars (founded in 1119), they became a powerful, landed Christian presence holding seven fortified castles and many other estates in the kingdom. By the mid–twelfth century, the order had split into members who fought and others who worked with the sick. So the Hospitaler who accompanies Godfrey is an amalgam of characteristics associated with his order, but the anachronism plays well in the film.

This man, whose name we never hear, seems to have been assigned as an advisor and armed guard, first to Godfrey, who as a baron of the kingdom of Jerusalem deserves such protection, and then to his son. When they are ambushed by Godfrey's nephew (who would like to be a landed baron), the Hospitaler fights expertly on horseback; and when Godfrey takes an arrow in the ribs, he extracts the arrow and matter-of-factly delivers a prognosis ("If the rib is broken, the marrow will enter the blood and you'll contract a fever and die. Or a cyst will form and you'll live. You're in the hands of God"). He continues to nurse Godfrey until he dies, and at that moment gives him last rights. This warrior-healer-confidant is played by David Thewlis, a gifted, sensitive actor. The character that emerges is an alert but quiet man who seems to understand the implications of every situation and chooses his words carefully. He is not directly involved when Godfrey or Balian deals with another baron or the king, but we come to realize that the intensity of these scenes and our sense of the pressure and significance of events derives partly from the way Thewlis attends to the primary characters: he listens and misses nothing, his face registers his understanding, and we too, as if by sympathetic magic, find ourselves acutely aware of the subtext—what it means that such a thing has been said.

In this way Thewlis's character becomes a normative presence, a center of moral awareness that offers a steady point of view on the violent and often chaotic world of the film. Paradoxically, this model crusader often seems to be smiling as he delivers his advice—as though in the much larger context of eternal things these matters of life and death are simple enough, and can be borne. When Balian says he has lost his religion, the Hospitaler replies, "I put no stock in religion. I have seen too much religion in the eyes of too many murderers." "By what you decide to do every day," he tells Balian, "you will become a good man. Or not." In the commentary that accompanies the film Scott says he intended Thewlis's character as a kind of angel figure, a divine counterpart in human form. Perhaps, but in the film the Hospitaler comes across more as an Everyman—not any man, of course, but the very man one would hope a crusader could be: wise, gentle, disciplined, strong, and absolutely dedicated to his faith—not in religion, but in something greater than he is, a God great enough for the faith of all men, whether Christian or Muslim.

But when the army of Jerusalem goes to war with Saladin, the Hospitaler's order leaves with the army. Is this a march to certain death, as Balian tells him? "All death is certain," says the Hospitaler. He honors his vow of obedience, riding away to join the dusty column of doomed men. Days later, when Balian sadly inspects the battlefield (the Horns of Hattin), he finds the man's head in a pile, along with many others. For better or worse, Balian is now the sole defender of the city (Tiberias, the Marshal, decides there is nothing left to fight for and leaves for Cyprus, where in later centuries the Hospitalers had their base). This places him in the company of Heraclius, the Christian Patriarch of Jerusalem, who is as weak and hollow as the Hospitaler was steadfast. The slant of the film is such that we might anticipate corruption in this high priest, but in this case the film seems to reflect history; at least it reflects the Chronicle of William of Tyre, who served the king in Jerusalem and experienced the Patriarch at close quarters.[12] Dressed in his formal white raiments, Heraclius appears beside Balian at just those moments when courage and leadership are needed. His advice is rather that he and Balian should find good horses and flee by one of the city's postern gates. Or that Balian should tell Saladin they will all convert to Islam—they can always recant later. The Patriarch is played by Jon Finch, a strong veteran actor who registers every nuance of high-echelon cowardice and self-seeking.[13] After the siege, as William of Tyre recalls, the historical Patriarch took advantage of Saladin's lenience by smuggling a fortune out of the city on a train of pack mules. In any event, Balian's noble qualities prove equal to those of his father and the Hospitaler, and the church recedes into history. We see it receding as Saladin's clerics repossess the Church of the Holy Sepulchre, reconsecrating it by scattering rose petals. The long Frankish banners fall one by one to the floor, and what had been for a hundred years a church is now a mosque.

The culture of the near East appears early in *Kingdom of Heaven* and remains to the end, not because the film is a travelogue or a venture into the mind of Islam, but because it is centrally the story of Balian's experience of the East. He goes there—driven across the perilous sea—because he must; in that, he is like many of the Franks and other Europeans who are impelled to follow the crusades by forces they probably do not understand. To begin with, in the late twelfth century France has too many restless knights, men who live to fight and have the money and men to do so. How much better if they went away to fight—to Spain, perhaps, where they can add their force to the *Reconquista*, or to the south of France where they can help root out the Cathars, or even farther away (therefore better) to the Holy Land, now a broad Christian beachhead in the heart of Islam. Moreover, the church of Rome has not forgotten the days when the Holy Roman Empire was a real power, holding out the promise of further growth toward the East; after one hundred years in possession of Jerusalem, the church clings tightly to what it considers a piece of Europe. And despite the social and economic progress in France during that century, there are many who do not share it—the poor, the disinherited, the malcontent, those crazed by intense faith—all of them craving an overwhelming purpose, a holy war that will somehow redeem their lives. The brief narrative that comes onscreen at the beginning of the film—"Europe suffers in repression and poverty"—gives some sense of this broad impulse.

What it does not mention is our own implicit hunger for experiencing the East—its exotic styles and customs, its elusive, arcane wisdom, its sensualities of silk, ivory, spices and perfumes, the strange intricacies of its religion and politics, the forbidden beauty of its women, the age-old horrors of its poverty and disease. This hunger, along with the subtle assumption of western superiority that often comes with it, has been called Orientalism. It is the fascination the Greeks and Romans had for Egypt, and an attitude we continue to share with the European Middle Ages. It is a powerful mind-set, for, in effect, we project our own fears, desires and fantasies onto the canvas of the East where they call to us in ways that seem compelling and significant.[14] Let us admit it: *Kingdom of Heaven* is unashamedly a celebration of Orientalism. Balian goes to Jerusalem because he believes he will find *himself* there. Godfrey of Ibelin, the war-weary crusader, Baldwin the leprous king in his inscrutable, god-like mask[15]—these are excellent men who have projected their highest ideals onto the kingdom of Jerusalem and died in its defense. If we, along with Balian, are thrilled by such a projection, we know at least that in this surrogate, filmic way, our ideals are still alive.

The privileging of eastern culture begins as soon as the crusaders reach Balian's village. As Godfrey and the Hospitaler are negotiating with him about supplies and the shoeing of their horses, another man from their small band entertains a gang of delighted children. He is tall and strong, very dark, and has a friendly look. "Did you kill anybody?" they want to know, but he just laughs and plays with them. At their camp in the forest, he is the one who tells Godfrey's young squire (in Arabic) not to urinate upstream, fouling their watering place. And in the ambush, he fights hard, taking several painful wounds before we see him laid out, beautiful in death, alongside his German comrade-in-arms.

Arriving at Messina, Balian gazes at the port where the Italians carry on a brisk trade, shipping supplies to Acre, Tripoli, Tyre, and Ascalon, all the coastal cities held by Christians in the eastern Mediterranean. "So the Italians grow rich, as God intended,"[16] says his companion dryly (he too will die, drowned in the shipwreck). Balian notices some men kneeling on the rocky beach. "Muslims," the companion tells him—"Saracens. They are praying." And he translates the prayer for Balian, having recited it in Arabic, though he is blond and blue-eyed. "It sounds like our prayers," Balian says, and receives a measured look. He is learning about the East, but there is much more still to be learned.

Balian's initiation, where he finally steps through the eastern looking glass, is the ritual scene of his father's death. He is summoned, dressed in a simple linen gown and brought to Godrey's bed in an area closed off by muslin hangings and lit by many candles. It is a sacred place of death prepared by the Hospitaler and guarded by members of his order. "Kneel—on your knees!" he is told, and Godfrey somehow stands long enough to make his son a knight and swear him to the service of the king before he faints into death and receives last rites. The rite is Christian, of course, but the setting, the costumes, the lighting, the score (with motifs drawn from the music of the East)—all this implies that Balian has entered the chivalry of the eastern Mediterranean, and is now a culture straddler bound to serve a king who rules over Christian, Muslim and Jew, the people of Jerusalem he has now sworn to protect.

His father dead, Balian sails for the Holy Land, is shipwrecked in a gale and wakes in a fragment of their ship, surrounded by drowned men. He is alone on this desert shore, and the score is unmistakably eastern, announcing the culture of the East. A fine black stallion has also survived the wreck, and after trekking through the sandy waste for part of a day, he captures the horse at a waterhole. Two Arabs are watching. One of them wants the horse and tries to skewer him with a lance before Balian's sword rips out his throat; the other Arab, thrown from his terrified horse, lies on the sand waiting for death. We see Balian struggle with himself, but, revealingly, he thrusts his sword into the sand, telling the astonished Arab to take him to Jerusalem. The medium-range shot that follows is one of the most stirring in the film, as, paced by zither music (another road song), the ragged Christian and his Arab companion in swirling robes canter through the haunting beauty of the desert land and sky, headed for the holy city. Balian is in country, and we sense his bonding with it. The Arab he spared will turn out to be the refined, aristocratic Imād ad–Dīn, Saladin's commander of cavalry and ultimately one of his biographers.[17] In Jerusalem, Balian releases this Arab and gives him the black horse he won with his sword. And so Imād becomes his friend, later saving his life in turn and becoming the symbol of how, in fairness and courtesy, good men can honor each other across the culture wars.

Jerusalem itself is waiting for war. The Templars, led by men like Sibylla's despicable husband Guy de Lusignan and the casually murderous Reynald de

Châtillon, are raiding Arab caravans, provoking Saladin to war; and Saladin himself would like nothing better than to sack Jerusalem and drive its Franks back to Europe.[18] After one raid too many, his army arrives at Reynald's fortress of Kerak on the caravan route from Syria to Egypt. Balian is living at Ibelin by this time, guarding Jerusalem's pilgrim road to the sea, but is called east and south to the defense of Kerak. He and perhaps fifty riders arrive in time to attack Saladin's enormous force of advance cavalry before it can ride down the villagers fleeing to the fortress. "We cannot attack that and live," says one of his men; and, in fact, their charge is overwhelmed in a short, brutal combat. The episode establishes Balian as one who cares more for honor and for the safety of the defenseless than he does for his life; and if Reynald is unmoved, Sibylla, watching from the battlements, is not. When Balian is carried from the field, bloody and unconscious, Imād the commander of cavalry honors his courage by sparing his life.

It is logical that Balian's chivalric excellence is first noted by the Muslims, because the measure of ethical authority in this film is ultimately the culture of the East. Godfrey of Ibelin and Baldwin IV are fine men, but they die, and the civil harmony they sought fades like a dream. Tiberius is tough and fair, but his time is past; the new arrivals in the Holy Land, aided by the Templars,

Velibor Topić as Amalric, and Orlando Bloom as Balian, in Ridley Scott's *Kingdom of Heaven* (2005).

will have their war. And the Hospitaler, the moral icon of the film, remains until his death a telling observer of events he cannot alter. That leaves Balian to defend Jerusalem against the moral fury of the Arabs, who have been badly wronged, first by the bloody conquest of Jerusalem and now by skirmishes with the war-like Franks.[19] That defense is heroic from anyone's point of view, but we value it not in relation to the deeds of his father or other Christian warriors, but by comparison to the sober determination of Saladin, with the weight of the aroused Islamic world behind him.

We have our first look at Saladin after Baldwin's Christian army emerges from the heat haze on the plains before Kerak. Saladin wheels his horse, commanding his staff to wait, then rides out to meet Baldwin, who is by this time so weakened by his disease he can scarcely ride. Then comes a long shot of the two men sitting their horses head to head, alone on the plain, the waste of sand and rock stretching out beyond them, massed armies lying to either side with their forest of long lances, banners snapping in the endless desert wind. It is a breathtaking moment, partly because of the solemn beauty and palpable threat of this perfectly composed scene, but also because by this time we know the character of both men, their utter dedication to avoiding casualties if they can, and—the battle being crucial for both of them—fighting to the last man if they must.

The next shot gives us Saladin from close up, and we are not disappointed. Played by the acclaimed Syrian stage and film actor Ghassan Massoud, Saladin has the thin, almost starved features and the piercing gaze we would expect of a general who has campaigned for years in the desert. His presence is compelling because of his intensity, and because he offers a reasoned choice: "I pray that you will retire from this field unharmed and leave this business to me." Baldwin is close to fainting, and his voice, issuing from the tooled steel mask, is lighter, but the words of a dying man have the weight of certainty: "And I pray that you will retire with your army unharmed to Damascus, or we will all die here. I will punish the men who did this thing. I swear it." And then, "Do we have terms?" Saladin glances aside at the Christian army, then the terrible eyes return to Baldwin like gunsights: "We have terms."

With that, Baldwin releases an exhausted sigh and slumps a little—he will die, but he has saved Kerak as well as his own city. The shot–reverse shot returns us to Saladin's gaze, which softens, gaining depth and a different kind of power as he tells Baldwin, "I—will send you my physicians."[20] Then they return to their armies, which immediately begin to withdraw. In its cryptic way, this confrontation carries the whole message of *Kingdom of Heaven*. Balian's renowned defense of Jerusalem, which takes up a good part of the second half of the film, will only be a restatement—or, more precisely, an acting out of the selfless dedication and humanity shown by these hard but thoughtful men.

Saladin does not reappear until the opening of the second half, when he is visited by a Muslim cleric, or mullah, who wants to know why he withdrew his forces at Kerak. After all, God is great, Islam must conquer. Saladin acerbically replies that the success of armies depends of course on God's will—but also upon the preparation of the army, the absence of an enemy to the rear of a siege, and the availability of water. "Thank you for your visit," he says, then repeats it, dismissing the bearded young nobleman in his black clerical robes. Saladin, like Baldwin, finds himself between the necessity to defend his people and the pressure of church politics (which are also regional politics) for ever more victories in battle. Again like Baldwin, he was born a warrior, but for both of these men, war is no longer the reason for life but a means only, and sometimes only a distraction. Consequently, as we witness the Frankish run-up to war, enabled by Sibylla's pride and Guy de Lusignan's lust for power, we are increasingly conscious of war's pointlessness, its endless waste of life; and that is how we are prepared for the siege of Jerusalem, where so many lives are lost on both sides to win a holy city which would have been better off had it never been fought for.

The scope of the siege justifies calling *Kingdom of Heaven* an epic, for it is vast, the kind of event which, in our times, can only be filmed with considerable aid from computer graphics. The danger of this largely unscripted series of violent scenes is its tendency to distort the film, flattening it into an action adventure. That does not happen in Scott's director's cut, partly because of the scenes where Sibylla grieves over her son and brother, agonized with guilt over losing the army and thus the city. But the siege, with its bitter human cost, is also meaningful as a contest between the wills of two men who must win a battle they did not want. For Saladin, winning Jerusalem will satisfy Muslims all over the Islamic world, but it will not help him defeat the Franks, whose significant holdings are ports like Acre and Tyre, safe havens for ships arriving from Europe with more supplies, weapons and knights. Nor has Balian anything to gain from its defense. His tenure as lord of Ibelin is hopeless, now that Saladin has gone to war, and Jerusalem itself is no kingdom without an army. All he can hope to accomplish by his defense of the city is to save the lives of the people in it, many of whom would be massacred in the blind fury of a successful siege—as in the Christian conquest of the city one hundred years past. That is what he swore to his dying father that he would do: "Defend the king. If the king is dead, defend the people."

In itself, the siege is fascinating. The section of the wall of Jerusalem where the action occurs is apparently the largest movie set in history (shot from the other side, it was the castle of Kerak), and the massive catapult, or trebuchet, needed for close-up shots of Saladin's artillery was built from Roman plans and could hurl stones hundreds of yards. The fighting on this enormous set goes on for many minutes, of course, with its hail of arrows, boiling and burning oil, siege towers, men falling from them in flames, and finally the siege towers toppling, slowly, catastrophically onto the men swarming beneath them. Most memorable, and relatively new in medieval film, is the night bombardment that begins the siege. Balian and his men peer into the darkness: "When will it begin?" "Soon"—and at that moment a line of small fires appears across the enemy front. The fires begin to rise and grow—they are in-coming catapult stones on a high, flat trajectory, blazing with naphtha; when they crash into the city, walls collapse, buildings fall and fire spreads everywhere. Ridley Scott films so close to these flaming bombs that we can see debris speeding by the camera. Inside the cathedral, Sibylla is praying for her city, perhaps for her soul, and through the clerestory windows we can see the fiery arc of the stones as they pound the city.[21]

Still, it is the leaders who give this battle its meaning. Here is Balian with his range-finder, engineering the defenses; and here he is with the rest of the wounded, as Sibylla and other women change the bloody bandages by lamplight and bind new ones for the next day's assault; and here again, as he rallies his men and then, in one of the film's finer (and more democratic) moments, knights every one of them. Saladin watches, first the bombardment, then the assault on the walls, as his men fall to Balian's carefully prepared catapult shots, arrows, boiling oil, and spring-loaded guns that harpoon the siege towers and pull every one of them down. He silently absorbs the mounting damage, his hard face expressionless under the battle helmet. And when he nods his head slightly, we feel the loss. That night the Christians are burning their dead (the Patriarch's objections are ignored), and Saladin is praying over the scores of shrouded bodies the Muslims are about to bury. He sadly, silently touches his eyes, his mouth—a farewell to so many.[22]

After the wall shatters and the attackers and defenders fight to a standstill in the rubble, we see Balian rising painfully from among the corpses where he fainted from exhaustion. He walks out to confront Saladin's proposal: "Will you yield the city?" By this time we have seen enough of the siege from both Christian and Muslim points of view that not yielding would be horrible for both sides. As Balian says, if we have to fight, we will die, but your army will be destroyed and you will never raise another one—"You offer terms. I ask none." At this point, Saladin enters the role he played in history, offering Balian passage to the sea, along with every other man, woman and child in the city.[23] Given what both the army and the city have suffered, it is a wise solution. What has Saladin to gain from slaughtering the Christians, as Christians slew Muslims a century ago? And why risk even more casualties when there are so many other cities he needs to take?

The decision is noble and its outcome weighty because it will not be praised by the Muslim clerics who are with the army, urging on the troops with religious slogans, or, just as pressingly, by the Islamic states from Syria to Egypt whose allegiance to Saladin depends on continued successes in war. Saladin, however, is a Kurd from the mountains of what is now northern Iraq, set aside from Arab politics by his language and his pious, unbending character. He does not break promises. "When the Christians took Jerusalem they spared no one," Balian says. "I am Saladin. *Saladin*," is the reply. Here, as in the treaty with Baldwin, peace is made with many lives at stake. The intolerable pressure of religious and political necessity that lies behind both of them is disregarded for the moment—perhaps, very briefly, this *is* a kingdom of conscience—while they do something that is humane and if not exactly friendly, then mutually respectful. "Salaam Aleichoum," Saladin says. "And peace be with you," says Balian.

The road to the sea, of course, is no path to redemption, any more than Jerusalem could be Balian's or even Sibylla's permanent home. For both of them the siege is a proof of character, but the promise of life lies—in France? We know only that Balian was briefly happy at one point in the film, and that takes us back to his first arrival at Ibelin.

In many ways, the emotional center of *Kingdom of Heaven* is the sequence of scenes beginning with the long shot of Balian's column of retainers riding toward us in the desert, pennants flying, coming into his hereditary lands in early evening. Here he sees that although his father was an important man, as one of the men says, his lands were not. Ibelin is small, hot, dusty—1000 acres, one hundred families, 50 oxen. "It will suit me," he replies, and slowly we see that it does. Proceeded by his houseman, he enters the main room of his house, long unoccupied: a chicken is standing on the central table. It is humorous and touching; we have not seen chickens since Balian left his village home in France. He looks up at the walls—a series of figures are painted there, skeletons hand in hand, with an inscription: "Quod sumus, hoc eritis." What we are, this you will be: a memento mori and another echo of home, where he had carved on the beams of his smithy "What man is a man who does not make the world better." It seems that both father and son were given to long thoughts, and were aware of their place in things. Balian goes out onto the veranda and looks off across his lands. He seems to like what he sees.

The next day, perhaps, he has everyone—his guard, the villagers, their children—digging for water at various spots in this hot and dusty place. As Professor Madden noted in his review, irrigation is no novelty in the fertile crescent[24]; but however it is that Ibelin is dry, the film requires water at this point, because Balian himself badly needs re-greening. The king has returned, as it were, and the barren fields must bloom. So, indeed, there is wet clay in one of their holes—"Go find the master!"—and when Balian arrives there is already water standing around their ankles. "Right, stone the walls," he says, the soldier-engineer well satisfied. Here, with the coming of the water, we first hear the Ibelin theme, a tender, lyrical melody that builds as we watch the troughs built and trenches dug until they open the gate and the flood sluices down toward the fields and gardens. Little boys make a boat from a chip and float it down the stream.

These motifs of homecoming are reinforced by Sibylla as she arrives with her women about her. She is on the way to Canaan (Ibelin is not on the road to Canaan) and expects his hospitality. "It is given," Balian says quietly, but that is a rather grand thing to say, and we see he is proud to be the master of Ibelin. She takes up residence, and her little flock of attendants carefully set out the beautiful, delicate things that make up a noblewoman's household. He goes out to supervise the irrigation; her eyes follow him. He comes back with his men in the evening, weary but happy and spattered with mud; she has set out a bowl of water with rose petals, and when he enters, begins to wash his face. Time goes by. We see Balian walking through his lands, where plots of rice and other green, growing things spread out in an orderly way, divided by channels of water glinting in the sun. A new theme enters the soundtrack, a busy little tune hurrying to keep pace with the water, urging the growth of all good things. He stops by one of the irrigation sluices, which widens, becoming a small brook. In the mud he finds the little boat we saw earlier, sets it right and sends it down the current. Watching it go, we think of Balian's sea voyage to the Holy Land, and are aware once more that he has passed through peril and come home to cultivate his garden.

This in-between time, as the gardens of Ibelin begin to flourish and Balian and Sibylla are coming nearer to being lovers, is the film's earthly image of the Kingdom of Heaven. Paradise is not too strong a word for what it represents to a young man who has lost wife, home, country, and innocence, but somehow won it all back again in a charmed haven—in fact, an oasis—in the Levant. A moist, fertile new land has appeared amidst the old land where Romans, Greeks, Phoenicians, Hebrews, and Muslims lived and died for two millennia, and a new man has shed his armor and the bitterness of exile to dwell in it. Watching this film, we recognize the Edenic myth of our own new world, and for a moment, Balian the builder is as much the American Adam as any of us. But only for a moment. For we reflect that Balian and Sibylla are French expatriates in the Holy Land, and their time in Eden will be short. And, sadly, however much we might also wish that the American presence in the middle East will bring the flowering of peaceful communities and stable alliances instead of blood, broken cities and broken lives, that is not the reality of our time or of the film.

Sibylla lies in bed, waking up beside Balian, and, educated princess that she is, she can read the skeleton frieze: *Quod sumus, hoc eritis*. Balian wakes, and while they delay rising she shows him her rings, one from her brother, one to remind her of death, one she put on when she met him, and so on—endearments, but really they are her ties with family, royalty and privilege. She feeds him a bit of rich red fruit—a pomegranate seed to make him her prisoner, as in the ancient myth—but clearly they are both hostages to their situation, and the next scene brings news of Saladin's advance on Kerak. "What will happen to us?" she asks him. "The world will decide," he replies, "it always decides." Indeed they are soon swept away by world-historical forces that care nothing for love. The crusaders will keep sailing to the Holy Land for the next hundred years, and the Muslims will counter them until Baybars' invincible Mamluk army rises in the East and puts a lasting end to the kingdom of Jerusalem.[25] But because both Balian and Sibylla choose not to cling to eastern wealth and position, they win a measure of autonomy, and in that freedom, in their life together, they will have as much of the kingdom of heaven as anyone can.

Epilogue

So ... the medieval filmscape. The films we have looked at together embody, in their various ways, what's medieval about it; and along the way I have tried to suggest why we might care—why we enter the world of a medieval film as if returning to a part of ourselves that we embrace with a kind of grim joy. But such things are most keenly and precisely understood through the movies themselves (and, hopefully, through our discussion of them) and need no repetition. Now let us briefly sight the axis of medievalism from the other direction, this time from the past, looking at the way modern hopes and worries pull at the medieval narrative, reshaping its dynamic while being themselves transformed and reshaped. Too long a look would be tedious—worse, it would reduce the medieval to a modern flavor or decorative motif. But for a moment we will see ourselves this way, for it may lend insight into the medieval movies we have seen, as well as those to come.

Easter has recently come and gone at this writing, and the new Argentinian Jesuit pope, Francis I, has endeared himself to some and appalled others by washing the feet not of priests but of criminals in the Roman prisons, some of them women or Muslims. Was this a strict interpretation of an ancient tradition? A personal sense of what his new role requires? I don't know. But, necessarily, this ritual act sheds a crosslight on what has become the secular faith of the western world—namely, its fearful, conflicted worship of consumer capitalism. Like St. Francis, the Pope has grasped the essential humanity of the outcast, and for a tiny moment the world of things trembles and becomes transparent as a dream. But only for a moment. Medieval moviegoers enjoy, perhaps endure, the dominance of an intensely material culture,[1] and its pressure is virtually never absent. For such people, the medieval film world may offer a certain lightness of being—a time when hunger is real, money is coin, and the future, lacking investment or actuarial extension, is now.

We suffer each our own shadow. Yet probably any viewer will discover that the bottom-line question ("What does it cost?") feels a little different in the medieval film world. In our world as well, it can cost sweat, blood, years, a broken heart. But in a medieval movie one is less buffered by the constraints and defenses of a credit economy. One is up against it in a physical and even a spiritual sense. Greed and great wealth do exist in medieval films, naturally, and men will do practically anything for money ... and yet it is a different wealth, a more naked greed and want. Rich men are pompous, cruel, full of pride and sometimes generosity, a grandness of spirit; the poor want their blood. The immediacy charms us. And when in reaction to such avarice the medieval story enters the spiritual life, there too we find the tangibly real, the tempted priest, the martyr in her chains, the lawyer straining to live his moral philosophy. It doesn't matter, your attitude toward material life: since you are engaged in the struggle, you will be drawn to such matters in medieval film—indeed, you will find yourself there, strangely mirrored.

What else does medieval film see in us? Our very lives, I think, our vow to succeed at work and play. We—and Europe, and many others—see ourselves as democratic, every man a citizen, and every citizen in a small way a governor. But is democracy a person's right to achieve whatever possible, or is it a person's right to equality in regard to certain basic needs? One could argue that freedom presupposes equality, or that equality presupposes freedom. In practice, we argue both at the same time. As a consequence, we have two political parties which profess to stand for freedom, tradition (and an earned place in the hierarchy), and equality, fairness and a decent life (no matter one's place in the hierarchy). Fundamental to this eternal debate is the right to (and need for?) private property, of course, but purpose, motivation and worth are also entailed—in other words, the substance of and reason for our lives. Can you imagine viewers of a medieval movie not wanting to see these issues played out on what I earlier called "the violent medieval turf?" Freedom and equality, both are there, as well as the inevitable tension between them. In *Kingdom of Heaven*, for instance, Balian the simple blacksmith is suddenly known as the natural son of a baron: we watch him enter the privileged hierarchy. Later he must defend a defenseless Jerusalem—and so he calls every able-bodied man in the city to kneel and then "Rise a knight!"

Where are our sympathies in this? Surely we find it thrilling when every beggar and tradesman in Jerusalem rises proudly to knighthood: that is the democratic myth. Yet I think we also feel Balian's pride as the gardens of Ibelin, his small barony, begin to green, and he comes closer to being the lover, and finally husband, of an Oriental-French princess. I wouldn't argue that Ridley Scott imposed his western democratic cultural bias on the eastern world of *Kingdom of Heaven*, merely that the tensions between freedom and equality, between those who would have and those who would distribute, are inherent in our western view of things. That tension emerges (even) in the monarchical world of medieval film. It appears in *The Advocate*, where Richard Courtois, the idealistic young lawyer, goes to live in Abbeville, far from litigious Paris. There he encounters the order and rule imposed on the region by the Seigneur d'Auferre, a mild, ironic man with an iron will. D'Auferre is himself a site of contention. A wealthy businessman, he bought his castle and the lordship that went with it. He uses the secret meetings of the local Cathar brotherhood (his family has belonged for generations) to fix local prices, and if Courtois mentions it to anyone else his life is forfeit. Where does aristocracy end and democracy begin? In medieval film, it seems, they are bound eternally to co-exist.

What other demands do we make on the medieval film world? In the Introduction I argued that identity is a point of convergence in medieval film, given its ideals and the temptations that assail them. Identity is beleaguered in any age, and we empathize with Richard Courtois, or William of Baskerville, as they struggle against becoming someone they are not. Our own challenge comes from a different direction. We live in a complex period, bombarded (no?) by advertising, offers, opportunities, and motivations, but threatened as well by what folktale scholars call *lack*—not the plague, or Godfather Death,

Jof's vision in Bergman's *The Seventh Seal* (1957): The knight and others follow Death toward the dark lands.

but the lack of jobs, the dearth of fantasy once called "purpose," the fading of illusion (some call it hopefulness). We fight back. Lacking the stability of lifelong careers, extended families, and gendered responsibilities, we adapt to instability, "cloning" ourselves, multi-tasking, developing skill sets, jumping to successive careers like pony express riders. If the corporate world produced the self-made man, post-industrialism seems to create the "man-made self," a clever, shape-shifting, artistic entity which can "harmonize the bewildering multiplicity of experiences by filtering them through the integral, originary self where order is brought out of chaos through the agency of creativity."[2]

Perhaps every age of transition promotes what Stephen Greenblatt calls "Renaissance Self-Fashioning." I do not lament its appearance. But neither is it strange to find this liquid identity in the mirror of medieval film—in Richard Courtois, who tries to find himself as a lawyer by entering a country practice; or Balian, the blacksmith baron without a barony, married to a princess without a crown (a Frenchwoman who has never seen France). In Arnaud du Tilh, the imposter of *The Return of Martin Guerre*, we see the man-made self in full flower. Martin fled wife, family and village, leaving behind an empty space— the function, manhood, or being we call "identity." With an actor's charm and an ambassador's guile, Arnaud moves into that space, feeling for the role, embodying, then extending it, becoming the strong, loving, ambitious Martin Guerre people had always hoped he could be. We internalize his striving—it is so like our own—and love his success. We remain aware that the new Martin's life is a juggling act (soon the fairy tale hero, the grim, crippled, dispassionate, "true" Martin will return), but we strain against the truth—and that may be our deepest understanding of the film.

Finally, it all comes down to identity—that is what fables are for. We seek ourselves in the mirror of medieval film. And find ourselves there. How could we not?

Filmography

Arthur's Quest, d. Neil Mandt, with Arye Gross, Alexandra Paul, Catherine Oxenberg. Crystal Sky Communications, 1998.

The Advocate, d. Leslie Megahey, with Colin Firth. France/Great Britain: BBC Films, CiBy 2000, British Screen, European Co-production Fund, 1994.

Becket, d. Peter Glenville, with Peter O'Toole, Richard Burton. Great Britain/USA: Keep Films, Paramount, 1964.

A Boy and His Dog, d. L.Q. Jones, with Don Johnson. USA: LQ/JAF, 1975.

Braveheart, d. Mel Gibson, with Mel Gibson. USA: Icon Productions, Ladd, 20th Century–Fox, 1995.

Conan the Barbarian, d. John Milius, with Arnold Schwartzenegger. Universal City Studios, 1982.

A Connecticut Yankee in King Arthur's Court, d. Tay Garnett, with Bing Crosby. USA: Universal, 1949.

Camelot, d. Joshua Logan, with Richard Harris, Vaness Redgrave. USA: Warner Seven Arts, 1967.

El Cid, d. Anthony Mann, with Charleton Heston and Sophia Loren. Allied Artists, 1961.

Excalibur, d. John Boorman, with Nicol Williamson. USA: Orion, 1981

The Fellowship of the Ring, d. Peter Jackson, with Ian McKellan. USA: New Line Cinema, 2003.

First Knight, d. Jerry Zucker, with Richard Gere, Sean Connery. USA: Zuckers Brothers, Columbia, 1995.

Henry V, d. Kenneth Branaugh. BBC, Renaissance Films, 1989.

High Plains Drifter, d. Clint Eastwood. USA: Universal, 1973.

Ivanhoe, d. Richard Thorpe, with Robert Taylor, Elizabeth Taylor. USA: MGM, 1952.

Joan of Arc, d. Christian Duguay, with Leelee Sobieski. Canada: Alliance Atlantis Communications/ Canadian Broadcasting Corp., 1999.

Joan the Woman, d. Cecil B. DeMille, with Geraldine Farrar. USA: Paramount, 1917.

King Arthur, d. Antoine Fucqua, with Clive Owen. USA: Touchstone/Jerry Bruckheimer, 2004.

A Knight's Tale, d. Brian Helgeland, with Heath Ledger. USA: Columbia, Escape Artists/Finestkind Productions, 2001.

Ladyhawke, d. Richard Donner, with Rutger Hauer, Michelle Pfeiffer, Matthew Broderick. 20th Century–Fox, 1985.

Lancelot du Lac, d. Robert Bresson, with Luc Simon. France: Compagnie Française de Distribution Cinematographique, 1974.

The Lion in Winter, d. Anthony Harvey, with Katharine Hepburn, Peter O'Toole. Great Britain: Haworth Productions, 1968.

Lionheart, d. Franklin J. Schaffner. USA: Orion/Warner Studios, 1987.

Mad Max II: The Road Warrior, d. George Miller, with Mel Gibson. USA: Warner Bros., 1982.

The Magnificent Seven, d. John Sturges, with Yul Brynner. USA: Universal/UA, 1960.

Medieval England: The Peasants' Revolt, d. John Irvin, with Anthony Hopkins. USA: Learning Corporation of America, 1975.

Monty Python and the Holy Grail, d. Terry Gilliam, Terry Jones. USA: Columbia/TriStar, 1975.

The Name of the Rose, d. Jean-Jacques Annaud, with Sean Connery. German Federal Republic/Italy/France: Neue Constantin, Cristaldifilm, Ariane Productions, 1986.

Orlando, d. Sally Potter, with Tilda Swinton. Columbia, Tri Star, 1993.

La Passion de Jeanne d'Arc, d. Carl Dreyer, with Renée Falconetti, Antonin Artaud. France: Société Générale des Films, 1928.

The Passion of the Christ, d. Mel Gibson, with James Caviezel. USA: Icon Productions, 2004.

Perceval le gallois, d. Eric Rohmer, with Fabrice Lucchini. Germany: Bayerisches Rundfunk, 1979.

Le Procès de Jeanne d'Arc, d. Robert Bresson, with Florenz Carrez. Agnès Delahaie Productions, 1962.

Quest for Fire, d. Jean-Jacques Annaud, with Ron Perlman. France: ICC, 1981.

The Return of Martin Guerre, d. Daniel Vigne, with Gerard Depardieu, Nathalie Baye. France: Société Française de production cinematograhique, 1982.

Rob Roy, d. Michael Caton-Jones, with Liam Neeson. USA: MGM/UA, 1995.

Robin Hood, Prince of Thieves, d. Kevin Costner. USA: Morgan Creek, 1991.

Saladin, d. Yussef Chahine. Egypt: Lotus Films, 1963.

The Seventh Seal, d. Ingmar Bergman. Sweden: Svensk Film-industri, 1957.

Shane, d. George Stevens, with Alan Ladd. USA: Paramount, 1953.

The Sword of Lancelot, d. Cornel Wilde. Great Britain/USA: Emblem/Universal, 1963.

The Thirteenth Warrior, d. John McTiernan, with Antonio Banderas. USA: Touchstone, 1999.

Timeline, d. Richard Donner. USA: Paramount, 2003.

The Vikings, d. Richard Fleischer, with Kirk Douglas. United Artists, 1958.

Chapter Notes

Introduction

1. Critics writing about film genres tend to distinguish between accidental and essential forms: the film's content (its accidental or surface features), and its inner, or essential, form (typically oppositions, such as man vs. nature) that creates the fundamental dynamic of the film. The essential features are harder to isolate and harder to defend as necessary to the genre. Hence some critics pragmatically define genre in terms of its recurring "generic" images. See Rick Altman for "A Semantic/Syntactic Approach to Film Genre," *Cinema Journal* 23.3 (1984): 6–18, and Edward Buscombe, "The Idea of Genre in American Cinema," *Screen* 11.2 (1970): 33–45, for a discussion of inner and outer form. Robert Stam, "Interrogating Authorship and Genre," *Film Theory: An Introduction* (Oxford: Blackwell, 2000), 123–30, provides a useful overview of genre criticism.

2. Cf. Sarah Berry, "Genre," in *A Companion to Film Theory*, ed. Toby Miller and Robert Stam (Oxford: Blackwell, 1999), 40: "A text that cannot be located within some sort of genre is, for practical purposes, unreadable."

3. Ordinary life in these films can have a simple, idyllic quality, creating a medieval world sheltered from the dissonance of modern (or medieval) complexity. Mikhail Bakhtin's essay on "Forms of Time and Chronotope in the Novel" (*The Dialogic Imagination: Four Essays*, trans. Caryl Emerson and Michael Holquist [Austin: University of Texas Press, 1981]), which discusses late-classical Greek romance, is useful for thinking about medieval film, many of whose generic features derive from the romance tradition:

[D]istinctive for the idyll is the fact that it is severely limited to only a few of life's basic realities. Love, birth, death, marriage, labor, food and drink, stages of growth—these are the basic realities of idyllic life. They are brought into close proximity in the crowded little world of the idyll (225).

4. Geoffrey Chaucer, *The Canterbury Tales*, ed. Larry D. Benson (Boston: Houghton-Mifflin, 2000).

5. Even the glossier medieval films like *Camelot* or *Ladyhawk* usually include a form of primitivism—a violent near-death, a snarling (enchanted) black wolf—that conveys unmediated risk.

6. Elaine Scarry, *The Body in Pain: The Making and Unmaking of the World* (New York: Oxford, 1985): "The physical pain is so incontestably real that it seems to confer its quality of 'incontestable reality' on that power that has brought it into being. It is, of course, precisely because the reality of that power is so highly contestable, the regime so unstable, that torture is being used" [27].

7. *Oedipus at Colonus* takes place many years after *Oedipus Rex*, so Oedipus has had time to meditate on his unthinkable past. He is still the fierce and tragic man he was in *Oedipus Rex*, but he is no longer ashamed of what he is, and he makes the most of his hard fate.

8. Mark Twain, *Letters from the Earth*, ed. Bernard DeVoto (New York: Harper and Row, 1962).

9. Cf. Bakhtin's discussion of the "static" world of Greek romance: "Greek adventure-time ... leaves no traces .... No changes of any consequence occur, internal or external, as a

result of the events recounted in the novel.... And yet people and things have gone *through* something, something that did not, indeed, change them but that did affirm what they, and precisely they, were as individuals, something that did verify and establish their identity, their durability and continuity" [106].

10. John Aberth, *A Knight at the Movies: Medieval History on Film* (New York: Routledge, 2003). Aberth believes the *Monty Python and the Holy Grail* parody of film technique, Arthurian legend, and historians who study it provides a revealing view of medieval film as a representation of history.

11. Bakhtin identifies the "chronotope [minor genre] of the road" as a distinctive feature of narrative about metamorphosis and identity: "[*The Golden Ass*] fuses the course of an individual's life ... with his actual spatial course or road—that is, with his wanderings. Thus is realized the metaphor 'the path of life.' ... An intersection always signifies some turning point in the life of the folklore character" [120].

12. Cf. Bakhtin's analysis of the "spatial world" of the idyll: "The immanent unity of folkloric time ... finds expression predominantly in ... an organic fastening-down, a grafting of life and its events to a place, to a familiar territory with all its nooks and crannies, its familiar mountains, valleys, fields, rivers and forests, and one's own home.... This little world is limited and sufficient unto itself, not linked in any intrinsic way with other places, with the rest of the world" [225].

13. Michael Crichton, *Timeline* (New York: Alfred A. Knopf, 1999).

14. This section benefits from Jane Tompkins' remarkable *West of Everything: The Inner Life of Westerns* (New York: Oxford, 1992).

15. *Poem of the Cid*, trans. W.S. Merwin (New York: Meridian, 1975), laisse 86:

> He who was born in good hour did not delay:
> he put on his silk tunic, his long beard hung down;
> they saddled for him Babieca and fastened the caparisons.
> My Cid rode out upon him bearing wooden arms.
> On the horse they called Babieca he rode, rode at a gallop; it was a wonder to watch.

In the final scene of *El Cid*, Babieca charges out of the gates of Valencia bearing his dead master, who sits straight in the saddle, his right arm holding out the banner of Castile. This scene does not appear in the *Poem of the Cid*, but in a 13th-century ballad about the Cid, written, it is said, by the monks of Cardeña, where the Cid was entombed (see Aberth, *A Knight at the Movies*, 134, and *The Poem of the Cid*, trans. Rita Hamilton and Janet Perry [1975; New York: Penguin, 1984], 2).

16. *Sir Gawain and the Green Knight*, trans. Marie Borroff (New York: Norton, 1967):

> Then was Gringolet girt, that was great and huge,
> And had sojourned safe and sound, and savored his fare;
> He pawed the earth in his pride, that princely steed.
> The good knight draws near him and notes well his look,
> And says sagely to himself, and soberly swears,
> "Here is a household in hall that upholds the right!
> The man who maintains it, may happiness be his!
> Likewise the dear lady, may love betide her!" [2047–54]

17. See Johan Huizinga, *The Waning of the Middle Ages*, trans. Fritz Hopman (1924; New York: Doubleday Anchor, 1954), Ch. IV: "The Idea of Chivalry," 67–77, esp. 77.

18. Cf. Tompkins, *West of Everything*: "Horses are there to galvanize us. More than any other single element in the genre, they symbolize the desire to recuperate some lost connection to life" [94].

19. Lesley Megahey, who wrote and directed *The Advocate*, drew the lines (see note 14 to Ch. 4) from the fourteenth-century French poem *Le Dit de Franc Gontier* by Philippe de Vitri, "bishop of Meaux, musician and poet, and a friend of Petrarch" (Johan Huizinga, *The Waning of the Middle Ages*, trans. Fritz Hopman [1924; New York: Doubleday, 1954], 130n).

20. Merlin enters medieval literature in the twelfth century, in the works of Geoffrey of Monmouth, but his archetype is probably akin to the images of the clown and the fool, in the "depths of a folklore that pre-exists class structures." As Bakhtin says: "[The clown and fool] are life's maskers.... Essential [to them] is ... the right to be 'other' in this world, the right not to make common cause with any single one of

the existing categories that life makes available" [159].

21. See Northrop Frye, *The Secular Scripture: A Study of the Structure of Romance* (Cambridge: Harvard University Press, 1976), 24. I have borrowed from Frye's third chapter title: "Our Lady of Pain: Heroes and Heroines of Romance."

22. Cf. Bakhtin on identity in Greek romance: "No matter how impoverished, how denuded a human identity may become in a Greek romance ... one always senses a faith in the indestructible power of man in his struggle with nature and with all inhuman forces" [105].

23. Scarry, *The Body in Pain*: "Whatever pain achieves, it achieves in part through its unsharability, and it ensures the unsharability through its resistance to language" [4].

24. See Torben Grodal, "The Experience of Realism in Audiovisual Representation," *Realism and "Reality" in Film and Media*, ed. Anne Jerslev (Copenhagen: Museum Tusculanum Press [University of Copenhagen], 2002): "The bias in realist representations for describing suffering or deprived people may not only reflect a political wish for advocating empathy, but also a feeling that pain and deprivation are more real than pleasure" [87].

25. See Sigmund Freud, *Complete Psychological Works*, ed. James Strachey, Vol. XVIII (1922; London: Hogarth Press, 1955), 8–11.

26. Cf. Bakhtin on the trials and the identity of the hero in Greek romance: "The ... adventures in a Greek romance are ... trials of the hero and heroine, especially ... of their chastity and mutual fidelity. But other things may also be tested: their nobility, courage, strength, fearlessness, and—more rarely—their intelligence" [106].

27. David B. Morris, *The Culture of Pain* (Berkeley: University of California Press, 1991), 129.

28. Morris, *Culture of Pain*, 135.

29. Ibid.

30. The assumption that the medieval world view remains "implicit" in our own and other cultures is an idea that Domenico Pietropaulo attributes to Ovidio Capitani ("Eco on Medievalism," *Studies in Medievalism* 5 [1993]: 127–38): "Wherever modern man, prompted by the failure of human history to deliver the sense of existence and burdened by the feeling of cosmic pessimism that inevitably follows the discovery of that fact, responds to the call of reason to seek a meaningful realization of being, there the medieval *Erlebnis* emerges from the darkness of consciousness to color his self-understanding and his perception of the scheme of things" [136].

Chapter One

1. Johan Huizinga, *The Waning of the Middle Ages*, trans. F. Hopman (1924; New York: Doubleday, 1954), 9.

2. Ibid., 10.

3. Umberto Eco, "Dreaming of the Middle Ages," in *Travels in Hyperreality* (1967; London: Picador, 1987), 69.

4. Torben Grodal, "The Experience of Realism in Audiovisual Representations," in *Realism and "Reality" in Film and Media*, ed. Anne Jerslev (Copenhagen: Museum Tusculanum Press [University of Copenhagen], 2002), 84.

5. Ibid., 83.

6. Ibid., 86.

7. Ibid., 87.

8. Ibid.

9. Ibid., 70 (italics mine).

10. Ibid., 81.

11. Ibid., 82.

12. Robert S. Blanch and Julian N. Wasserman, "Fear of Flyting: The Absence of Internal Tension in *Sword of the Valiant* and *First Knight*," *Arthuriana* 10.4 (2000): 28.

Chapter Two

1. Here I mean to suggest the primitive imaginary from which the Conan story is drawn, not actual scenes from the film.

2. *The Lais of Marie de France*, trans. Robert W. Hanning and Joan Ferrante (New York: Dutton, 1978).

3. W.H. Auden, "In Memory of W.B. Yeats," line 8.

4. *Iliad*, XVIII: 109–10.

5. Richard W. Kaeuper and Elspeth Kennedy, *The Book of Geoffroi de Charny* (Philadelphia: University of Pennsylvania Press, 1996).

6. Sidney Painter, *William Marshal, Knight-Errant, Baron, and Regent of England* (1933; Toronto: University of Toronto Press, 1982).

7. Sir Thomas Malory, *Le Morte Darthur: The Winchester Manuscript*, ed. and abr. Helen Cooper (New York: Oxford University Press, 1998).
8. John Steinbeck, *The Acts of King Arthur and His Noble Knights* (New York: Noonday, 1986).
9. J.R.R. Tolkien, *The Lord of the Rings*, 2nd ed. (Cambridge: Houghton-Mifflin, 1965).
10. T.H. White, *The Once and Future King* (New York: Putnam, 1958).
11. See Emmanuel Le Roy Ladurie, *The Peasants of Languedoc*, trans. John Day (Chicago: University of Illinois Press, 1974), Ch. 1–5.
12. See Jean-Louis Flandrin, *Families in Former Times: Kinship, Household and Sexuality*, trans. Richard Southern (Cambridge: Cambridge Univesity Press, 1976), and Robert Mandrou, *Introduction to Modern France 1500–1640: An Essay in Historical Psychology*, trans. R.E. Hallmark (New York: Holmes and Meier, 1975).
13. Natalie Zemon Davis, *The Return of Martin Guerre* (Cambridge: Harvard University Press, 1983).
14. Stephan Greenblatt, *Renaissance Self-Fashioning: From More to Shakespeare* (Chicago: Chicago University Press, 1980).
15. Geoffrey Chaucer, *The Canterbury Tales*, ed. Larry D. Benson (Boston: Houghton-Mifflin, 2000), I: 2777.

Chapter Three

1. Aristotelis, *De Arte Poetica Liber*, ed. Rudolf Kassel (Oxford: Clarendon Press, 1965), 1450b, 16–18.
2. Stephen Halliwell, *The Poetics of Aristotle*, trans. and comm. (Chapel Hill: University of North Carolina Press, 1987), 98–9.
3. Stephen Halliwell, *Aristotle's Poetics* (Chicago: University of Chicago Press, 1998), 64.
4. Kevin J. Harty, *The Reel Middle Ages: Films About Medieval Europe* (Jefferson, NC: McFarland, 1999), 313.

Chapter Four

1. Umberto Eco, *Travels in Hyperreality*, trans. William Weaver (1986; London: Picador, 1987): 61–72.
2. *The Advocate*, dir. Lesley Megahey. Screenplay Leslie Megahey. Cinematography John Hooper. Music Alexandre Desplat. A Miramax release of a BBC/CiBy 2000 production, 1994.
3. In his review for *Sight and Sound* 4 (February 1994), Phillip Strick said: "Part whodunnit, part rustic comedy and part historical pageant, *The Hour of the Pig* embraces its opportunities with an enthusiastic but precarious grasp, seemingly reluctant to decide on a main argument." The unusually close attention to authenticating detail that creates the solidly medieval look and feel may result from Leslie Megahey's having written and directed the film, but the production company, BBC/CiBy 2000, and shooting the picture on location in northern France, might also have helped.
4. Peter Rainer, *Los Angeles Times* (3/31/94): 11.
5. Thelma Adams, *New York Post* (8/24/94): 35.
6. *Magill's Cinema Annual 1995* (Englewood Cliffs, NJ: Salem Press, 1996), 10.
7. Kim Newman, *Empire* 56 (February 1994): 30.
8. Lisa Nesselson, *Variety* 25 (October 1993): 82.
9. Marianne Gray, *Film Review* (February 1994): 19
10. Nesselson, *Variety*: 82.
11. Linda E. Mitchell, *American Historical Review* 100 (1995): 1221–22.
12. Legal issues, legal language and legal procedures are central to the film, but one reviewer (see note 11) thought the movie did not clarify the differences between Roman law and the "Custom" of Ponthieu:

Roman law creates a chasm between male and female on the same rational basis by which it differentiates between human and animal. Thus women, according to Roman law, are closer to animals than they are to men: they, too, are incapable of rational decision-making and can be exploited and abused like chattels. [Yet] [j]ust as customary law makes few distinctions between human and animal, it makes few distinctions between male and female. Unfortunately, the debate between these concepts is not an element of *The Advocate* [1222].

13. Johan Huizinga, *The Waning of the*

Middle Ages, trans. F. Hopman (1924; New York: Doubleday, 1954), 30.

14. Here Megahey presents the Middle Ages in ways reminiscent of Huizinga's account, but there are even stronger resemblances. When Courtois, the naïve urbanite, orders his first supper at the Abbeville Inn, he somewhat absurdly quotes Phillipe de Vitri's *Le Dit de Franc Gontier*, a fourteenth-century poem on the simple joys of country life: "Under green leaves ... near a noisy brook ... Gontier took his meal with dame Helayne on fresh cheese ... garlic and onions [and] chopped shallots on a brown crust with coarse salt, to drink the better." These lines appear in Huizinga's chapter on "The Idyllic Vision of Life" (130n) in support of his commentary on the late-medieval pastoral ideal. Certain tableau scenes in the film may imply a familiarity with later chapters on the Van Eycks as well.

15. In *Coming to Terms: The Rhetoric of Narrative in Fiction and Film* (Ithaca, NY: Cornell University Press, 1990), ch. 8–9, Seymour Chatman distinguishes between the implied author in a film, the film's narration, its slant, and its filtration. The implied author represents the film's intentions—aesthetic, ideological and so forth. Narration is how the film is presented, and narration produces slant, the ideological or other commentary implicit in the presentation. Filtration, however, is commentary "filtered through" a particular character's sensibilities and point of view. We often share Courtois's earnest, reasonable point of view (his filtration), but the film retains its own narrative slant, or implied commentary, an interface between medieval times and our own. It reminds us that Courtois is intelligent but rather inexperienced in this country setting, that his thinking is reasonable yet legalistic (he is a *medieval* lawyer, after all), and that while we may sympathize with his brand of enlightened discontent, we cannot really share it.

16. See R. Howard Bloch, *Medieval French Literature and Law* (Berkeley: University of California Press, 1977): "Trials of barnyard animals were not uncommon. Under the assumption that the responsibility of domestic animals is identical to that of humans, the *Registre Criminel de Saint-Martin* reports the case of a sow which, having killed a young child, was executed at Noisi according to the procedure reserved for murderers" [33]. See also Yvonne. Bongert, *Cours d' histoire de droit penal français de la seconde moitié du XIIIe siècle à 1493* (Paris, 1970), 350.

17. This metaphor was in fact known to medieval legal discourse. Cf. Walter Ullmann. *The Medieval Idea of Law as Represented by Lucas de Penna: A Study in Fourteenth-Century Legal Scholarship* (1946; New York: Barnes and Noble, 1969), 45, who quotes Lucas de Penna, a fourteenth-century Neapolitan jurist, on law as "the reflection of the divine will": "*Lex est divinae voluntatis imago*" (*Commentarium* XI, 18, 1, no. 12).

18. The following discussion is derived from Gaines Post, *Studies in Medieval Legal Thought: Public Law and the State, 1100–1322* (Princeton: Princeton University Press, 1964), 508–12, 539ff., 548ff., 552f.

19. On the Continental witch trials, see Richard Kieckhefer, *European Witch Trials: Their Foundations in Popular and Learned culture, 1300–1500* (Berkeley: University of California Press, 1976). Kieckhefer argues that "the drastic increase [during the fourteenth and fifteenth centuries] in trials for sorcery came about because of anxieties felt throughout society, but ... the more fantastic charge of diabolism ... built on a foundation that was already laid. The jurists and theologians who suggested this charge supplied a new dimension to the craze that was already underway, adding fuel to an already blazing fire. The masses and the intellectual elite combined their energies in a task of common concern—and demonstrated that the fruits of such cooperation are by no means necessarily salutary" [105].

20. Latin *aufero* (infinitive *auferre*) means "remove," "take," and in some cases "seduce" or even "steal." It suits this grasping lord well.

21. Marjorie K. McIntosh, "Finding Language for Misconduct" in Barbara A. Hanawalt and David Wallace, eds., *Bodies and Disciplines: Intersections of Literature and History in Fifteenth-Century England* (Minneapolis: University of Minnesota Press, 1996), provides a suggestive account of what was probably a parallel situation in mid-fifteenth-century France:

For local jurors, the need to maintain control in the face of [the social and economic changes following the hundred years' war] was paramount: they sought both to regulate the life of their communities and to retain their own power.

They were faced with the presence of new kinds of people and styles of behavior that undermined traditional patterns of good order, yet they lacked specific legal authority with which to address many of the issues that seemed most threatening ... their sense of urgency in responding to the problems can only have been intensified by the political uncertainties of the higher levels of government [112–13].

22. The predations of d'Auferre's son have their medieval precedent in the notorious acts of Gilles de Rais, a young nobleman of Anjou (1404–40) whose early military career included commanding a part of the troops that Joan of Arc led against the English at Orleans (1429). Shortly after, at the coronation of Charles VII, he was named Marshal of France. In the decade that followed, rumors circulated, but no one pursued them because Gilles's cousin, Georges de La Trémoile, was then the king's favorite. But in 1440, constrained by indebtedness caused by his profligate spending, Gilles committed the sacrilege of disrupting a mass in Brittany and kidnapping a priest, with the hope of repossessing a castle he had previously sold to the priest's brother. The Duke of Brittany, who was his suzerain, then had him brought to trial. Faced with torture, Gilles de Rais "spontaneously" confessed to sodomizing and murdering, during the preceding eight years, at least 128 children—all or mostly boys—who, at his command, were kidnapped from the streets and fields, from the ranks of his pages and choirboys, and especially from the numbers of beggar children who came to his residence hoping to receive alms. Gilles de Rais was sentenced to death for his crimes on October 25, 1440, after several lengthy and impassioned confessional speeches. The next day he was hanged and burned, but asked to be executed first, before his accomplices, to provide them with an example of how to die well. See *Laughter for the Devil: The Trials of Gilles de Rais, Companion-in-Arms of Joan of Arc (1440)*, trans. Reginald Hyatte (Rutherford, NJ: Fairleigh Dickinson University Press, 1984).

23. According to the credits, Courtois's character is based on the life of Barthélemy de Chasseneuz (sometimes spelled Chassanée) (1480–1541). See M. Michaud, ed., *Biographie Universelle, Ancienne et Moderne*, Nouvelle Edition (Paris: Madame C. Desplaces, 1854), VII: 699–700. Chasseneuz, a prominent jurist, did defend animals and became president of the Parlement d'Aix in 1540, where he presided during the notorious judgment of the villagers of Mérindol, who were suspected of heresy. Some had been condemned to death for their failure to present themselves at court (*contumace*), others to be banished and their houses destroyed. Chasseneuz prevented this judgment from being carried out by arguing that since one could not excommunicate rats before they were arraigned and their testimony heard, then even the heretics of Mérindol should not be treated more harshly (*rigoureusement*) than these animals.

Some historians believe this to be a mere story drawn from a Protestant martyrology. Yet it is true that Chasseneuz had previously reported a case in Beaune (see his *Consilia*, Lyon, 1531) in which beetles had attacked the vines, but then as well he had refused to uphold a judgment that the beetles leave the territory under threat of excommunication: the beetles would not come to court, yet neither had they refused counsel. In his judgment at Mérindol, Chasseneuz cited several other similar cases against harmful animals (*animauz nuisibles*), such as rats and snails in Autun, Lyon and Macon. On these grounds, he obtained an order from the king that the Mérindol defendants should remain free from judgment until arraigned. This order remained in force until the following year (1541) when Chasseneuz died suddenly, some say by poison in a bouquet of flowers, and the unfortunate villagers suffered their cruel judgment.

In retrospect, it seems that the underlying strategy of Chasseneuz may have been to establish precedents which, since they concerned animals, were clearly an illustration of natural law (i.e. first principles), and would retain their authority in judgments concerning humans.

24. Barbara W. Tuchman, *A Distant Mirror: The Calamitous 14th Century* (New York: Knopf, 1978).

25. On the differences between the laws in the North and the South of France in the Middle Ages, see Joseph R. Strayer, ed., *Dictionary of the Middle Ages* (New York: Scribner, 1986), VII: 457–68.

26. Richard W. Kaeuper, *War, Justice and Public Order: England and France in the Late Middle Ages* (Oxford: Clarendon Press, 1988),

378–380, makes the point that whereas the English crown's active attempts to adjudicate legal issues during the Hundred Years War helped to create regional (parliamentary) resistance to central rule, the French crown during that time tended to allow legal issues to be dealt with by the powerful nobles, through long-established feudal practices. Consequently, when the French king consolidated his rule in the late fifteenth century, no effective parliamentary system existed, and the French monarchy enjoyed an uninterrupted absolutist rule until the eighteenth century.

27. Henry David Thoreau, *Walden* (1854; New York: New American Library, 1960), 66.

28. *Corpus Iuris Civilis* D. 9, 2, 4. More broadly, "All laws (natural and human) sanction the use of force to repel force": "*Vel enim vi defendere, omnes leges, omniaque iura permittunt*" (D. 9, 2, 45, 4). Both passages quoted in Post, *Studies in Medieval Legal thought*, 509.

29. Huizinga, *The Waning of the Middle Ages*, 232.

Chapter Five

1. *The Seventh Seal*, d. Ingmar Bergman. Screenplay Ingmar Bergman. Cinematography Gunnar Fischer. Music Erik Nordgren. Swedish with English subtitles. Svensk Filmindustri, 1957.

2. Cf. Jesse Kalin, *The Films of Ingmar Bergman* (Cambridge: Cambridge University Press, 2003): "[Bergman's] morality tale is ... a version of *Everyman* in which each person represents some aspect of human being—greed, sexual desire, egotism, patience, tenderness, generosity.... They are [the] ways and possibilities of our lives" (66). But Laurie A. Finke and Martin B. Shichtman, in *Cinematic Illuminations: The Middle Ages on Film* (Baltimore: The Johns Hopkins University Press, 2010), argue for a broader social perspective: "Block is both a medieval knight and an allegorical figure for the body politic; the health of the body represents the health of society itself" (303).

3. Cf. Marc Gervais, *Ingmar Bergman: Magician and Prophet* (Montreal: McGill-Queens University Press, 1999): "Can anything be more representative of post-war Europe than life as a chess game between Man and Death, with the stakes nothing less than the meaningfulness or absurdity of existence" (53).

4. Cf. Kalin, *Films*: "In fact, God and the Devil are everywhere [in *The Seventh Seal*] and as real as other people" (61).

5. On these two characters as reflecting the two sides of Bergman's personality, see Frank Gado, *The Passion of Ingmar Bergman* (Durham, NC: Duke University Press, 1986), 210.

6. Gado, *Passion*, 198.

7. Cf. John Orr, "Bergman, Nietzsche and Hollywood," in *Ingmar Bergman Revisited: Performance, Cinema and the Arts*, ed. Maaret Koskinen (London: Wallflower Press, 2008): "A ludic riposte to all deathly metaphysics" (153).

8. Cf. Gervais, *Ingmar Bergman*: "Death [is] quite naturally ... surrounded by somewhat expressionistic effects—the extreme contrasts, the dark costumes, the disorienting of space into the more or less abstract, complemented by confrontational editing, and of course, the added "Dies Irae" motifs" (205).

9. Cf. Arthur Gibson, *The Silence of God: Creative Response to the Films of Ingmar Bergman* (New York: Harper & Row, 1969): "Chess is of all human games the most perfect paradigm of the freedom mystery and of the God-man relationship" (30).

10. Cf. Gervais, *Ingmar Bergman*: "There is as never before in a film an almost formal existentialist philosophical debate going on" (204). But Gado, in *Passion*, says the connection is "more apparent than real; examining the film through an existentialist lens does not clarify its meaning" (206).

11. Gervais, in *Ingmar Bergman* (156–200), provides a meticulous technical description of this key scene.

12. Ibid., 206–10.

13. *La Passion de Jeanne d'Arc*, d. Carl Theodor Dreyer. Screenplay Carl Theodor Dreyer. Cinematography Rudolph Maté. Société Générale des Films, 1928.

14. Richard Einhorn's oratorio, *Voices of Light* (1995), has become an integral part of the silent film *La Passion de Jeanne d'Arc*. The libretto is a montage of medieval writings, mainly female mystics, including letters by Jeanne herself.

15. Cf. Tom Milne, *The Cinema of Carl Dreyer* (New York: A.S. Barnes, 1971): "The action itself is reduced to what is virtually a

symphony of faces" (94); Laurie A. Finke and Martin B. Shichtman, *Cinematic Illuminations: The Middle Ages on Film* (Baltimore: The Johns Hopkins University Press, 2010): "[Joan's] judges confront us like so many medieval gargoyles" (119); and David Bordwell, *The Films of Carl-Theodore Dreyer* (Berkeley: University of California Press, 1981): "The film's intelligibility hinges upon our connecting one close-up with another" (66). On Dreyer's expressionism, see Paul Schrader, *Transcendental Style in Film: Ozu, Bresson, Dreyer* (Berkeley: University of California Press, 1972), 113–26, esp. 116–18: "German expressionism featured rich chiaroscuro, jutting and oblique angles, surreal architectonics, antirealistic sets, distorted faces—techniques which are present to a greater or lesser degree in all of Dreyer's films" (117). See also Bordwell, *Films*, 81.

16. See Dreyer's comment in. Bordwell, *Films*: "My idea of telling the passion of Jeanne in close-up did not fit into the framework of what was then understood as a 'normal film'" (234n4).

17. Cf. Bordwell, *Films*: "What the close-up as spatial fragment destroys, the expressive face seeks to rebuild. The plenitude of Jeanne's character as a focusing unity and the tiny second-by-second fluctuations of expression are structural necessities" (85).

18. Cf. Milne, *Cinema*: "Inexorably, Dreyer highlights his heroine's isolation, her helplessness to counter the weight massed against her, so that the dry, chapped lips, the face streaked with sweat and tears, the eyes shadowed with intolerable pain, the head thrown back in supplication, can still move an audience to tears today" (103).

19. Ibid., 105.

20. Cf. Finke and Shichtman, *Illuminations*: "And this is perhaps the genius of the film, this intense concentration on the hero's existential suffering" (117).

21. Carl Dreyer, "Realized Mysticism," in *Dreyer in Double Reflection*, edited by Donald Skoller, 47–50 (New York: E.P. Dutton, 1973): "[In *La Passion de Jeanne d'Arc*] I wanted to interpret a hymn to the triumph of the soul over life" (50). See also Amédée Ayfre, *Le Cinema et sa vérité* (Paris: Cerf, 1969): "What the body is to the soul, what the sacraments are to grace ... the films of Dreyer are to a mysterious world which normally escapes us" (175; translated by Bordwell, *Films*, 2).

22. Ebbe Neergaard, *Carl Dreyer: A Film Director's Work*, New Index Series, No. 1 (London: BFI, 1950), qtd. in Milne, *Cinema*, 94.

23. See Bordwell, *Films*, 72–4.

24. See Bordwell's extended treatment in *Films*, 66–80.

Chapter Six

1. *Perceval le gallois*, d. Eric Rohmer. Screenplay Eric Rohmer. Cinematography Nestor Almendros. Music Guy Robert. Costumes Jacques Schmidt. French with English subtitles. Gaumont-Films du Losange, 1978.

2. Lesley Coote, "The Art of Arthurian Cinema," in *A Companion to Arthurian Literature*, edited by Helen Fulton, 511–24 (Malden, MA: Wiley-Blackwell, 2009), believes that Rohmer has reproduced on film the medieval "dance-play," a "widespread practice across Europe ... in which actor/dancers would perform all or part of a sung narrative, miming the actions while speaking or singing part of the musical accompaniment" (516).

3. On distancing, see Jeff Rider, Richard Hull and Christopher Smith, "The Arthurian Legend in French Cinema: *Lancelot du Lac* and *Perceval le gallois*, in *Cinema Arthuriana: Essays on Arthurian Film*, ed. Kevin J. Harty (New York: Garland, 1991), 42, 44, 49. See also Joan Tasker Grimbert, "Distancing Techniques in Chrétien and Rohmer," *Arthuriana* 10.4 (2000): 33–44.

4. Cf. Joseph Marty, "Perceval le Gallois d'Eric Rohmer, un itinéraire roman," *Les Cahiers de la cinémathèque* 42–43 (Summer 1985): 125–32: "Rohmer, then, like the romance poets, gives permanent articulated form to a meticulous and almost punctilious realism through a stylization which is imaginary to a degree bordering on the extreme" (127) (my translation).

5. Nadja Tesich-Savage, "Rehearsing the Middle Ages" [Interview of Eric Rohmer], *Film Comment* 14.5 (September/October 1978): 50–52, 54–56, 80; http://search.proquest.com, 1–5. "[Rohmer:] 'Look, I am not trying to show the Middle Ages as we would see it if we could go back in a time machine and photograph it; I am searching to rediscover the vision of the Middle Ages as it saw itself'" (1); 'I believe that one can judge a period by the idealized image that it offers of

itself, and often the period is better described by an idealized image than a 'truthful' one" (5); '[A] society reveals itself more through its myths than through a summary of events'" (5).

6. Grimbert, 36.
7. Ibid., 40.
8. Rider, et al., 41–2.
9. Cf. Coote, "Art": "What matters is not the naturalism of the image, but what is signified. The stylized gesture reminds the viewer of the signified emotion in the natural, the 'real' world, and this is what the viewer 'reads'" (517).
10. Grimbert believes that "the scene is meant as a visual representation of the lesson Perceval receives" (44). Rider, Hull and Smith consider it "Rohmer's profoundly Catholic, highly moralized interpretation of Chrétien's romance" (53).
11. Cf. Bruce A. Beattie, "The Broken Quest: The 'Perceval' Romances of Chrétien de Troyes and Eric Rohmer," in *The Arthurian Revival: Essays on Form, Tradition and Transformation*, edited by Debra N. Mancoff, 248–65 (New York: Garland, 1992): "If Perceval is a type of Christ, he is also the ultimate 'errant knight' whose wanderings ... have no end. He is ... the quest hero whose object is 'the impossible dream.'... The 'broken quest' becomes a metaphor of transcendence" (262). See also Linda Williams, "Eric Rohmer and the Holy Grail," *Literature and Film Quarterly* 11.2 (1983). *ProQuest Research Library*, 71–82: "We see Perceval both as himself and as Christ" (77).
12. Tesich-Savage, "Rehearsing": "[Rohmer:] 'Romanesque churches are very "deep." ... I want to give great importance to the third dimension and had thought of using the wide-angle lens.... Space will be presented through enormous sets with a sky as background which should make everything even bigger.... Vast empty landscapes should correspond more to the idea of the Middle Ages" (2).
13. *Lancelot du Lac*, d. Robert Bresson. Screenplay Robert Bresson. Cinematography Pasqualino de Santis. Music Philippe Sarde. French with English subtitles. Mara Films, 1974.
14. On Bresson's treatment of blood and body in *Lancelot du Lac*, see Keith Reader, *Robert Bresson* (Manchester: Manchester University Press, 2000), 118–20.
15. Cf. Lesley Coote, "The Art of Arthurian Cinema," *A Companion to Arthurian Literature*, edited by Helen Fulton, 511–24 (Malden, MA: Wiley-Blackwell, 2009): "Bresson represents the prophetic presence from his source text in terms of a souciant nature" (514).
16. See Jonathan Rosenbaum, "The Rattle of Armor, the Softness of Flesh," *Movies as Politics* (Berkeley: University of California Press, 1997): "The destinies of the horses are bound to those of the men who ride them" (205).
17. See Kristin Thompson, "The Sheen of Armour, the Whinnies of Horses: Sparse Parametric Style in *Lancelot du Lac*," *Robert Bresson*, edited by James Quant, 339–71 (Toronto: Toronto International Film Festival Group, 1998): "Much of the interest of the film's style remains independent of narrative functioning" (339).
18. See Thompson, "Sheen of Armour," 350–53, on the recurring motifs of armor, tents, shields, leggings, pennants and sounds. See also Rosenbaum, "Rattle of Armour," 205–206, and Michael Dempsey, "Despair Abounding: The Recent Films of Robert Bresson," *Robert Bresson*, edited by James Quant, 373–91 (Toronto: Toronto International Film Festival Group, 1998), 380.
19. Cf. Coote, "Art," 512.
20. On horses in *Lancelot du Lac*, see Coote, "Art," 511–12.
21. Cf. Thompson, "Sheen of Armour": "In this film, the tiniest gestures and glances become expressive.... Such moments gain not only in emphasis but in intensity through their comparative rarity" (346).
22. Cf. Coote, "Art": "Frequently what we see in the film is simply spaces" (514).
23. Cf. Jeff Rider, Richard Hull, and Christopher Smith, "The Arthurian Legend in French Cinema: *Lancelot du Lac* and *Perceval le Gallois*," *Cinema Arthuriana: Essays on Arthurian Film*, edited by Kevin J. Harty, 43–56 (New York: Garland, 1991): "What *Lancelot du Lac* shows us is ... medieval literature transformed into a cinematic mask for twentieth-century alienation" (52). See also Reader, *Robert Bresson*, 120.
24. On Guinevere, see Dempsey, "Despair Abounding," 381–82.
25. See, for example, Jonathan Rosenbaum, "The Last Filmmaker: A Local, Interim Report," *Robert Bresson*, 17–24 (Toronto: Toronto International Film Festival Group, 1998), 21.

Chapter Seven

1. *The Name of the Rose*, dir. Jean-Jacques Annaud. Screenplay Andrew Birkin, et al. Music James Horner. Cinematography Tonino delli Colli. Neue Constantin/Twentieth Century–Fox, 1986. Umberto Eco, *The Name of the Rose*, trans. William Weaver (New York: Harcourt Brace Jovanovich, 1983). Originally published in Italian in 1980. See also Theresa Colletti, *Naming the Rose: Eco, Medieval Signs and Modern Theory* (Ithaca, NY: Cornell University Press, 1988); the retrospective by Eco, *Postscript to The Name of the Rose*, trans. William Weaver (New York: Harcourt Brace Jovnovich, 1984); and the helpful volume by Adele J. Haft, et al., *The Key to The Name of the Rose: Including Translations of the Non-English Passages* (Harrington Park, NJ: Ampersand Associates, 1987).

2. Barbara Tuchman, *A Distant Mirror: The Calamitous 14th Century* (New York: Ballantine, 1979).

3. See Jean Leclercq, *The Love of Learning and the Desire for God: A Study of Monastic Culture*, trans. Catharine Misrahi (New York: Fordham University Press, 1961). Originally published in French in 1957. See also Jean Leclercq, et al., *The Spirituality of the Middle Ages* (New York: Seabury Press, 1968).

4. Saint Augustine, *The City of God Against the Pagans*, trans. R.W. Dyson (Cambridge: University of Cambridge Press, 1998).

5. See Gordon Leff's landmark study, *Heresy in the Later Middle Ages: The Relation of Heterodoxy to Dissent, 1250–1450*, 2 Vols. (Manchester: Manchester University Press, 1967).

6. See, for example, John Moorman, *A History of the Franciscan Order* (Oxford: Clarendon Press, 1968).

7. See Brian Clegg, *The First Scientist: A Life of Roger Bacon* (New York: Carroll & Graff, 2003).

8. See Stephen Ozment's lucid *The Age of Reform 1250–1550* (New Haven: Yale University Press, 1980).

9. See Gordon Leff, *William of Ockham* (Manchester: Manchester University Press, 1975.). See also Leff's useful overview, *The Dissolution of the Medieval Outlook* (New York: New York University Press, 1976).

10. This irresistibly quotable phrase was apparently coined by John of Jandun, a contemporary of Ockham's.

11. In addition to Leff, *Heresy*, see David Burr, *The Spiritual Franciscans* (University Park: Pennsylvania State University Press, 2001).

12. Leff, *Heresy*, 241.

13. Quoted in Leff, *Heresy*, 242.

14. Leff, *Heresy*, 242. See also Lester K. Little, *Religious Poverty and the Profit Economy in Medieval Europe* (Ithaca, NY: Cornell University Press, 1978).

15. Leff, *Heresy*, 152. For samples of Ubertino's text, see Ubertinus de Casali, *The Tree of the Crucified Life of Jesus, Book Five (excerpts)*, translator unknown. In *The Prophet*, Vol. 3 (Hyde Park, NY: New City Press, 2001), 141–206.

16. Leff, *Heresy*, 152.

17. My translation. See Eco, *Name*, 222.

18. Eco, *Name*, 222–26.

19. See Decima L. Douie, *The Nature and the Effect of the Heresy of the Fraticelli* (Manchester: At the University Press, 1932).

20. Bernardus Guidonis, *The Inquisitor's Guide: A Medieval Manual on Heretics*, trans. Janet Shirley (Walwyn Garden City, UK: Ravenhall Books, 2006).

Chapter Eight

1. *The Return of Martin Guerre*, d. Daniel Vigne. Screenplay Jean-Claude Carriere and Daniel Vigne. Photography Andre Neau. Music Michel Portal. French with English Subtitles. Société de Production Cinematographique, 1982.

2. For an overview of the economy of Languedoc in the fourteenth to sixteenth centuries, see Le Roy Ladurie, *The Peasants of Languedoc*, trans. John Day (Urbana: University of Illinois Press, 1974), Part I, Ch. 1–2.

3. See Natalie Zemon Davis, *The Return of Martin Guerre* (Cambridge: Harvard University Press, 1983), Ch. 1.

4. Ibid., 74, 96.

5. Ibid., 97.

6. Ibid., 127.

7. *The Return of Martin Guerre* won César awards for Best Original Score, Best Original Screenplay, and Best Production Design. For his performance in this film, Gérard Depardieu won the National Society of Film Critics Best Actor award.

8. In real life, Martin's first trial was held in the town of Rieux, on the Garonne, perhaps

a day's ride to the northwest of Artigat. Firmin Vayssière, who assists Coras in both the film's trials, was probably the judge at Rieux in 1560. "[A] licentiate in law and a staunch Catholic, he was later in charge of investigating Huguenot attacks on church property in the diocese" (Davis, *Return*, 62). In the film, Vayssiére becomes a Protestant sympathizer for the sake of narrative economy.

9. See Robert Mandrou, *Introduction to Modern France, 1500–1640: An Essay in Historical Psychology*, trans. R.D. Hallmark (New York: Holmes and Meier, 1976), 124–6; Peter Burke, *Popular Culture in Early Modern Europe* (New York: New York University Press, 1978), 200; Natalie Zemon Davis, *Society and Culture in Early Modern France* (Stanford: Stanford University Press, 1975), 104–9.

10. Ladurie, 205.
11. Mandrou, 211.
12. Ibid., 209.
13. See Davis, *Return*, Ch. 4.
14. Ibid., 40–41.
15. Mandrou, 53.
16. Nicolas Malebranche, qtd. in Mandrou, 55.
17. Georges Duby, *Medieval Marriage: Two Models from Twelfth-Century France* (Baltimore: Johns Hopkins University Press, 1978), qtd. in Martha Howell, "The Properties of Marriage in Late Medieval Europe: Commercial Wealth and the Creation of Modern Marriage," 17–61, in Isabel Davis, et al., eds., *Love, Marriage, and Family Ties in the Later Middle Ages* (Tournhout: Brepols, 2003), 23.
18. Lawrence Stone, *The Family, Sex and Marriage in England 1500–1800*, abridged edition (New York: Harper and Row, 1977), qtd. in Howell, 24.
19. Howell, 37–47.
20. Antoine Héroët, qtd. in Mandrou, 86.
21. Jean-Louis Flandrin, *Families in Former Times: Kinship, Household and Sexuality*, trans. Richard Southern (Cambridge: Cambridge University Press, 1979), 163.
22. Qtd. in Flandrin, 164.
23. Pierre de Bourdeille, Abbé and Seignure de Brantôme, *Les Dames Galantes*, first treatise, ed. Maurice Rat (Paris, 1955), 25–6, qtd. in Flandrin, 165.
24. See Davis, *Society*, Ch. 5.
25. Mandrou, 226.
26. Davis, *Return*, Ch. 10.
27. Flandrin, 163.

Chapter Nine

1. *Kingdom of Heaven*, dir. Ridley Scott. Screenplay William Monahan. Music Harry Gregson-Williams. Cinematography John Mathieson. Twentieth Century–Fox, 2005. All references will be to the director's cut (194 minutes), which was Scott's initial print of the film. On May 6, 2005, Fox released an edited version (shorter by 45 minutes) which earned $47 million in the U.S. against a budget of $130 million. On December 23, 2005, Scott released his director's cut, which was more successful in Europe and the rest of the world. Total sales rose to more than $211 million.
2. "Truth Is the First Victim," *The Times* (online edition), May 5, 2005.
3. "The real Crusades began in 1095 as a response to centuries of Muslim conquests of Christian lands. Their purpose was to restore those territories, including the Holy Land, to Christian control." "Onward PC Soldiers: Ridley Scott's *Kingdom of Heaven*," *National Review* (online edition), May 27, 2005.
4. Amin Maalouf. Qtd. in Charlotte Edwardes, "Ridley Scott's New Crusades Film Panders to Osama bin Laden," *The Telegraph* (online edition), December 17, 2004.
5. "Haya binna"—roughly, "get going"—is an Arabic command that Eva Green (twice) and Jeremy Irons (once) use when they want mounted attendants to move out briskly. It tells us that they have grown up or grown old in the culture of the East. Richard Francaviglia, "Crusaders and Saracens: The Persistence of Orientalism in Historically Themed Pictures about the Middle East," in *Lights, Camera, History: Portraying the Past in Film*, ed. Richard Francaviglia and Jerry Rodnitzky (College Station: Texas A&M University Press, 2007), calls Sibylla "the perfect trope for the exoticized Eastern woman" (79).
6. Thomas F. Madden, "Onward PC Soldiers."
7. See Greg Mortenson and David Oliver Relin, *Three Cups of Tea: One Man's Mission to Promote Peace...One School at a Time* (New York: Penguin, 2006), and Greg Mortenson, *Stones into Schools: Promoting Peace with Books, Not Bombs, in Afghanistan and Pakistan* (New York: Viking, 2009).
8. Dana C. Munro, trans., "Speech of Urban II at the Council of Clermont, November 26, 1095," in *Urban and the Crusaders:*

Translations and Reprints from the Original Sources of European History, ed. Dana C. Munro, 3rd edition (Philadelphia: Department of History of the University of Pennsylvania, 1901), 7. Several quite different versions of Urban's speech survive. This widely influential version was recorded by Robert the Monk of Rheims some eleven years after the actual speech. On the date of Robert's *History*, see Carol Sweetenham, trans., *Robert the Monk's History of the First Crusade, Historia Iberosolimitana* (Burlington: Ashgate, 2007).

9. See Sweetenham, *Robert the Monk's History*, 81, 81n12.

10. Cf. Thomas F. Madden, "Onward PC Soldiers": "*Kingdom of Heaven* ... performs the delicate operation of stripping religious piety completely out of the Crusades. Balian and his father appear to be agnostics. Other Crusaders, like the Hospitaler, are openly critical of religion."

11. See Jonathan Riley-Smith, *The Knights of St. John in Jerusalem and Cyprus c. 1050–1310* (New York: Macmillan, 1967), 37–43; and Alan John Forey, *The Military Orders: From the Twelfth to the Fourteenth Centuries* (Toronto: University of Toronto Press, 1992), 17–22.

12. See William, Archbishop of Tyre, *A History of Deeds Done Beyond the Sea*, trans. Emily Atwater Babcock and A.C. Krey, 2 vols. (New York: Columbia University Press, 1943), II: 508, 508n12.

13. The Patriarch is described by Christopher Tyerman as follows: "If not the gigolo of hostile memory, a brave and skilled politician if not a paragon of celibate virtue, Heraclius, originally from the Auvergne, reinforced the contempt some in the west felt for the *poulains*, as they derisively called those who lived in Outremer." *God's War: A New History of the Crusades* (Cambridge: Harvard University Press, 2006), 216. See also Kenneth M. Setton, ed., *A History of the Crusades*, 5 vols. (Madison: University of Wisconsin Press, 1969), I: 597: "Heraclius, a handsome though incompetent and immoral cleric."

14. See Edward Said's seminal treatment of this phenomenon in *Orientalism* (New York: Pantheon, 1978).

15. Kathleen Biddick provides an interesting interpretation of Edward Norton's performance as the masked leper king in "Unbinding the Flesh That Remains: Crusader Martyrdom Then and Now," *GLQ* 13:2–3 (2007): 213–216.

16. See Setton, *History of the Crusades*, 72–3, 96, and esp. 584.

17. See H.A.R. Gibb, *The Life of Saladin: From the Works of 'Imād ad-Dīn and Bahā' ad-Dīn* (Oxford: Clarendon Press, 1973).

18. On Reynald de Châtillon (a.k.a. Reginald of Châtillon, and later, Reginald of Kerak), see Setton, *History of the Crusades*, 603–606, 614.

19. Usāmah ibn–Munquidh, in his autobiography, provides some lively and unbiased anecdotes describing the Franks as he saw them. See *An Arab-Syrian Gentleman and Warrior in the Period of the Crusades: Memoirs of Usāmah ibn–Munquidh*, trans. Philip K. Hitti (New York: Columbia University Press, 2000).

20. On Imād ad-Dīn's account of Saladin, see H.A.R. Gibb, *Saladin: Studies in Islamic History* (Beirut: Arab Institute for Research and Publishing, 1974), 87: "That Imād ad-Dīn was a convinced admirer of Saladin cannot be denied, but he presents Saladin throughout as an entirely human figure, a personality naturally generous and humane beyond the ordinary run of princes, modest and not above making mistakes, but deeply in earnest and endowed with a serene conviction which upheld him in all conflicts and disappointments. But there is no exaggeration whatever in this; it is the true Saladin."

21. Imād ad-Dīn provides a vivid account of the bombardment: "The bases of the walls and the teeth of their battlements were battered and broken down by stones from the catapults' slings.... Their missiles were invincible, all precautions against them were useless.... How many boulders came down out of heaven upon them, how many blocks of sandstone plunged into the earth, how many firebrands bespattered them!" In Francesco Gabrieli, *Arab Historians of the Crusades* (Berkeley: University of California Press, 1969), 155.

22. Saladin's piety is emphasized by all of his biographers. The following is drawn from Bahā ad-Dīn's account: "Now Saladin was a man of firm faith, one who often had God's name on his lips. He drew his faith from the evidence duly studied in the company of the most authoritative scholars and greatest lawyers, acquiring sufficient competence to take part in a theological discussion should one

arise in his presence.... He never omitted the canonic prayer. ... If the hour of prayer came round while he was traveling he would dismount from his horse and pray." Gabrieli, *Arab Historians of the Crusades,* 87–88.

23. See Setton, *History of the Crusades*: "All who could pay at the rate of ten gold pieces for a man, five for a woman, and one for a child might have forty days time to depart. ... Saladin next offered to release all of the poor, of whom there were more than twenty thousand who could pay nothing, for the sum of one hundred thousand gold pieces.... Balian, fearful that the Templars and Hospitalers would not pay such an amount, was forced to accept freedom for seven thousand of the poorest ... for thirty thousand gold pieces. As a result there were several thousand unredeemed whose probable fate was slavery. The fault was presumably the Templars' and Hospitalers,' but Balian was blamed." However, "[a] great many apparently escaped over the walls or in disguise or successfully used bribery. Further, Saladin not only proved himself unusually liberal to prominent individuals like Stephanie of Kerak [the wife of Reginald], but he and his emirs personally set free three or four thousand poor" (616–617).

24. Madden, "Onward PC Soldiers."

25. Riley-Smith, *The Knights of St. John*, 91 99–100.

Epilogue

1. Medieval film seems to be a first-world phenomenon. Even the richly-produced *Saladin* (d. Youssef Chahine. Egypt: Lotus Films, 1963) is more a national epic than a vehicle for medievalism.

2. Here I draw upon Paul Leinberger and Bruce Tucker, *The New Individualists: The Generation After the Organization Man* (New York: HarperCollins, 1991), 256. See Chapter 6: "Personal Artifice: From the Self-Made Man to the Man-Made Self."

Bibliography

Aberth, John. *A Knight at the Movies: Medieval History on Film.* New York: Routledge, 2003.

Altman, Rick. "A Semantic/Syntactic Approach to Film Genre." *Cinema Journal* 23.3 (1984): 6–18.

Aristotelis. *De Arte Poetica Liber.* Edited by Rudolf Kassel. Oxford: Clarendon, 1965.

———. *The Poetics of Aristotle.* Translation and commentary by Stephen Halliwell. Chapel Hill: University of North Carolina Press, 1987.

Augustine, Saint. *The City of God Against the Pagans.* Translated by R.W. Dyson. Cambridge: Cambridge University Press, 1998.

Ayfre, Amédée. *Le Cinema et sa vérité.* Paris: Cerf, 1969.

Bakhtin, Mikhail. *The Dialogic Imagination: Four Essays.* Translated by Caryl Emerson and Michael Holquist. Austin: University of Texas Press, 1981. Originally published in Russian in 1975.

Beattie, Bruce. "The Broken Quest: The 'Perceval' of Chrétien de Troyes and Eric Rohmer." In *The Arthurian Revival: Essays on Form, Tradition and Transformation,* edited by Debra N. Mancoff, 248–65. New York: Garland, 1992.

Bernardus Guidonis. *The Inquisitor's Guide: A Medieval Manual on Heretics.* Translated by Janet Shirley. Walwyn Garden City, UK: Ravenhall Books, 2006.

Berry, Sarah. "Genre." In *A Companion to Film Theory,* edited by Toby Miller and Robert Stam, 25–44. Oxford: Blackwell, 1999.

Biddick, Kathleen. "Unbinding the Flesh That Remains: Crusader Martyrdom Then and Now." *GLQ* 13: 2–3 (2007): 197–225.

Biographie Universelle, Ancienne et Moderne. Edited by M. Michaud. Nouvelle ed. Paris: Madame C. Desplaces, 1854.

Blanch, Robert J., and Julian N. Wasserman. "Fear of Flyting: The Absence of Internal Tension in *The Sword of the Valiant* and *First Knight.*" *Arthuriana* 10.4 (2000): 15–32.

Bloch, R. Howard. *Medieval French Literature and Law.* Berkeley: University of California Press, 1977.

Bongert, Yvonne. *Cours d'histoire du droit pénal: Le droit pénal français de la seconde moitié du XIIIe siècle à l'ordonnance de 1493.* Paris: Cours de droit, 1973.

Bordwell, David. *The Films of Carl-Theodore Dreyer.* Berkeley: University of California Press, 1981.

Brantôme, Pierre de Bourdeille. *Les Dames Galantes.* Edited by Maurice Rat. Paris: Éditions Garnier Frères, 1960.

Burke, Peter. *Popular Culture in Early Modern Europe.* New York: New York University Press, 1978.

Burr, David. *The Spiritual Franciscans.* University Park: Pennsylvania State University Press, 2001.

Buscombe, Edward. "The Idea of Genre in American Cinema." *Screen* 11.2 (1970): 33–45.

Capitani, Ovidio. "Eco on Medievalism." *Studies in Medievalism* 5 (1993): 127–38.

Chatman, Seymour. *Coming to Terms: The Rhetoric of Narrative in Fiction and Film.* Ithaca, NY: Cornell University Press, 1990.

Chaucer, Geoffrey. *The Canterbury Tales.* Edited by Larry D. Benson. Boston: Houghton-Mifflin, 2000.

Clegg. Brian. *The First Scientist: A Life of Roger Bacon.* New York: Carroll & Graff, 2003.

Colletti, Theresa. *Naming the Rose: Eco, Medieval Signs and Modern Theory.* Ithaca, NY: Cornell University Press, 1988.

Coote, Lesley. "The Art of Arthurian Cinema." In *A Companion to Arthurian Literature*, edited by Helen Fulton, 511–24. Malden, MA: Wiley-Blackwell, 2009.

Crichton, Michael. *Timeline.* New York: Alfred A. Knopf, 1999.

Davis, Natalie Zemon. *The Return of Martin Guerre.* Cambridge: Harvard University Press, 1983.

Dempsey, Michael. "Despair Abounding: The Recent Films of Robert Bresson." In *Robert Bresson*, edited by James Quant, 373–91. Toronto: Toronto International Film Festival Group, 1998.

Dictionary of the Middle Ages. Edited by Joseph R. Strayer. 13 Vols. New York: Scribner, 1982–89.

Douie, Decima L. *The Nature and the Effect of the Heresy of the Fraticelli.* Manchester: At the University Press, 1932.

Dreyer, Carl. "Realized Mysticism." In *Dreyer in Double Reflection*, edited by Donald Skoller, 47–50. New York: E.P. Dutton, 1973.

Duby, Georges. *Medieval Marriage: Two Models from Twelfth-Century France.* Baltimore: Johns Hopkins University Press, 1978.

Eco, Umberto. "Dreaming of the Middle Ages." In *Travels in Hyperreality*, 61–72. Translated by William Weaver. London: Picador, 1987.

———. *The Name of the Rose.* Translated by William Weaver. New York: Harcourt Brace Jovanovich, 1983. Originally published in Italian in 1980.

———. *Postscript to The Name of the Rose.* Translated by William Weaver. New York: Harcourt Brace Jovanovich, 1984. Originally published in Italian in 1983.

Edwards, Charlotte. "Ridley Scott's New Crusades Film Panders to Osama Bin Laden." *The Telegraph* (online edition). December 27, 2004.

Einhorn, Richard. *Voices of Light* (oratorio). Stereo music track for *The Passion of Joan of Arc*, dir. Carl Dreyer. 1928. Criterion Collection, 1999.

Finke, Laurie A., and Martin B. Shichtman. *Cinematic Illuminations: The Middle Ages on Film.* Baltimore: The Johns Hopkins University Press, 2010.

Flandrin, Dean-Louis. *Families in Former Times: Kinship, Household and Sexuality.* Translated by Richard Southern. Cambridge: Cambridge University Press, 1976.

Forey, John Alan. *The Military Orders: From the Twelfth to the Fourteenth Centuries.* Toronto: University of Toronto Press, 1992.

Francaviglia, Richard. "Crusaders and Saracens: The Persistance of Orientalism in Historically Themed Pictures about the Middle East." In *Lights, Camera, History: Portraying the Past in Film*, edited by Richard Francaviglia and Jerry Rodnitzky, 53–90. College Station: Texas A&M University Press, 2007.

Freud, Sigmund. *Complete Psychological Works.* Edited by James Strachey. Vol. XVIII. 1922. Reprint London: Hogarth Press, 1955.

Frye, Northrop. *The Secular Scripture: A Study of the Structure of Romance.* Cambridge: Harvard University Press, 1976.

Gabrieli, Francesco. *Arab Historians of the Crusades.* Berkeley: University of California Press, 1969.

Gado, Frank. *The Passion of Ingmar Bergman.* Durham, NC: Duke University Press, 1986.

Gervais, Marc. *Ingmar Bergman: Magician and Prophet.* Montreal: McGill-Queens University Press, 1999.

Gibb, H.A.R. *The Life of Saladin: From the Works of 'Imād ad-Dīn and Bahā' ad-Dīn.* Oxford: Clarendon Press, 1973.

———. *Saladin: Studies in Islamic History.* Beirut: Arab Institute for Research and Publishing, 1974.

Gibson, Arthur. *The Silence of God: Creative Response to the Films of Ingmar Bergman.* New York: Harper & Row, 1969.

Greenblatt, Stephen. *Renaissance Self-Fashioning: From More to Shakespeare.* Chicago: Chicago University Press, 1980.

Grimbert, Joan Tasker. "Distancing Techniques in Chrétien and Rohmer." *Arthuriana* 10.4 (2000): 33–44.

Grodal, Torben. "The Experience of Realism in Audiovisual Representation." In *Realism and "Reality" in Film and Media,* edited by Anne Jerslev, 67–91. Copenhagen: Museum Tusculanum Press, 2002.

Halliwell, Stephen. *Aristotle's Poetics.* Chicago: University of Chicago Press, 1998.

Harty, Kevin J. *The Reel Middle Ages: Films About Medieval Europe.* Jefferson, NC: McFarland, 1999.

Howell, Martha. "The Properties of Marriage in Late Medieval Europe: Commercial Wealth and the Creation of Modern Marriage." In *Love, Marriage, and Family Ties in England 1500–1800,* edited by Isabel Davis, et al., 17–61. Tournhout: Brepols, 2003.

Huizinga, Johan. *The Waning of the Middle Ages.* Translated by Fritz Hopman, 1924. New York: Doubleday, 1954.

Ibn-Munquidh, Usāmah. *An Arab-Syrian Gentleman and Warrior in the Period of the Crusades: Memoirs of Usāmah ibn-Munquidh.* Translated by Philip K. Hitti. New York: Columbia University Press, 2000.

Kaeupper, Richard W. *War, Justice and Public Order: England and France in the Late Middle Ages.* Oxford: Clarendon Press, 1988.

_____, and Elspeth Kennedy. *The Book of Geoffroi de Charny.* Philadelphia: University of Pennsylvania Press, 1996.

Kalin, Jesse. *The Films of Ingmar Bergman.* Cambridge: Cambridge University Press, 2003.

Kieckhefer, Richard. *European Witch Trials: Their Foundations in Popular and Learned Culture, 1300–1500.* Berkeley: University of California Press, 1976.

Ladurie, Emmanuel Le Roy. *The Peasants of Languedoc.* Translated by John Day. Chicago: University of Illinois Press, 1974.

The Lais of Marie de France. Translated by Robert W. Hanning and Joan Ferrante. New York: Dutton, 1978.

Laughter for the Devil: The Trials of Gilles de Rais, Companion-in-Arms of Joan of Arc (1140). Translated by Reginald Hyatte. Rutherford, NJ: Fairleigh Dickinson University Press, 1984.

Leclercq, Jean. *The Love of Learning and the Desire for God: A Study of Monastic Culture.* Translated by Catharine Misrahi. New York: Fordham University Press, 1961. Originally published in French in 1957.

_____, et al. *The Spirituality of the Middle Ages.* New York: Seabury Press, 1968.

Leff, Gordon. *The Dissolution of the Medieval Outlook.* New York: New York University Press, 1976.

_____. *Heresy in the Middle Ages: The Relation of Heterodoxy to Dissent, 1250–1450.* 2 Vols. Manchester: Manchester University Press, 1967.

_____. *William of Ockham.* Manchester: Manchester University Press, 1975.

Leinberger, Paul, and Bruce Tucker. *The New Individualists: The Generation After the Organization Man.* New York: HarperCollins, 1991.

Lewis, Janet. *The Wife of Martin Guerre.* San Francisco: Colt Press, 1941.

Little, Lester K. *Religious Poverty and the Profit Economy in Medieval Europe.* Ithaca, NY: Cornell University Press, 1978.

Madden, Thomas F. "Onward PC Soldiers: Ridley Scott's *Kingdom of Heaven.*" *National Review* (online edition). May 27, 2005.

Malory, Sir Thomas. *Le Morte d'Arthur: The Winchester Manuscript.* Edited and abridged by Helen Cooper. New York: Oxford, 1998.

Mandrou, Robert. *Introduction to Modern France 1500–1640: An Essay in Historical Psychology.* Translated by R.E. Hallmark. New York: Holmes and Meier, 1975.

Marty, Joseph. "Perceval le Gallois d'Eric Rohmer, un itinéraire roman." *Les Cahiers de la cinématèque* 42–43 (Summer 1985): 125–32.

McIntosh, Marjorie K. "Finding Language for Misconduct." In *Bodies and Disciplines: Intersections of Literature and History in Fifteenth-Century England*, edited by Barbara A. Hanawalt and David Wallace, 87–122. Minneapolis: University of Minnesota Press, 1996.

Michell, Linda E. "Review of *The Advocate*." *American Historical Review* 100 (1995): 1221-2.

Milne, Tom. *The Cinema of Carl Dreyer*. New York: A.S. Barnes, 1971.

Moorman, John. *A History of the Franciscan Order*. Oxford: Clarendon Press, 1968.

Morris, David B. *The Culture of Pain*. Berkeley: University of California Press, 1991.

Mortenson, Greg. *Stones Into Schools: Promoting Peace with Books, Not Bombs, in Afganistan and Pakistan*. New York: Viking, 2009.

_____, and David Oliver Relin. *Three Cups of Tea: One Man's Mission to Promote Peace ... One School at a Time*. New York: Penguin, 2006.

Munro, Dana C., trans. "Speech of Urban II at the Council of Clermont, November 26, 1095." In *Urban and the Crusaders: Translations and Reprints from the Original Sources of European History*, 3rd Edition, edited by Dana C. Munro. Philadelphia: Department of History of the University of Pennsylvania, 1901.

Neergaard, Ebbe. *Carl Dreyer: A Film Director's Work*. New Index Series, No. 1. London: BFI, 1950.

Orr, John. "Bergman, Nietzsche and Hollywood." In *Ingmar Bergman Revisited: Performance, Cinema and the Arts*, edited by Maaret Koskinen, 143–60. London: Wallflower Press, 2008.

Ozment, Stephen. *The Age of Reform, 1250-1550*. New Haven: Yale University Press, 1980.

Painter, Sidney. *William Marshall, Knight-Errant, Baron, and Regent of England*. 1933. Toronto: University of Toronto Press, 1982.

Poem of the Cid. Translated by W.S. Merwin. New York: Meridian, 1975.

The Poem of the Cid. Translated by Rita Hamilton and Janet Perry. New York: Penguin, 1984.

Post, Gaines. *Studies in Medieval Legal Thought: Public Law and the State, 1100–1322*. Princeton: Princeton University Press, 1964.

Reader, Keith. *Robert Bresson*. Manchester: Manchester University Press, 2000.

Rider, Jeff, Richard Hull, and Christopher Smith. "The Arthurian Legend in French Cinema: *Lancelot du Lac* and *Perceval le gallois*." In *Cinema Arthuriana: Essays on Arthurian Film*, edited by Kevin J. Harty, 41–56. New York: Garland, 1991.

Riley-Smith, Jonathan. *The Knights of St. John in Jerusalem and Cyprus c.1050–1310*. New York: Macmillan, 1967.

_____. "Truth Is the First Victim." *The Times* (online edition). May 5, 2005.

Rosenbaum, Jonathan. "The Rattle of Armor, the Softness of Flesh." In *Movies as Politics*, 201–207. Berkeley: University of California Press, 1997.

_____. "The Last Filmmaker: A Local, Interim Report." In *Robert Bresson*, edited by James Quant, 17–24. Toronto: Toronto International Film Festival Group, 1998.

Said, Edward. *Orientalism*. New York: Pantheon, 1978.

Scarry, Elaine. *The Body in Pain: The Making and Unmaking of the World*. New York: Oxford, 1985.

Schrader, Paul. *Transcendental Style in Film: Ozu, Bresson, Dreyer*. Berkeley: University of California Press, 1972.

Setton, Kenneth M., ed. *A History of the Crusades*. 5 Vols. Madison: University of Wisconsin Press, 1969.

Sir Gawain and the Green Knight. Translated by Marie Borroff. New York: Norton, 1967.

Stam, Robert. "Interrogating Authorship and Genre." In *Film Theory: An Introduction*, 123–30. Malden, MA: Blackwell, 2000.

Steinbeck, John. *The Acts of King Arthur and His Noble Knights*. New York: Noonday, 1986.

Stone, Lawrence. *The Family, Sex and Marriage in England, 1500–1800*. Abridged ed. New York: Harper and Row, 1977.

Strick, Phillip. "Review of *The Hour of the Pig [The Advocate]*." *Sight and Sound* NS 4 (February 1994), 53.

Sweetenham, Carol, trans. *Robert the Monk's History of the First Crusade, Historia Iberosolimitana.* Burlington, VT: Ashgate, 2007.

Tesich-Savage, Nadja. "Rehearsing the Middle Ages." *Film Comment 14.5* (September/October 1978): 50–52, 54–56, 80. http://search.proquest.com. [Interview with Eric Rohmer].

Thoreau, Henry David. *Walden.* 1854. Reprint New York: New American Library, 1960.

Tolkien, J.R.R. *The Lord of the Rings.* 2nd ed. Cambridge: Houghton-Mifflin, 1965.

Tompkins, Jane. *West of Everything: The Inner Life of Westerns.* New York: Oxford, 1992.

Thompson, Kristin. "The Sheen of Armour, the Whinnies of Horses: Sparse Parametric Style in *Lancelot du Lac.*" In *Robert Bresson*, edited by James Quant, 339–71. Toronto: Toronto International Film Festival Group, 1998.

Tuchman, Barbara W. *A Distant Mirror: The Calamitous 14th Century.* New York: Knopf, 1978.

Twain, Mark. *Letters from the Earth.* Edited by Bernard DeVoto. New York: Harper, 1962.

Tyerman, Christopher. *God's War: A New History of the Crusades.* Cambridge: Harvard University Press, 2006.

Ubertinus de Casali. *The Tree of the Crucified Life of Jesus, Book Five (Excerpts).* Translator unknown. In *The Prophet*, Vol. 3, 141–206. Hyde Park, NY: New City Press, 2001.

Ullman, Walter. *The Medieval Idea of Law as Represented by Lucas de Penna: A Study in Fourteenth-Century Legal Scholarship.* 1946. Reprint New York: Barnes and Noble, 1969.

White, T.H. *The Once and Future King.* New York: Putnam, 1958.

William, Archbishop of Tyre. *A History of Deeds Done Beyond the Sea.* Translated by Emily Atwater Babcock and A.C.Krey. 2 Vols. New York: Columbia University Press, 1943.

Index

Aberth, John 182*n*10, 182*n*15
Abraham, F. Murray 131
ad-Dīn, Bahā 192*n*22
ad-Dīn, Imād 192*n*20, 192*n*21
Adams, Thelma 184*n*5
The Advocate 5–6, 9, 11, 17–18, 24–25, 27, 36, 59–75, 60, 177, 184*n*2; Accursius (*Glossa Ordinaria*) 66; animal theme 35–36, 66–70; fears and threats 17, 62–65, 68; human image in 59, 62, 65- 75; immediacy in 25; Inquisition 65, 67, 71; justice (*iustitia*) 65, 68; Justinian (*Corpus Iuris Civilis*) 66, 74; law of nature (*ius naturale*) 65–66, 74–75; law of peoples (*ius gentium*) 65–66, 70, 74–75; Law of the State (*ius civile*) 65–66; *lex talionis* (eye for an eye) 68; *maleficium* (witchery) 63, 67, 74; narrative filtration 64; narrative slant 74; order and rule 67, 70–71; reflective hero 27–28; reviews 61–62; simplicity in 40; suffering for an ideal 21
Altman, Rick 181*n*1
Andersson, Bibi 77
Angela of Foligno 125
Annaud, Jean-Jacques 117, 119, 121, 122, 127, 128, 133, 190*n*1
Antolek, Vladimir 109
Apostles (of Gherardo Segarelli) 127
Aristotle 128–129; *Poetics* 46, 184*n*1, 184*n*2, 184*n*3; *Poetics* (of comedy) 129
Arnold, Matthew 104
Artaud, Antonin 90
Arthur's Quest 27
Auden, W.H.: *Ode in Memory of W.B. Yeats* 36, 183*n*3
authenticity 23–34; *see also* realism
Ayfre, Amédée 188*n*21

Bacon, Roger 45, 116, 123, 133
Bakhtin, Mikhail 181*n*9, 182*n*11, 182*n*12, 182*n*20, 183*n*22, 183*n*26

Baldwin IV, King of Jerusalem 158, 168–169
Balsan, Humbert 106
Baybars 174
Baye, Nathalie 138, 144
Beattie, Bruce A. 189*n*11
Becket 28, 33
Becket, Thomas 19–20, 49, 54
Benedictine Order 116–122, 127–128, 132
Bergman, Ingmar 8, 21, 59, 76, 81, 86, 187*n*1
Bergman, Ingrid 56
Berry, Sarah 181*n*2
Bettany, Paul 38
Biddick, Kathleen 192*n*15
Björnstrand, Gunnar 78
Blanch, Robert J. 183*n*12
Bloch, R. Howard 185*n*16
Bloom, Orlando 155
Bongert, Yvonne 185*n*16
Bonnaire, Sandrine 56
Bordwell, David 188*n*15, 188*n*16, 188*n*17, 188*n*23, 188*n*24
Bourdeille, Pierre de 191*n*23
Braveheart 7, 21, 31
Brembre, Nicholas 5
Bresson, Robert 6, 14, 15, 26, 33, 52, 89, 95, 105–107, 112–113, 115, 199*n*13
Brueghel, Pieter, the Elder 137, 146
Burke, Kenneth 11
Burke, Peter 191*n*9
Burr, David 190*n*11
Burton, Richard 19, 28
Buscombe, Edward 181*n*1

Camelot 18, 28, 37, 95, 104, 181*n*5
Capitani, Ovidio 183*n*30
Carrière, Jean-Claude 136
Carter, Helena Bonham 49
Chahine, Youssef 193*n*1
Chaliapin, Feodor, Jr. 132
Charles VII 186*n*22

199

Charny, Geoffroi de 36
Chasseneuz, Barthélemy de 186n23
Chatman, Seymour 185n15
Chaucer, Geoffrey 6, 10, 38, 70, 141, 181; *The Canterbury Tales* 6, 10, 181, 184n15
chivalry 15, 36–39, 106, 109, 112, 114–115; Geoffroi de Charny 36; and spectacle 50–54; Thomas Malory 36–37; William Marshall 36; woman in chivalry 53–54
Chrétien de Troyes: *The Knight of the Cart* 107; *Perceval* 51, 94–104
El Cid 12
El Cid 46, 182n15
cinematic medievalism 23–25, 32
Clare of Montefalco 125
Cleff, Brian 190n7
Colletti, Theresa 190n7
Conan the Barbarian 35
Condominas, Laura Duke 49, 110
A Connecticut Yankee in King Arthur's Court 7
Connery, Sean 8, 18, 24, 28, 37, 121
The Cook's Tale 6
Coote, Lesley 188n2, 189n15, 189n19, 189n20, 189n22
Coras, Jean de 136
Corpus Iuris Civilis 187n28
Costner, Kevin 31
Crichton, Michael: *Timeline* 10, 182n13
crusades 8
Csokas, Marton 158

Dante Alighieri 9, 38
Davis, Natalie Zemon 136, 144, 184n13, 190n3, 190n4, 190n5, 190n6, 190n8, 191n10, 191n13, 191n14, 191n24, 191n26
DeMille, Cecil B. 7
Dempsey, Michael 189n18, 189n24
Dench, Judi 27
Depardieu, Gérard 11, 143
A Distant Mirror 70
Dolcinites 127–128, 131
Dominican Order 117, 131
Douglas, Kirk 29–30
Douie, Decima L. 190n19
Dreyer, Carl 20, 42, 76, 85–86, 88, 188n21
Duby, George 146–147, 198n17

Eco, Umberto 59, 116–117, 124, 128, 133, 183n3, 184n1, 190n1, 190n17, 190n18; *The Name of the Rose* 116, 190n1; *Il nome della rosa* 116; *Postscript to The Name of the Rose* 190n1
Edward I 21
Einhorn, Richard 187n14
Ekerot, Bengt 81
Eleanor of Aquitaine 5, 9, 46, 50

Euripides 96
Everyman 59
Excalibur 9, 18, 26, 30, 37, 49, 94, 104

fairy tales 4
Falconetti, Renée 20, 28, 56, 86
Finch, John 165
Finke, Laurie A. 187n2, 188n15, 188n20
Firth, Colin 6, 62
First Knight 8, 18, 27, 33, 37
Flandrin, Jean-Louis 184n12, 191n21, 191n22
Forey, Alan John 192n11
Fra Dolcino 127
frame story 4
Francaviglia, Richard 191n5
Francis I, Pope 175
Franciscan Order 43, 116–117, 120, 123–131; conventuals 104, 132; spirituals 116–117, 124–125, 128
Fraticelli 128
Freud, Sigmund 21, 183n25; pleasure principle 29; reality principle 29
Frye, Northrop 182n21

Gabrieli, Francesco 192n21, 193n23
Gado, Frank 189n5, 189n6, 189n10
Gandalf 18
Geoffrey of Monmouth 182n20
Gere, Richard 4, 33
Gervais, Marc 83, 187n3, 187n10, 187n11, 187n12
Gibb, H.A.R. 192n17, 192n19
Gibson, Arthur 187n8
Gibson, Mel 7, 21
Goldman, James 50
Grail quest 8
Gray, Marianne 184n9
Green, Eva 158, 191n5
Greenblatt, Stephen 41, 178, 184n14
Grimbert, Joan Tasker 188n3, 189n6, 189n10
Grodal, Torben 25, 28, 30, 33, 183n24, 183n4, 183n5, 183n6, 183n7, 183n8, 183n9, 183n10, 183n11
Gui, Bernardo (Bernardus Guidonis) 129–131, 133; *Practica Inquisitionis Heretice Pravitatis* 131, 190n20

Haft, Adele J. 190n1
Halliwell, Stephen: *Aristotle's Poetics* 184n3; *The Poetics of Aristotle* 184n2
Harris, Richard 28, 37
Harty, Kevin J. 50, 184n4
Hauer, Rutger 35
Henry II 19, 46–47, 50, 54
Henry V 24
Hepburn, Katharine 9, 50
Héroët, Antoine 191n20

Index

Hickey, William 125
High Plains Drifter 10
Holm, Ian 56, 63
Holmes, Sherlock 116, 122–123
Homer: *Iliad* 7, 36, 183n4
Hopkins, Anthony 5
horses 11–15
The Hour of the Pig (*The Advocate*) 59, 62, 184n3
Howell, Martha 147, 191n17, 191n18, 191n19
Huizinga, Johan 23–24, 63, 75, 182n16, 182n19, 183n1, 183n2, 184n13, 187n29
Hull, Richard 188n3, 189n10, 189n23

Ibn-Munquidh, Usāma 192n19
identity 15–21, 30, 177; *see also* medieval film world
Irons, Jeremy 158, 191n5
Ivanhoe 9, 15, 31

Joan of Arc 7, 10, 17, 21–22, 24, 30, 33, 42, 56, 85–86; as spectacle 56
Joan of Arc 10, 14
Joan the Woman 7
John of Jandun 190n10
John XXII, Pope 45, 117, 124–125, 129

Kaeuper, Richard W. 183n5, 186n26
Kalin, Jesse 187n2, 187n4
Kempe, Margery 27
Kennedy, Elspeth 183n5
Kieckhefer, Richard 185n19
King Arthur 12, 50, 54, 94
Kingdom of Heaven 39, 54–55, 155–174, 176, 191n1; the Church 55, 161–166; Ibelin 166, 168, 170, 172–173, 176; kingdom of conscience 158–160, 172; Knights Hospitalers 55, 163–167, 192n23; Knights Templars 158, 163–164, 167- 168, 192n23; Orientalism 166; Saladin 158–160, 163, 165, 168–172, 174, 192n22, 193n23
Knightley, Keira 50
A Knight's Tale 5–6, 12, 27, 32, 37–38

Ladurie, Emmanuel Le Roy 140, 184n11, 190n2, 191n10
Ladyhawke 31, 35, 181n5
Lancelot du Lac 7, 14–15, 18, 49, 51–53, 104–115, 189n13; armor 107; colors 107; distant relationships 111; enclosures 113–114; fears 108–109; forest metaphor 104–105, 109; horses 104, 106, 108–109, 112; identity 111, 114; "models" (actors) 109–110; reversals 114; rituals of pride 108–109; spectacle 50–52; war and despair 112
La Trémoile, Georges de 186n22
Leclercq, Jean 190n3

Ledger, Heath 12, 37
Leff, Gordon 125, 190n5, 190n9, 190n11, 190n12, 190n13, 190n14, 190n15, 190n16
Leinberger, Paul 193n2
Lewis, Janet 136
lex naturalis 20
The Lion in Winter 5, 9, 27, 46
Little, Lester K. 190n14
Locke, John 33
Lonsdale, Michael 121
The Lord of the Rings 18
Louis IV of Austria (Holy Roman Emperor) 44, 116–117, 123
Luchini, Patrice 51, 96, 101–103

Maalouf, Amin 191n4
Mad Max II: The Road Warrior 10
Madden, Thomas F. 155, 172, 191n3, 191n6, 192n10, 193n24
Magill's Cinema Annual (1995) 184n6
Malebranche, Nicolas 191n16
Malory, Thomas 18, 28; apprenticeship of knights 36–37; Arthur 57–58; *Le Morte d'Arthur* 37, 184n7; names of knights 37; the Round Table 37
Mandrou, Robert 147, 152, 184n12, 191n9, 191n11, 191n12, 191n15, 191n25, 191n27
Marie de France: *Bisclavret* 35, 183n2
Marshall, William 36
Marty, Joseph 188n4
Massoud, Ghassan 169
McIntosh, Marjorie K. 185n21
medieval film world: an animal world 35–36; communal life 57; faith and being 19, 21, 25, 35, 41; fears 17; felt experience 6, 25; frame story 4, 25; horses 11–15; identity 15–20, 25, 35; love and loyalty 18–19, 25, 35, 43; nature 54; necessity 17; sex 32; ways of being (estates) of knights, monks, peasants 36, 39
medieval hero 15–20, 26–28; agency 26; choices 26–27; female heroes 53–54, 57; as a focusing presence 32; pain 27; recantation 34; reflective nature 27; self-fashioning 41
medievalism 3, 16–17, 24, 26
Megahey, Leslie 182n19, 184n2, 185n14
Mérindol 186n23
Merlin 9, 18, 25, 104, 182n20
Meury, Anne-Laure 101
Michael of Cesena 123–124, 132
Milne, Tom 187n15, 188n18, 188n19
Mitchell, Linda E. 184n11
Monahan, William 156
Montaigne, Michel Eyquem, Seigneur de 141, 148, 152
Monty Python and the Holy Grail 8, 27, 59, 182n10

Moorman, John 190*n*6
Morgana 27
Morris, David 21, 183*n*27, 183*n*28, 183*n*29
Mortenson, Greg 191*n*7
Munro, Dana C. 191*n*8

The Name of the Rose 5, 9, 17–18, 20, 24, 26–28, 30, 39, 55, 116–134, 190*n*1; apocalypse 122, 125–126, 132; apprenticeship 39; Benedictine Rule 55, 124; heresy 119, 122, 124–126, 128–130; inquisition 122, 124, 129–131; *mise en abyme* 119, 122; nature 54; poor use (*usus pauper*) 130; scholasticism 123; simple use (*simplex usus facti*) 124; simplicity 44–45; spectacle (the Church) 55–56
Neergaard, Ebbe 188*n*22
Nero, Franco 32, 49
Nesselson, Lisa 184*n*8, 184*n*10
Newman, Kim 184*n*7

Oedipus at Colonnus 181*n*7
Oedipus Rex 7, 181*n*7
The Once and Future King 37
Orlando 28
Orr, John 187*n*7
Othello 16
O'Toole, Peter 19, 50
Ovid 128
Ozment, Stephen 198*n*8

pain 20–22, 28–30; *see also* realism
Painter, Sidney 183*n*6
La Passion de Jeanne d'Arc 20, 27–28, 42, 76, 85–93, 187*n*13, 187*n*14; close-ups 87; *contemptu mundi* 93; Dreyer's "cinema of the soul" 90–91; expressionism 86; simplicity 42; spectacle 56; spiritual axis 89; transcendence 90–91; weight of inevitability 88
Paston, Margaret 27
The Peasants' Revolt 5
Penna, Lucas de 185*n*17
Perceval le gallois 5, 51, 94–104; courtly love 96, 98–99; inner development 102–104; irony 95–96, 99; spectacle 51–52; stylized realism 95–104
Perlman, Ron 121, 127
Pfeiffer, Michelle 31, 35
Philippe de Vitri 182*n*19, 185*n*14
Pietropaulo, Domenico 183*n*30
Planchon, Roger 138
Plato idealist tradition 33
The Poem of the Cid (Rita Hamilton and Janet Perry, trans.) 82*n*15
Poem of the Cid (W.S. Merwin, trans.) 182*n*15
Poppe, Nils 79

Post, Gaines 185*n*18, 187*n*28
Prechtel, Volker 121
Le Procès de Jeanne d'Arc 26, 33, 89

Quest for Fire 121, 133
quest narrative 8, 14

Rainer, Peter 184*n*4
Rais, Gilles de 186*n*22
Reader, Keith 189*n*14, 189*n*23
realism, authenticating 21, 23–24; emotional extremes 23; faces 31; filtration 64, 185*n*15; gazes 28; generic images 181*n*1; immediacy 24; inner form 4, 181*n*1; pain as 20–22, 28–30; primitivism 24–25, 35; prototypical acts 26; range of specificity 32; sense of the typical 32; spiritual poignancy 25; stereotypes of medieval life 32; themes and ideas 32–34; truth claim 25
realism, cognitive ("schematic") 32–34; decorum 31; details of mundane experience 23; fables of identity 15–20, 33, 178; freedom, dignity, loyalty, identity 33–34; ideology 32; Locke (complex ideas) 33; recantation abandonment of self 33–34
realism, perceptual 26, 30–32; perceptual uniqueness and complexity 30–32
Redgrave, Vanessa 49
Relin, David Oliver 191*n*7
"Renaissance Self-Fashioning" 178
The Return of Martin Guerre 5, 11, 24–25, 27, 30, 36, 39, 135–154, 178, 190*n*1, 190*n*7; *aiguillette* 140; animal life 36; Charivari ritual 39, 57, 139–140, 148; companionate marriage 147; life of peasants 40–41, 56–57; nature 54; priests 55–56; protestants 138, 140–141, 146, 148–149, 154; self-fashioning 41, 178; simplicity 40–41; spectacle, 56–57; witch trials 152
Reynald de Châtillon 159, 167–168, 192*n*18
Richard Lionheart 9
Richard II 6
Rider, Jeff 188*n*3, 189*n*10, 189*n*23
Riley-Smith, Jonathan 155, 191*n*2, 192*n*11, 193*n*25
Rob Roy 7
Robert the Monk (of Rheims) 192*n*8
Robin Hood 27, 56
Robin Hood, Prince of Thieves 31
Rohmer, Eric 5, 51, 97, 99–100, 102–103, 188*n*1, 189*n*10
Le Roman de Renart 70
romance 20
Ronsard, Pierre de 152
Rosenbaum, Jonathan 189*n*16, 189*n*18, 189*n*25
Roth, Tim 7

Index

Said, Edward 192*n*14
Saint Augustine 69, 119, 190*n*4
Saint Bartholomew's Day massacre 138
Saint Catherine 21
Saint Francis 24, 35, 56, 175; and simple life 44, 125; as spectacle 56
Saint Teresa 21
Saladin 158–160, 163, 165, 168–172, 174, 192*n*20, 192*n*22
Saladin (film) 193*n*1
Scarry, Elaine 7, 21, 181*n*6, 183*n*23
Schrader, Paul 188*n*15
Schutz, Maurice 88
Schwarzenegger, Arnold 35
Scott, Ridley 155, 161–162, 170–171, 176, 191*n*1, 191*n*3, 191*n*4
Segarelli, Gherardo 127
Setton, Kenneth M. 192*n*13, 192*n*15, 192*n*18, 193*n*23
The Seventh Seal 8, 10, 17–18, 21, 25, 27, 30–31, 33, 36, 76–85, 86, 187*n*1; character archetypes 43; dialectic of life and death 80–81; Jof and Mia 44, 79–80; sense of immanence 77; and simplicity 43–44; symbolic forms 84
Shane 10
Sheen, Michael 161
Shichtman, Martin B. 187*n*2, 188*n*15, 188*n*20
Silvain, Eugène 87–88
Simon, Luc 106, 112
simplicity 35–45; atavism 45; chivalry 36–38; faith and being 41–43; monks 39–40; peasants 40–41; the simple life 44–45; ways of being 36
Sir Gawain and the Green Knight 14, 182*n*16
Slater, Christian 18, 121
Smith, Christopher 188*n*3, 189*n*10, 189*n*23
Sobieski, Leelee 10, 14, 56
Society for Creative Anachronism 16, 24
spectacle **70–83**; Aristotle, *Poetics* 46; castles 46–49; chivalry 50–54; the Church 55- 56; kings 49; nature 54; peasants 56–57; queens 49–50
Stam, Robert 181*n*1
Steinbeck, John 37, 184*n*8
Stone, Lawrence 147, 191*n*18
Strayer, Joseph R. 186*n*25
Strick, Phillip 184*n*3
subjectivity 25–26
Sweetenham, Carol 192*n*8, 192*n*9
Swinton, Tilda 28
The Sword of Lancelot 18, 32, 49

Taylor, Elizabeth 31
Taylor, Robert 9, 15
Terry, Nigel 37

Tesich-Savage, Nadja 37
Thewlis, David 164
The Thirteenth Warrior 9; chivalry 51; nature 54
Thompson, Kristin 189*n*17, 189*n*18, 189*n*21
Thoreau, Henry 6, 35, 60, 72–73; *Walden* 72–73, 90, 187*n*27
Timeline 10, 182*n*13
Tolkien, J.R.R. 37, 116, 184*n*9
Tompkins, Jane: *West of Everything* 182*n*14, 182*n*18
Tuchman, Barbara 70, 117, 186*n*24
Tucker, Bruce 193*n*2
Twain, Mark: *A Connecticut Yankee in King Arthur's Court* 7–8; *Huckleberry Finn* 8; *Letters from the Earth* 181*n*814
Tyerman, Christopher 192*n*13
Tyler, Wat 5

Ubertino da Casale (Ubertinus de Casali) 124–127, 129, 133; *Arbor vitae crucifixae Jesu* 125–126, 190*n*15
Ullmann, Walter 185*n*16
Unset, Sigrid 16
Unsworth, Barry 116
Urban II, Pope 163, 191*n*8
Uther Pendragon 9, 18

Van Gogh, Vincent 150
Vargas, Valentina 128
Vayssière, Firmin 138, 190*n*8
Vermeer, Jan 138
Vigne, Daniel 136, 190–191*n*1
The Vikings 20
Virgil 128
Vitri, Philippe de 182*n*19, 185*n*14
von Eschenbach, Wolfram *see* Wolfram von Eschenbach
Von Sydow, Max 78

Wallace, Jean 49
Wallace, William 7, 11, 21–22, 31, 33
The Waning of the Middle Ages 23, 63, 75
Wasserman, Julian 183*n*12
White, T.H.: *The Once and Future King* 37, 184*n*10
Wilde, Cornel 32, 49
William of Ockham 45, 116, 123, 133
William of Tyre 165, 192*n*12
Williams, Linda 189*n*11
Williamson, Nicol 18, 63, 67
wisdom 18–19
witch trials 152
Wolfram von Eschenbach 96

www.ingramcontent.com/pod-product-compliance
Ingram Content Group UK Ltd.
Pitfield, Milton Keynes, MK11 3LW, UK
UKHW042006140426
5217IPUK00015B/1014